A SHORT REFERENCE GRAMMAR OF GULF ARABIC

A SHORT REFERENCE GRAMMAR OF GULF ARABIC

HAMDI A. QAFISHEH

in consultation with

Ernest N. McCarus

THE UNIVERSITY OF ARIZONA PRESS
Tucson, Arizona

About the Author . . .

HAMDI A. QAFISHEH, member of the University of Arizona Oriental Studies faculty, specializes in Arabic and linguistics. Holder of degrees from the University of Baghdad and the University of Michigan, he also has taught at universities and language schools throughout the Middle East. His numerous other publications include *A Basic Course in Gulf Arabic*, published by the University of Arizona Press, and *An Introduction to Gulf Arabic, A Course in Levantine Arabic,* and *Beginning English: A Basic Course for Arab Students.*

The research reported herein was performed pursuant to a contract with the United States Office of Education, Department of Health, Education, and Welfare, under the provisions of Title VI, Section 602, NDEA.

THE UNIVERSITY OF ARIZONA PRESS

I.S.B.N. 0-8165-0570-5
L.C. No. 76-55465

Dedicated to

K.S.Q.

in affection and gratitude

FOREWORD

The Arabic dialects of the Arabian Peninsula have long been of great interest to scholars because of their academic importance; they have recently come to be of great interest to individuals in business and government as well because of the strategic importance of the area. Saudi and Gulf dialects remain, however, among the least studied and least known of Arabic dialects. Dr. Hamdi A. Qafisheh has made several important contributions in the field of Gulf Arabic studies, the United Arab Emirates in particular, in the field of basic course materials for those who wish to speak Gulf Arabic. The present work is in a sense the culmination of all his previous work – a reference grammar which systematically presents the linguistic structures of Gulf Arabic. It will be invaluable for learning to speak the dialect but also for the linguist specializing in Arabic dialects. Based on extensive field work, it contains comprehensive coverage of the phonology, morphology and syntax of Gulf Arabic, presented in a straightforward manner that is easily accessible to the layman yet with the disciplinary rigor required by the scholar. This is an important contribution to Arabic dialect studies.

Ernest N. McCarus
University of Michigan

ACKNOWLEDGMENTS

I would like to express my thanks and appreciation to all those who helped in the preparation of this study. First, to the administrators of the Office of Education of the Department of Health, Education, and Welfare, Title VI, Section 602, for the contract which made the present study possible. To Professor Ernest N. McCarus, Chairman, Department of Near Eastern Studies, University of Michigan, goes my deepest appreciation for having carefully read the entire manuscript and made a number of corrections and instructive suggestions, and for having provided valuable counsel and editorial consultation; to Professor Wallace M. Erwin, Chairman, Department of Arabic, Georgetown University, for his corrections and constructive criticism of the phonology and the morphology parts. I am very grateful to President John P. Schaefer and Vice President for Research, Dr. A. Richard Kassander Jr., who arranged for some travel expenses and an Institutional Grant and for their encouragement. I wish to express my deep gratitude to H.E. Dr. Ezzeddin Ibrahim, Cultural Advisor, Ministry of Presidential Affairs, Abu Dhabi, U.A.E., for having unfailingly provided support and assistance in too many ways to mention. I must mention the kindness and generosity of the Ministry of Presidential Affairs and the Ministry of Education of Abu Dhabi, which made it possible for me to meet with useful language informants and helped in many other ways. To Linda S. Hunt for a typing job well done and for text transcribing and proofreading; to Mrs. Joyce Drennen of The University of Arizona Bureau of Printing and Reproductions for an efficient production of the final copy of the manuscript; and to Mr. Mark Sanders of The University of Arizona Press for having helped expedite the final stages of the production process. To my main language informants, Abdalla Kaddas, Mrs. Fatima Kaddas, Mohammad Mijrin Al-Rumaithi, Mrs. Kaltham Al-Rumaithi, Hamad Bin Tamin, Salim Khamis, Mahdi Al-Tajir, and my students in

Tucson and Abu Dhabi for their intelligence, patience, humor, and warm hospitality. To Mr. Carl N. Hodges, Director of The University of Arizona Environmental Research Laboratory and the resident staff members of the Arid Lands Research Center in Abu Dhabi for their steady interest and encouragement. Last, but not least, my hearty thanks go to the Head of the Department of Oriental Studies and the Dean of the College of Liberal Arts of The University of Arizona for having provided adequate office facilities and released time needed for the completion of the project.

H.A.Q.

Tucson, Arizona

CONTENTS

PART TWO
THE MORPHOLOGY OF GULF ARABIC

PART THREE
THE SYNTAX OF GULF ARABIC

PART FOUR
TEXTS

APPENDICES AND BIBLIOGRAPHY

INTRODUCTION

1. Preliminary

The language which the present work defines is to be commonly known as Gulf Arabic: it is the language used in informal situations by the indigenous populations of Bahrain, Qatar, and the United Arab Emirates of Abu Dhabi, Dubai, Sharja, Ajman, Umm al-Qaiwain, Ras al-Khaima, and Fujaira. These territories have much in common. Geographically, they lie on the southern coast of the Gulf. Most of them are coastal settlements, although some, such as Ajman, are inland territorial enclaves which presumably originated from settlements around watering places and summer gathering centers of nomads. Historically, the whole area came into the orbit of European influence in the sixteenth century, when the Portuguese established settlements for their trading ports. In the eighteenth century, traders from Holland, France, and Britain began vigorously to attack the Portuguese monopoly. Dutch predominance was gradually overtaken by the British in the late eighteenth century. Britain became paramount in the area, and the Gulf became an important link in the chain of her communications with India. In 1853 the rulers of the Shaikhdoms signed a treaty in which they agreed to the cessation of plunder, raids, and piracy. The most recent developments in the Gulf are the formation of the United Arab Emirates, the establishment of a U.S. naval base in Bahrain, and the opening of American embassies and consulates in the U.A.E., Bahrain, and Qatar. Socially, the indigenous populations of the Gulf states is made up of Arabs. A high degree of mutual intelligibility exists among the dialects of these states. There are differences, of course, but "the fact that these differences exist, however, should not be allowed to obscure the fact of their essential unity as a dialect group." (T.M. Johnstone, *Eastern Arabian Dialects,* London: Oxford University Press, 1967, p. 18.)

2. Summary of Relevant Studies

Much has been written on the history and politics of the Gulf area; a few linguistic studies have been published, but almost nothing of the scope of the present work has been previously attempted or published. *BASIC GULF ARABIC* (by this author), based on the dialect of Abu Dhabi, was first published by The University of Arizona Environmental Research Laboratory and later by Khayats, Beirut, Lebanon, 1970. It was written while the author was Linguistics Specialist and Training Director of the Abu Dhabi Program, which The University of Arizona administers in Tucson and in Abu Dhabi. This book was intended to serve the specific language needs of The University of Arizona Environmental Research Laboratory staff. The kind of Arabic described in this textbook is basically that of Abu Dhabi, modified by contact with the speech of Arab immigrants–Palestinians, Lebanese, Syrians, Iraqis, etc. Designed with practical and specific goals in mind, this textbook provides the learner with approximately 600 vocabulary items, of which 100 are specialized terms of importance to project members. The topics around which the dialogs are centered partially serve the needs of people with a wide variety of interests.

Some textbooks have been prepared by the oil companies for the use of their personnel. The Bahrain Petroleum Company has produced a *Handbook for the Spoken Arabic of Bahrain* (n.d. or place). In Qatar the government has published a small textbook *Spoken Arabic of Qatar* (K. Dajani, Beirut, 1956). A member of the American Mission in Kuwait has published a textbook *Spoken Arabic of the Arabian Gulf* (E. de Jong, Beirut, 1958). It should be stated that all of those handbooks and texts are very much limited in scope and lack a modern linguistic treatment. They adopt either the grammar-translation method or no method at all. The grammar notes are flimsy and sketchy; the grammar drills, if any, are limited in number and type and are unsuitable for classroom use. Furthermore, the authors tend to give preference to pan-Arabic *koine* over Bahraini or Qatari in the matter of vocabulary, and they themselves say of their appended texts that they are "closer to 'Classical Arabic' " than ordinary speech. Aramco's *Spoken Arabic* (Dhahran, 1957), *Conversational Arabic* (Beirut, n.d.), and its *English-Arabic Word List* (Beirut, 1958) are all in pan-Arabic *koine.*

This researcher has produced *A Basic Course in Gulf Arabic,* The University of Arizona Press and Librairie de Liban, Beirut, Lebanon, 1975, under the auspices of the U.S. Office of Education, which is a basic language course based on the dialect of Abu Dhabi, U.A.E., as modified by the dialects of Bahrain, and Qatar. It comprises forty-two lessons from spontaneous conversations of unsophisticated Gulf Arabs. The dialogs cover a wide variety of interests, such as greetings, getting acquainted, directions, shopping, banking, mailing letters, etc.

Linguistic studies of the related dialects are rather better represented. Cantineau's "Études sur quelques parlers de nomades arabes d'Orient," *Annales de l'Instituit d'Études Orientales d'Alger,* ii (1936), 1-118 and iii (1937), 119-237. These studies give a detailed phonological and a useful morphological analysis of a large number of dialects of different Bedouin groups. A more recent work is that of T.M. Johnstone, *Eastern Arabian Dialects,* London: O.U. Press, 1967. Cantineau's work lacks a modern linguistic treatment and reflects theory and practice of 35 years ago; Johnston's is a more scientific work, but it is limited in scope, fragmented and repetitious in presentation. Furthermore, it does not bear directly on the present work, as it is not a description of the present urban semi-educated and unsophisticated Gulf Arab. *A Short Reference Grammar of Iraqi Arabic* by Wallace M. Erwin and *A Reference Grammar of Syrian Arabic* by Mark C. Cowell were useful in setting up grammatical categories.

It is hoped that the present study would contribute to future studies of Penisular Arabic, particularly the varieties of Arabic spoken in Eastern Arabia, and to comparative studies of Arabic dialects.

3. The Present Study

A Short Reference Grammar of Gulf Arabic, based on the dialect of Abu Dhabi, U.A.E., presents an explicit outline of the phonology, morphology, and syntax of Gulf Arabic. It is the result of the author's field work in Abu Dhabi, Bahrain, and Qatar during the periods of February through May of 1970, September 1970 through June 1971, and the following summer months (June through August) of 1972 through 1975. Initially, a frequency word list of about 3,000 items for *A Basic Course in Gulf Arabic* was compiled from recordings which this investigator had made of spontaneous, unprepared narratives and conversations of unsophisticated Gulf

Arabs in different situations, such as greetings, telephone conversations, comments, interviews, etc. Later, there was an active search for tales, fables, anecdotes, and stories from storytellers, poets, and other native speakers.

The present work seeks to fill some of the important gaps that presently exist in linguistic and language studies of Peninsular Arabic, especially that of the United Arab Emirates. It is linguistically oriented and the analysis uses different techniques for the description of language. The book is usable to students who have already acquired (or are acquiring) a knowledge of Gulf Arabic; to teachers who intend to use it as a checklist of grammatical points; and to Arabic linguists and dialectologists who will use it as a source of information about this dialect. It will also serve larger groups, namely, petroleum company employees, government consultants, technical experts, and others who have communicative and linguistic interests in the Arabian Gulf area. It will be useful, for instance, to the staff and personnel of the U.S. Naval bases in Bahrain and Dhahran and the newly established American embassies in Abu Dhabi, Bahrain, and Qatar.

4. The Native Speakers

The native speakers ("informants") whose speech served as the basis for the language of the present work are semi-educated and unsophisticated bona fide Gulf Arabs in Abu Dhabi. They have relation ties with other Gulf Arabs in Bahrain and Qatar and have come in contact with a great number of Arab immigrants working in the Gulf: Jordanians, Palestinians, Lebanese, Syrians, Iraqis, Egyptians, etc. The influence of the dialects of those immigrants on the local dialects has been so great that Gulf Arabs tend to emulate other dialects, especially Levantine and Egyptian. The author has frequently run across contrast of styles in the same speaker on different occasions.

TRANSCRIPTION

Consonants

Symbol	*Approx. Sound*	*Symbol*	*Approx. Sound*
’	(glottal stop)	p	*p* in *pen*
b	*b* in *big*	q	———
č	*ch* in *church*	r	Spanish *r* in *caro*
d	*d* in *dog*	s	*s* in *sip*
f	*f* in *fat*	ṣ	———
g	*g* in *God*	š	*sh* in *ship*
ġ	Parisian *r* in *Paris*	t	*t* in *tall*
h	*h* in *hat*	ṭ	*t* in *tot*
H	———	w	*w* in *win*
j	*j* in *jam*	x	German *ch* in *Nacht*
k	*k* in *skim*	y	*y* in *yet*
l	*l* in *lathe*	z	*z* in *zeal*
ḷ	*l* in *bell*	θ	*th* in *thin*
m	*m* in *mat*	ð	*th* in *this*
n	*n* in *nap*	ð̣	———
		q	———

Vowels

Short	*Approx. Sound*	*Long*	*Approx. Sound*
i	*i* in *sit*	ii	*ea* in *seat*
a	———	aa	*a* in *hat*
		ee	———
u	*u* in *put*	uu	*oo* in *food*
o	British *o* in *pot*	oo	British *aw* in *law*

Symbols and Abbreviations

→	item on the left is changed into item on the right
←	item on the right is derived from item on the left
*	indicates an ungrammatical utterance
AP	active participle
PP	passive participle
C	consonant
C_1	first consonant
C_2	second consonant
C_3	third consonant
N	noun
N	noun head
V	vowel
V-ed	passive participle
GA	Gulf Arabic
MSA	Modern Standard Arabic
( )	item enclosed is optional, e.g., *mu(u)(b)* can be read as *mu, muu, muub,* or *mub,* or explanatory, e.g., (English) is from English, (m.s.) is masculine singular, (p.) is plural, etc.

adj.	adjective	neg.	negative
adv.	adverb	obj.	object
alt.	alternate	p.	plural
coll.	collective	s.	singular
dim.	diminutive	s.th.	something
f.	feminine	s.o.	some
imp.	imperative	subj.	subject
intra.	intransitive	tra.	transitive
lit.	literally	var.	variant
loc.	locative	vd	voiced
m.	masculine	vl	voiceless

PART ONE

THE PHONOLOGY OF GULF ARABIC

Diagram I
CONSONANTS

		Bilabial	Labiodental	Interdental	Pharyngealized	Dental	Alveolar Pharyngealized	Alveolar	Alveo-Palatal	Velar	Uvular	Pharyngeal	Glottal
Stops	vl vd	p b				t d	ṭ			k g	q		'
Fricatives	vl vd		f	θ ð	 ð̣	s z	ṣ		š	x ġ		H 9	h
Affricates	vl vd							č j					
Nasals	vd	m						n					
Laterals	vd					l	ḷ						
Flap	vd							r					
Semivowel	vd								y	w			

Diagram II
VOWELS

1. Short

	Front	Central	Back
High	i		u
Middle			o
Low		a	

2. Long

	Front	Central	Back
High	ii		uu
Middle	ee		oo
Low		aa	

1. CONSONANTS

The consonant sounds below are described in terms of point of articulation (e.g., bilabial, labiodental, etc.) and manner of articulation (e.g., stops, fricatives, etc.). Among the consonant sounds of Gulf Arabic, the stops, fricatives, and affricates may be either voiceless or voiced. The voiceless sound is one which is produced without vibration in the vocal cords, e.g., the *t* sound in English *pat.* A voiced sound is produced with vibration in the vocal cords, e.g., the *d* sound in English *pad.* The voiceless-voiced pairs in American English are:

1. Stops: p-b, t-d k-g
2. Fricatives: f-v, θ-ð, s-z, š-ž
3. Affricates: č-j

Those of GA are:

1. Stops: p-b, t-d, k-g
2. Fricatives: θ-ð, s-z, x-ġ, H-9
3. Affricates: č-j

1.1 Stops: p,b,t,d,ṭ,k,g,q,'

A stop is a sound which is produced by halting the passage of air by a complete closure at some point along the vocal tract, and then releasing the air.

p: voiceless bilabial stop

Similar to English *p* as in *pin.*

This sound occurs rarely in GA. It is found in words of foreign origin:

pamp	'pump' (English)	peep	'pipe' (English)
parda	'curtain' (Persian)	pyaaḷa	'small glass' (Hindi)

b: voiced counterpart of *p*
Similar to English *b:*

b(i)9iir	'camel'
yabi	'he wants'
mu(u)(b)	'not'

t: voiceless dental stop
Similar to English *t:*

twannas	'he had a good time, enjoyed himself'
daxtar	'doctor'
kabat	'cupboard; wardrobe'

ṭ: pharyngealized counterpart of *t*

t and *ṭ* constitute the first pair of plain and pharyngealized consonants that we will take up. In the production of *t,* the tip of the tongue touches the back of the upper teeth; for the pharyngealized *ṭ* the tongue, instead of remaining relaxed as for plain *t,* is tense and a little retracted. *t* is a little aspirated, i.e., pronounced with a little burst of air, while *ṭ* is unaspirated. *ṭ,* like any other pharyngealized consonant sound, takes the backed pronunciation of adjacent vowels, while *t* takes the fronted variety.

ṭaaH	'he fell down'
9aṭni	'give (m.s.) me!'
banaaṭḷiin	'(pairs of) pants'
baṭṭal	'he opened'
ð̣aġṭ	'pressure'
gaṭṭ	'he threw away s.th.'

d: voiced counterpart of *t*
Similar to English *d:*

diriiša	'window'
'adri	'I know'
čabd	'liver'

k: voiceless velar stop
Similar to English *k*:

kuuli	'workman'
killa	'all of it'
seekal	'bicycle'
m(u)baarak	'blessed'

(For k → č, see APPENDIX III.)

g: voiced counterpart of *k*

This sound, similar to English *g* as in *good, bag,* etc., mainly occurs in foreign words:

garaaj	'garage' (English)
gafša	'spoon; ladle' (Turkish)
bugša	'envelope; bundle' (Persian)
jigaara	'cigarette' (English)
jimrig	'customs, duty' (Persian)
rig	'rig' (English)

In a few words it corresponds to MSA[1] *q:*

gaaḷ	'he said'	gaṭu	'cat'
gaṣṣaab	'butcher'	geeđ̣	'summer; (summer) heat'
gaḷam	'pencil; pen'	baag	'he stole'
ṣagir	'falcon, hawk'	naaga	'camel (f.)'
foog	'up; above'	'azrag	'blue'

q: voiceless uvular stop

This sound can be produced by trying to say a *k*-sound farther and farther back or by trying to pull the root of the tongue straight back as far as possible. It occurs in some words and classicisms in the speech of most educated Gulf Arabs.

Examples:

qadiim	'old; ancient'
qisim	'section, part'
l-qaahira	'Cairo (f.)'
ṣadiiq	'friend'

1. In this study MSA and literary Arabic are used interchangeably.

(For q → ġ and ġ → q, see APPENDIX II.)

': glottal stop

This sound does not exist in English as a distinctive sound. It is not a full-fledged phoneme in English, and it is not represented in regular writing. It is produced by all speakers of English in vowel-initial isolated words, e.g., *above, erase, ink,* etc. It sometimes occurs as a variant of *t* as in some dialects of English (e.g., *bottle, button,* etc., with the glottal stop instead of *-tt-*). It is also used, e.g., instead of the *h* in the English interjections: *oh-oh!* In GA ' is a distinctive sound; it occurs mainly in word-initial position:

'aana	'I'	'ubu	'father'
'ii na9am	'yes, certainly'	'ihni	'here'

It should be noted that in forms corresponding to MSA initially hamzated verbs, the glottal stop is sometimes not heard, e.g., *ya* 'he came' and *xað* 'he took' are heard rather than *'aya* and *'axað*. In postvocalic positions, however, it is retained, as in:

huwa 'arduni 'he is Jordanian' and *si'al* 'he asked'

It rarely occurs medially and finally: *l-'ardun* 'Jordan,' *si'al* 'he asked.' It usually changes into *l* when preceded by the definite article:

'ahil 'folks; relatives' + *l-* → l-lahil '(the) folks; (the) relatives'

'akil 'food; eating' + *l-* → l-lakil '(the) food; (the) eating'

1.2 Fricatives: f,θ,ð,ð̣,s,z,ṣ,š,x,ġ,H,9,h

During the production of a fricative, the air stream that passes along the vocal tract is not completely stopped as in the case of stops, but is allowed to pass with audible friction. The fricatives of GA are:

f: voiceless labiodental fricative

Similar to the English *f* sound in *fat* . The air stream is impeded between the lips and the teeth.

fannaš	'he quit work, resigned'
ftarr	'he turned around'
šifittum	'I saw them'

saalfa	'story, anecdote'
wilf	'valve'
Haaff	'dry'

θ: voiceless interdental fricative[2]
Similar to English *th* in *thin* and *Heath.*

θaani	'second'
l-laθneen	'Monday'
θilθ	'one third'

ð: voiced counterpart of θ
Similar to English *th* in *this, rather,* and *lathe.*

ðaak	'that (one)'
haðeel	'these'

ð̣: pharyngealized counterpart of ð

The dot under ð̣ represents pharyngealization, traditionally known as "emphasis." A pharyngealized sound is pronounced with the tongue farther back in the mouth; the lips are rounded or protruded slightly. In producing the plain non-pharyngealized ð the tongue is relaxed and its tip protrudes a little beyond the edges of the upper and the lower teeth. For the pharyngealized ð̣ on the other hand, the tongue is tense, lower in the middle, and more raised toward the back part. Note that this changes the quality of adjacent vowels, especially *a* and *aa,* and gives a 'hollow' or 'backed' effect. (The *aa* sound in *ðaa9* 'he broadcast,' for instance, is similar to the *a* in English *that,* but it changes to a sound similar to the *a* sound in *hard* in the GA word *ð̣aa9* 'he, it, got lost.') ð-ð̣ is the second pair of plain and pharyngealized consonants.

ð̣aaj	'he got fed up'
'abu ð̣abi	'Abu Dhabi'
gið̣ab	'he grabbed'
beeð̣	'eggs'

s: voiceless dental fricative
Similar to English *s* in *sip.*

---

2. It is interesting to note that in the speech of the Shiah sect in Bahrain, the sound θ does not exist; *f* is used instead. Thus, *faani, l-lafneen,* and *filf* are used instead of *θaani, l-laθneen,* and *θilθ*, respectively.

simač	'fish'
winsa	'fun, good time'
čiis	'bag; sack'

z: voiced counterpart of *s*

zeen	'well; fine, good'
ma9aaziib	'owners, proprietors'
raziif	'celebration; merry-making'
baariz	'ready'

ṣ: pharyngealized counterpart of *s*

s and *ṣ* constitute the third pair of plain and pharyngealized consonants. In the production of *ṣ* the front part of the tongue is in the same position for *s*, but the central part is depressed and the back part raised toward the velum. Pharyngealized *ṣ* has a lower pitch than plain *s*.

ṣbayy	'boy; servant'
ṣakk	'he shut, closed the door'
gaṣiir	'short, not tall'
girṭaas	'paper'

š: voiceless alveopalatal fricative
Similar to English *sh* in *ship*.

šayy	'thing; something'
šeeba	'old man'
š-šaarja	'Sharja'
diriiša	'window'
dašš	'he entered'
našš	'he woke up'

x: voiceless velar fricative

This sound is similar to Scottish *ch* in *loch* and German *ch* in *Nacht*. For the production of *x* the tongue is in the same position as for *k* but is allowed to move down just a little bit in order to let the air pass through. Examples:

xaliij	'gulf'	xuṭṭaar	'guests'
mixtilif	'different'	'uxu	'brother'

yiṭbax	'he cooks'	liix	'fishing net'

ġ: voiced counterpart of *x*

This sound is produced in gargling; it is close in quality to the Parisian r as in *Paris, rien,* etc.

In GA *ġ* sometimes corresponds to *q,* the voiceless uvular stop (see APPENDIX II).

ġašmar	'he joked with s.o.'
l-ġaaḏ̣i	'the judge; the magistrate'
laġa	'language'
faariġ	'empty'
ġitra	'head dress'
stiġlaal	'independence'
baġa	'he wanted, liked'
manaatiġ	'regions, districts'

H: voiceless pharyngeal fricative

For the production of *H* the muscles of the throat are tense and the passageway at the back of the throat becomes constricted. *x* has been described above as a voiceless velar fricative. In producing *x* the back of the tongue must come near the soft palate; for *H* the tongue must *not* approach it.

From the writer's own experience in teaching Arabic, *H* is one of the two most difficult sounds for native speakers of English. The other sound is *9,* which is described below. The following exercise has been tried with students in order to help them recognize and produce an acceptable *H* sound: whisper and repeat the phrase 'Hey you!' as loudly and as deep in your throat as you can; then say only 'Hey,' elongating the initial *h* sound, 'Hhhhhhhhhhhey.' Repeat this with the muscles used in gagging tensed up. This would be an acceptable approximation of *H.* An alternative suggestion is to start with 'ah!', whispering it as loudly as you can. Now repeat it and narrow the pharynx by moving the root of the tongue back, and raising the larynx.

Haaff	'dry, not wet'
Hammaam	'bathroom, latrine'
laHam	'meat'
mHassin	'barber'

yiHH	‘watermelons’
ṣ-ṣabaaH	‘(in) the morning’

9: voiced counterpart of *H*

There is nothing in the English sound system that is similar or even close to either *H* or *9*. In the production of *9* the muscles in the throat become very tense and the passageway at the back of the throat becomes constricted. The following exercises would yield an approximation of the *9* sound: say ‘ah,’ and then tense up the muscles of your throat as in gagging. Another exercise is to try to imitate the bleating of a sheep ‘baaa.’ Tighten your neck and throat muscles as if someone were choking you. The result would be a strangled or a squeezed sound, probably an acceptable *9* sound.

9aayla	‘family’	9eeš	‘rice’
maa9uun	‘dish; plate’	li9baw	‘they played’
ṣubi9	‘finger’	rabi9	‘(group of) people’

h: voiceless glottal fricative

Similar to English *h* as in *hat*. Contrary to English the GA *h* sound may occur in a pre-consonant position, a post-consonant position, or at the end of a word.

haaða	‘this’	hamba	‘mangoes’
bhaam	‘thumb’	karhab(a)	‘electricity’
hduum	‘clothes’	hini, hni	‘here’

’a9uuðu billaah! ‘God forbid!’

1.3 Affricates: *č* and *j*

č: voiceless alveopalatal affricate

This sound is similar to the English *ch* sound in *church* and *urchin*. In the following forms *č* is a variant of *k*:

čaan	‘he was’	Hači	‘talk, conversation’
čoočab	‘water spring’	čan9ad	‘kind of fish’
9ačwa	‘stick’	yabči	‘he cries, weeps’
diič	‘rooster’	simač	‘fish’

In the following forms only *č* occurs:[3]

9aṣaač	'your stick'
'asmič	'your name'
'uxuuč	'your brother'
ḍ̣arabč	'he hit you'
9aṭaač	'he gave you'

In foreign words *č* occurs as an original sound:

čaay	'tea' (Persian)
čingaaḷ	'fork' (Persian)
čuula	'fireplace' (Hindi-Urdu)
kalač	'(car) clutch' (English)
lanč	'launch (n.)' (English)
čayyak	'he checked' (English)

j: voiced counterpart of *č*

Similar to English *j* in *judge* and *dg* in *edge.* In most instances literary *j* corresponds to GA *y:*

yaahil	'child'	m(a)siid	'mosque'
yiit	'I came'	rayyaal	'man'
yaay	'(act. part.) coming'	mooy	'waves'

(See APPENDIX I for j → y and APPENDIX II for q → j.)

1.4 Nasals: *m* and *n*

Similar to the English sounds *m* and *n* in *man* and *night,* respectively.

m:	m(a)siid	'mosque'	'asmaač	'fishes'
	gḷaam(a)	'pens; pencils'	tamaam	'exactly'
n:	na99aaša	'dancing girl'	lanč	'small boat'
	flaan	'so and so'	leen	'when, as soon as'

3. See APPENDIX III.

1.5 Laterals: *l* and *ḷ*

l: dental lateral

While there is no similar sound in American English, there is an approximation of the GA *l* in words like *lean, lack, late,* etc., where the *l* sound is initial and prevocalic. In other positions the American *l* is more or less pharyngealized, depending upon the dialects of the speakers. GA *l* is a *plain* sound as opposed to the dark *l* as in American English *hill* and *belly*. In the production of GA *l* the tip of the tongue touches the tooth ridge (slightly farther forward than in English), and the middle of the tongue is low.

laHam	'meat'	leen	'when; until'
l-mi9ris	'the bridegroom'	yilas	'he sat down'
zuuliyya	'carpet'	čalma	'word'
naariil	'coconut'	9ayal	'therefore'

ḷ: pharyngealized counterpart of *l*

l-ḷ constitute the fourth pair of plain and pharyngealized consonants. *ḷ* is similar to the American English *l* sound in *tall, bill,* and *silly*. The occurrence of *ḷ* is more frequent in GA than in other Arabic dialects such as Syrian, Labanese, Jordanian, Palestinian, or Egyptian. Initially, it occurs only in the environment of pharyngealized consonants:

ḷ-ḷaṣil	'(the) origin'	ḷaṭiif	'nice'
gḷaaṣ	'glass (cup)'	'aḷḷa	'God'
magḷi	'fried'	gaḷam	'pen, pencil'
naxaḷ	'palm trees'	gabiḷ	'before'

1.6 Flap: *r*

GA *r* is not like American English *r;* the former is a consonant while the latter is more of a vowel than a consonant. For the production of *r* most Americans curl the tongue up toward the roof of the mouth as *car, far,* etc., and round their lips when the *r* sound is word-initial or syllable-initial, as in *ream, rock, marry,* etc. GA *r* is a tongue flap; it is produced by striking the tip of the tongue against the roof of the mouth. It is similar to the *r* in Spanish or Italian *caro* 'dear.' In the speech of most Americans, intervocalic *t* sounds similar to GA *r: city, pity, Betty,* etc.

raaH	'he went'	rasta	'paved road'
ribyaan	'shrimp'	rifiij	'friend; companion'
ġarbaḷ	'he bothered'	girṭaaṣ	'paper'
šakar	'sugar'	saar	'he left, went'

1.7 Semivowels: *w* and *y*

Similar to English *w* and *y* in *way* and *yet,* respectively. In most examples literary *j* corresponds to or is used interchangeably with GA *y.* For a discussion of this see APPENDIX I.

w:	waayid	'much, a lot'	wilda	'his son'
	zuwaaj	'marriage'	leewa	'folk dance'

For examples with final *w* see 3.1 below.

y:	yaabis	'dry'	yamm	'close to, near'
	ḍ̵iHiyya	'slaughter animal'	9ayyil	'child'

2. VOWELS

Short and Long. GA has in its sound system four short vowels *(i,a,u,o)* and five long vowels. Four long vowels correspond to the four short ones *(i-ii, a-aa, u-uu, o-oo)* and the fifth long vowel is *ee.* Unlike English, vowels in GA, as in most other dialects of Arabic, have a wide range of values, depending upon the environment in which the vowel is used, i.e., the type of consonants, other vowels, stressed or unstressed syllables, etc. In the sections below major variants of vowels will be described.

i: high front

Similar to English *i* in *bit,* though not so high and tense. This variant occurs when it is not word-final or preceded by semivowel *y* or in the contiguity of pharyngealized consonants. Examples:

killahum	'all of them (m.)'
simač	'fish'
finyaan	'(coffee) cup'
xašim	'nose'

Another variant of this sound is one between the *i* sound in *bit* and the *u* sound in *club:*

li-9raag	'Iraq'
('i)mbaarak	'Mubarak (male's name)'

i is often retracted and lowered in the environment of pharyngealized consonants:

ṣidj	'truth'	baṭin	'belly'
ġaaḏ̣i	'judge (n.)'	ḏ̣iHiyya	'slaughter animal'

ii: long counterpart of *i*

This long vowel is approximately twice as long as *i* and has a different quality. It is similar to the English sound *i* in machine, but is a monophthong and does not have any glide quality:

'ii na9am	'indeed, certainly'	fii	'there is; there are'
siččiin	'knife'	rayaayiil	'men'
tagriiban	'approximately'	ḏiib	'wolf'

ii is deeper and more audible in the environment of pharyngealized consonants:

mariiḏ̣	'sick'	basiiṭ	'simple'
naḏ̣iif	'clean'	ḷaṭiif	'nice'

a: short low front, central or back

a has a low back quality in the environment of pharyngealized consonants and frequently before or after /q/. This sound is similar to the *a* sound in *father* but shorter and farther back:

ṣakk l-baab	'he shut the door'
šanṭa	'bag, suitcase'
rṭab	'fresh dates'
rgaṣaw	'they danced'
qadiim	'old; ancient'
raqam	'number'

Before or after the pharyngeals *9* and *H,* or any other plain consonant, *a* is farther front than the *a* in *father;* its quality ranges between the *e* in *pen* and *a* in *pan:*

9adil	'correct(ly); just(ly)'
ba9ad	'too, also'
yim9a	'Friday'
9awar	'one-eyed'

Hamar	'red'
faHam	'charcoal, coal'
ribaH	'he gained'

aa: long counterpart of *a*

Long *aa* is more pharyngealized in GA than in most other dialects of Arabic because of the influence of other languages that are often heard, such as Persian and Urdu. It has a clear retracted and lowered quality in the contiguity of pharyngealized consonants, palatals, velars, pharyngeals, and glottals:

ṭaaH	'he fell down'
š-šaarja	'Sharja'
9ala hawaač	'as you wish'
nšaaḷḷa	'God willing'
gṣaar	'short (p.)'
ð̣aabiṭ	'(army) officer'
čaay	'tea'
biškaar	'servant'
xaayis	'rotten'
Haaḷa	'condition'
haadif	'Hadif (male's name)'

Elsewhere it has a more fronted quality:

saal	'it flowed'
rummaan	'pomegranates'
taab	'he repented'
saatt[4]	'sixth'
paariis	'Paris'
yaam9a	'university (f.)'

u: short high back rounded

Close to the *oo* sound in English *book*. This variant occurs in a medial or final position, not in the environment of a pharyngealized consonant:

4. Variant of *saadis*.

'uxu	'brother'
gabguuba	'crab; lobster'
murta	'his wife'
raadu	'radio'
'ubu	'father'
beettum	'their home'

In the environment of pharyngealized consonants or following *H* or *9*, *u* is more backed and lowered than in the examples above. Its quality is between *a* in *fall* and *u* in *full:*

ṣubi9	'finger'
buṭbuṭa	'motorcycle'
ð̣uhur	'noontime'
Hurma	'woman'
9ugiḷ	'head bands'

uu: long counterpart of *u*

uu is a monophthong. It is similar to English *oo* in *moon*. In *moon* the lips become more rounded toward the end of the vowel; but for GA *uu* the lips maintain the same rounded position throughout:

'ubuuy(a)	'my father'
buuz	'mouth'
ð̣ruus	'teeth'
mu(u)(b)	'not'
yithaawšuun	'they fight, are fighting'
yaryuur	'shark'
gabguuba	'crab; lobster'

o: short mid back rounded

This vowel occurs only in a few words. It is a less frequently used variant of *-aw*.

lo	'if' (var. *law*)
gaaḷo	'they said' (var. *gaaḷaw*)
twaag9o	'they quarreled with each other' (var. *twaag9aw*)

oo: long counterpart of *o*

GA *oo* is approximately twice as long as *o*. It is similar to the vowel *aw* in British English *law;* it does not have any off-glide quality. Examples:

yoom	'day'
9ood	'big, large'
gaaḷoo	'they said it'
zaxxoo	'they caught, found, him'
ṣoob	'in the direction of'

ee: long mid-front unrounded

This is the only long vowel that does not have a short counterpart. It is similar to, but not the same as, English *ai* in *main,* for example. In English *main* there is a glide toward the semi-vowel *y* at the end of the vowel; GA *ee* as in *θneen* 'two' is monophthongal and has no glide.

l-laθneen (var. *l-'aθneen*)	'Monday'
leet	'light'
naš̌šeena	'we woke up'
geeḏ	'summer (heat)'
ṣeef	'summer'
9alee	'on him'

3. SOUND COMBINATIONS

3.1 Diphthongs

A diphthong is a combination in one syllable of two vowel sounds, a vowel and a semivowel (*w* or *y*). The voice glides with a falling intonation from the first to the second sound and the mouth position is different at the end of the diphthong. There are five diphthongs in GA:

iw: This diphthong is not common:

9iwraan	'one-eyed (m.p.)'
('i)wlaad	'boys'
mla9iwzatni	'(she) having bothered me'

iy: This diphthong is used in free variation with the long vowel *ii:*

'iy na9am	'yes, indeed, certainly'
'iyda	'his hand'
wiyya	'with'

aw: This diphthong frequently occurs in the second or third person masculine plural suffixes:

gaaḷaw	'they said' (cf. *gaaḷoo* 'they said it')
riHtaw	'you went'
šribaw	'they drank' (cf. *šriboo* 'they drank it')
yaw (var. *jaw*)	'they came'
taww-	'just' (as in *tawwa ya* 'he has just come')

aaw is the long counterpart of *aw:*

yaaw	'they came' (var. *yaw* or *jaw*)
gṭaawti	'my cats'
daaw	'dhow, boat'

ay:	'ay(ya)	'which? any'
	maynuun	'crazy'
	9alayy(a)	'on me'
	mayy	'water'

aay is the long counterpart of *ay:*

šaayfa	'I have seen him'
maay (var. *mayy*)	'water'
waraay	'behind me'
čaay	'tea'
raay	'opinion; idea'
wiyyaay	'with me'

uw: This diphthong occurs only as a variant of the third person masculine plural suffix. See the diphthong *aw* above.

gaaḷuw	'they (m.) said'
šribuw	'they (m.) drank'
kaluw	'they (m.) ate'

3.2 Consonant Clusters

3.2.1 Double Consonants

In terms of length consonants in Arabic are referred to as single (i.e., short) or double (i.e., long) or doubled consonants.[5] Clusters of two identical consonants, traditionally known as geminates, occur frequently in GA. Double consonants in English occur across word boundaries, e.g., *straight to, hot tea, guess so,* etc., and occasionally within compound words and words with prefixes or suffixes, e.g., *cattail, unnamed, thinness,* etc. Double consonants in GA occur medially, finally, and, in a few cases, initially.

Initial

Initially, double consonants are usually those formed by the combination of a prefix (the article prefix, or a conjunction, or a verb prefix) and the first stem consonant. Examples:

r-rayyaal	'the man'
l-laHad	'Sunday'
d-dreewil	'the driver'
w-waṣix	'and dirty'
w-waafag	'and he agreed'
tčayyak	'it was checked'
jjaawib	'you (m.s.) answer'
ddarras	'it was taught'

Medial

Any double consonant may occur in an intervocalic position. -ġġ- and -*qq*- are rare, however.

dabba	'car trunk'	gaṭṭat	'she threw away'
madrasatta	'her school'	tfaððal	'please!'
('i)θ-θalaaθ	'Tuesday'	na99aaša	'female dancer'
najjaar	'carpenter'	ṣakkeet	'I closed'
naggaṣ	'he decreased'	tsallaf	'he borrowed'
maHHad	'nobody'	nšaaḷḷa	'God willing'
mitwaxxir	'late; belated'	naxxi(y)	'chick peas'

5. See Mark C. Cowell, *A Reference Grammar of Damascus Arabic,* Georgetown University Press, 1964, p. 23.

Haddaag	'fisherman'	xammaam	'garbage collector'
čaððaab	'liar'	bannad	'he shut'
ṭarraš	'he sent'	sahhal	'he made easy'
('al)Hazza	'now'	9awwar	'he hurt (s.o.)'
mHassin	'barber'	Hayya	'he greeted (s.o.)'
naššeet	'I woke up'	siččiin	'knive'
Haṣṣal	'he obtained'	ṣaffaj	'he clapped'

For the occurrence of a consonant sound after a double consonant see 4.3.2 below.

Final

Any double consonant may occur finally except for *g, q̇,* and *h,* which have not been noted. A final double consonant is not pronounced differently from a final single consonant, e.g., final *l* in *'aqall* 'less' is the same as final *l* in *tafal* 'he spat' as far as the sound itself is concerned. The difference is in stress: *'aqáll* and *táfal* (see 5. STRESS, below). A few examples are given below:

ð̣abb	'lizard'	'aqall	'less'
Hagg	'belonging to'	'ayann	'crazier'
lakk	'thousand'	maHall	'place'
nuṣṣ	'half'	'ayadd	'newer'
yximm	'he sweeps'	dagg	'he knocked'
zaxx	'he caught s.o.'	xaṭṭ	'letter'
9að̣ð̣	'he bit s.o.'	barr	'desert'
dašš	'he entered'	Haaff	'dry'
siHH	'dates'	ṣbayy	'young boy'
Hað̣ð̣	'luck'	saatt	'sixth'

If a suffix beginning with a consonant is added to a final double consonant, the double consonant is reduced to a single consonant. See 4.3.2 below.

3.2.2 Two-Consonant Clusters

A consonant cluster is here defined as any combination of two or more different consonants. In GA two-consonant clusters occur frequently.

Initial

Many two-consonant clusters occur initially. The following are examples:

y9arif	'he knows'	yHasid	'he envies'
rṭab	'fresh dates'	š-gadd	'how many (much)?'
nxaḷa	'palm tree'	ṣxaḷa	'young goat, kid'
štaġal	'he worked'	mxabbaḷ	'crazy'
bhaam	'thumb'	sbiil	'(smoking) pipe'
jnaaza	'funeral'	thaawaš	'he quarreled'
Hṭaba	'piece of wood'	fHama	'piece of coal'
rguba	'neck'	ntiras	'it was filled with s.th.'
gfaaš	'ladles'	hwaaša	'quarrel'
gmaaš	'pearl'	šyara	'tree'
stariiH	'rest!'	rweed	'radish'
msiid	'mosque'	štika	'he complained; he filed a suit'

Medial

Most two-consonant clusters may occur between two vowel sounds. Examples:

laġwiyya	'talkative'	parda	'curtain'
matruus	'filled with s.th.'	yamkin	'maybe, probably'
tagdar	'she can'	mixtilif	'different'
maṭaarzi	'bodyguard'	margad	'sleeping place'
čalma	'word'	ġatma	'mute'
'amlaH	'grey'	liHya	'beard'
bistaan	'garden; orchard'	'iϑra	'corn'
'afwaat	'feet'	dirwaaza	'doorway, gate'
naθya	'female'	maylis	'living room'
xašmič	'your nose'	bugša	'envelope'
d-dreewil	'the driver'	darzan	'dozen'
'aṣmax	'deaf'	la9waz	'he bothered'
9ibri	'passenger'	rubbiyya	'rupee'
9ačwa	'stick'	l-yim9a	'Friday'

Final two-consonant clusters are fairly common:

9awwart	'I, you, injured'	dirast	'I, you, studied'
farg	'difference'	wiṣṭ	'middle'
ṣidj	'truth'	9arafč	'he knew you'
9abd	'slave; negro'	čabš	'ram'
Halj	'mouth'	la9wazt	'I, you, bothered'
šarg	'east'	čabd(a)	'liver'
ð̣irs	'tooth'	waġt	'time'

3.2.3 Three-consonant Clusters

Three-consonant clusters are rare in GA. Initially they may occur in imperatives, e.g., *('i)striiH* (var. *stariiH*[6]) 'rest (m.s.).' Medially, they are very rare. The only example noted is *ġunṭraaz* 'contract.' Between word boundaries three- or four-consonant clusters (usually with the helping vowel *i*) are common (see 4.1 below). The following are examples of three-consonant clusters without the helping vowel:

gaṭ9 li-xšuum	'the cutting off of noses'
šarg 9uman	'east of Oman'
waladk jaasim	'your son, Jasim'
čabd xaayis	'rotten liver'
gilt-la	'I said to him; I told him'
farg waayid	'big difference'
bank bu ð̣abi	'Bank of Abu Dhabi'

4. MAJOR SOUND CHANGES

4.1 The Helping Vowel *i*

The helping vowel *i*, sometimes referred to as an anaptyctic or prosthetic helping vowel, is inserted within consonant clusters. Its occurrence does not affect meaning; it is used only as an aid to pronunciation. This feature is known as anaptyxis. In GA it is not usually used with an initial two-consonant cluster:

6. The variant *stariiH* is more commonly used.

šyara	'tree'
tguul	'you say' or 'she says'
rguba	'neck'
rṭab	'fresh (not very ripe) dates'
štaġal	'he worked'
stariiH	'(imp.) rest'
ḓraba	'he hit him'
n9aya	'ewe'
mṣaxxan	'running a temperature'
t9arif	'you know' or 'she knows'
yxadim	'he serves'

A three-consonant cluster is usually encountered in two cases:

A. When a word ends with a single consonant and is followed by a word beginning with a double consonant or a two-consonant cluster. In such a case the helping vowel is used after the first of three consonants or between word boundaries. Examples:

min-i-š-šaarja	'from Sharja'
fluus-i-d-dreewil	'the driver's money'
liHyat-i-r-rayyaal	'the man's beard'
leeš-i-d-diššʔ	'Why do you enter?'
leen-i-truuH	'when you go'
leeš-i-truuHiin	'Why do you (f.s.) go?'
ma yriid-i-xmaam	'he does not want garbage'
rayyaal-i-mxabbaḷ	'crazy man'
t9arfiin-i-š-kiθir?	'Do you (f.s.) know how many (much)?'
yriid-i-yruuH	'he wants to go'
yriiduun-i-ysaafruun	'they want to travel'
leen-i-truuHiin	'when you (f.s.) go'
raaH-i-štika	'he went and filed a suit'
ba9deen-i-t9arfiin	'you (f.s.) will know later on'

The forms *yriid yiruuH* and *yriiduun yisaafruun* are also heard.

B. When a word ends with a double consonant or a two-consonant cluster and is followed by a word beginning with a single consonant. In such a case no helping vowel is used. Examples:

Hagg 9ali	'belonging to Ali'
'ayann minnak	'crazier than you'
yximm wiyyaahum	'He sweeps with them.'
ṣikk Haljak!	'Shut your mouth!'

If the article prefix is used before a two-consonant cluster word, the helping vowel precedes the two-consonant cluster:

wiyya l-i-9yaal	'with the children'
min l-i-wlaad	'from the boys'
min l-i-mxabbaḷ	'from the crazy one'

Other examples are: *l-i-Hkuuma* 'the government,' *l-i-bdiwi* 'the Bedouin,' *l-i-gmaaš* 'the pearl,' *l-i-Hsaab* 'the bill, the (bank) account,' *l-i-fluus* 'the money,' *l-i-ṣxaḷa* 'the young goat, kid,' *l-i-fHama* 'the piece of coal, charcoal,' etc. Such examples are transcribed *li-Hkuuma, li-bdiwi,* etc., throughout this study.

A four-consonant cluster, which would be encountered when a word ending with a double consonant or a two-consonant cluster is followed by a word beginning with a double consonant or a two-consonant cluster, is prevented by inserting *i* between the two words. Examples:

bišt-i-bdiwiyya	'a Bedouin's dress'
min-i-dbayy	'from Dubai'
wild-i-kleeθim	'Kleithim's son, child'
čint-i-hnaak?	'Were you there?'
9abd-i-mxabbaḷ	'crazy slave'
Haṣṣalt-i-smiča	'I found, got, a fish'

4.2 Assimilation

In GA the feature of assimilation covers the sound *h* when preceded by the consonant *t* and both sounds occur medially and the sounds *d, s, z, j, θ, ṭ,* and *ð̣* when preceded by initial or medial *t.* In the latter case, the *t* is almost always an inflectional prefix of the imperfect tense or the first sound in a Class V verb. Examples:

beet + -hum	→ beettum	'their house'
+ -ha	→ beetta	'her house'
+ -hin	→ beettin	'their house'

t-	+ daa9maw	→	ddaa9maw	'they collided'
t-	+ duux	→	dduux	'you smoke; she smokes'
t-	+ sallaf	→	ssallaf	'he borrowed (money)'
t-	+ zixx	→	zzixx	'you lay hands (on s.o. or s.th.)'
t-	+ zigg	→	zzigg	'you deficate; she deficates'
t-	+ θamman	→	θθamman	'it was priced'
t-	+ ṭigg	→	ṭṭigni	'you hit me; she hits me'
t-	+ ð̣aHHač	→	ð̣ð̣aHHač	'he laughed'
t-	+ θallaθ	→	θθallaθ	'it was tripled'
t-	+ ṭarraš	→	ṭṭarraš	'it was sent'

The above examples involve only assimilation. Below are some other examples that involve both anaptyxis and assimilation:

číft	+ -hum	→	*čifithum	→	čifíttum 'I saw them'
ð̣arábt	+ -ha	→	*ð̣arabitha	→	ð̣arabítta 'I hit her'
ð̣aHHákt	+ -hin	→	*ð̣aHHakithin	→	ð̣aHHakíttin 'I made them laugh'

Forms with -V*t* where V is a short vowel change *t* into *č* before a -*č* suffix. Examples:

ð̣aHHakat 'she made s.o. laugh'	+ -č	→	ð̣aHHakáčč 'She made you laugh.'
xaabarat 'she telephoned you'	+ -č	→	xaabaráčč 'She telephoned you.'
9rafat 'she knew'	+ -č	→	9rafáčč 'She knew you.'

4.3 Elision

4.3.1 Vowel Elision

A word that ends with -VC, where -V- is any unstressed vowel, drops its -V- when any vowel-initial suffix is added to it, unless -V- is stressed in the resultant form. Examples:

'ásim 'name'	+ -a	→	'ásma 'his name'
	+ -ak	→	'ásmak 'your name'
	+ -i	→	'aśmi 'my name'
	+ -ič	→	'aśmič 'your (f.s.) name'
	+ -een	→	'asméen 'two names'

'ux́ut 'sister'	+	-a	→	'úxta 'his sister'
ftáham 'he understood'	+	-aw	→	ftáhmaw 'they understood'
	+	-at	→	ftáhmat 'she understood'
	+	-an	→	ftáhman 'they (f.) understood'

However, words of the *fá9al* pattern change into *f9ál-* when a vowel initial suffix is added except for the suffix *-een.* Examples:

gáḷam 'pen'	+	-a	→	gḷáma 'his pen'
	+	-ak	→	gḷámak 'your pen'
	+	-i	→	gḷámi 'my pen'
	+	-ič	→	gḷámič 'your (f.) pen'
	+	-een	→	gaḷaméen 'two pens'

The forms *gḷúma, gḷúmak* (or *gaḷámk*), *gḷúmi,* and *gḷúmič* (or *gaḷámč*) are also heard. Other examples are:

fáHam 'coal, charcoal':

fHáma	'his coal'
fHámi	'my coal'
fHámak (var. *faHámk*)	'your coal'
fHámič (var. *faHámč*)	'your (f.s.) coal'

báġaḷ 'mule':

bġáḷa	'his mule'
bġáḷi	'my mule'
bġáḷak (var. *baġáḷk*)	'your mule'
bġáḷič (var. *baġáḷč*)	'your (f.s.) mule'

wálad 'boy' is irregular:

wílda	'his son'
wíldi	'my son'
wíldak (var. *waládk*)	'your son'
wíldič (var. *waláčč*)	'your (f.s.) son'

9áraf 'he knew':

9ráfa	'he knew him'
9ráfak (var. *9aráfk*)	'he knew you'
9ráfič (var. *9aráfč*)	'he knew you (f.s.)'

qátal 'he killed':

qtála	'he killed him'
qtálak (var. *qatálk*)	'he killed you'
qtálič (var. *qatálč*)	'he killed you (f.s.)'

4.3.2 Consonant Elision

When a double consonant is followed by a single consonant in the same word or between word boundaries, the double consonant is reduced to one single consonant:

kill (var. *kull*) 'all; each'	+ -hum	→	kilhum (var. *kulhum*) 'all of them'
yamm 'near, close to'	+ saalim	→	yam saalim 'near Salim'
bass 'only, just'	+ maay	→	bas maay 'only water'
gaṭṭ 'he threw away'	+ -hum	→	gaṭhum[7] 'he threw them away'
	+ -ha	→	gaṭha 'he discarded her'
	+ -hin	→	gaṭhin 'he discarded them (f.)'
ywaffij 'he makes s.o. successful'	+ ak	→	ywafjak[8] 'he makes you successful'
ṣakk 'he closed'	+ -ha	→	ṣakha 'he closed it (f.)'
ṣikk '(imp.) close'	+ Haljak	→	ṣikk Haljak 'Shut your mouth!'

4.4 Pharyngealization[9]

We have seen above (see the pharyngealized consonants *ṭ,ð̣,ṣ,ḷ*) that pharyngealization is not limited only to a pharyngealized sound, but affects neighboring consonants and vowels and sometimes the whole word. Compare, e.g., *fatar* 'it became warm' and *faṭar* 'he had breakfast.' *f* in *fatar* is similar to English *f* in *fat*, but in *faṭar* the *f* sound is similar to that in *father*, i.e., it is backed and 'pharyngealized.' The quality of the vowel sound *a* is different in *fatar* from that in *faṭar*. In some analyses of Arabic *f* in *faṭar*, for

7. Such words will be transcribed with one single consonant, except between word boundaries, e.g., *kilhum* 'all of them' and *kill yoom* 'everyday.'

8. As in *'aḷḷa ywafjak!* 'good luck!' said to a man. It literally means 'May God make you successful.' *ywafjak* involves vowel elision.

9. The feature of pharyngealization is sometimes referred to as "emphasis" (see, for example, Erwin, Wallace M., *A Short Reference Grammar of Iraqi Arabic*, Georgetown University Press, Washington, D.C., 1963, pp. 13-14) or "pharyngealization" (see Cowell, *op. cit.*, p. 6, footnote).

example, would also be considered as a pharyngealized consonant. In this analysis, however, only *ṭ*, *ϑ̣*, *ṣ*, and *ḷ* are the pharyngealized consonants and other sounds affected by these pharyngealized consonants are considered plain and thus transcribed without subscript dots. In fact, pharyngealization varies from one region to another and from speaker to speaker.

5. STRESS

The stressed syllable in any given word is the one that is pronounced the loudest. In GA, stress is generally predictable, i.e., you can deduce which syllable in a word is stressed from the consonant-vowel sequence in that word. There are some exceptions, which will be pointed out as they occur. You should note the following general comments on syllable structure in GA:

1. Every syllable contains a vowel, short or long.
2. Every syllable begins with a consonant sound. The first syllable may have one, two, or three consonants initially.
3. If a word has two consonants or a double consonant medially, syllable division is between these two consonants.

There are three types of syllables in GA: short, medium, and long. A short syllable is composed of a consonant followed by a short vowel (CV). A medium syllable is composed of a consonant followed by a short vowel followed by a consonant (CVC), or a consonant cluster followed by a short vowel ($C_1 C_2 V$). A long syllable is of the following structures: CVVC, CVCC (or $CVC_1 C_2$), CCVC (or $C_1 C_2 VC$), CCVVC (or $C_1 C_2 VVC$), and CCVV (or $C_1 C_2 VV$). Other structures of syllables do not normally occur in GA, except for CVV.

Stress in GA is governed by the following two rules: (1) All words are stressed on the penultimate syllable, i.e., on the next to the last syllable, unless (2) the ultimate or final syllable is long, i.e., CVVC, CVCC (or $CVC_1 C_2$), or CCVC (or $C_1 C_2 VC$), CCVVC or $C_1 C_2 VVC$), CCVV (or $C_1 C_2 VV$), or CVV, in which case it is stressed. In the discussion below examples of the kinds of syllables in GA are cited.

A. Examples of one long syllable and one or more short or medium syllables:

Initial:	šáaffin	'he saw them'
	zóojha	'her husband'
	tlá9waz	'he was bothered'
	béettum	'their house'
	ṭṭárraš	'it was sent'
Medial:	tabíinha	'you want it'
	mitháawša	'having (f.s.) quarreled with s.o.'
	Hayáattin	'their life'
	maHáasna	'barbers' (pl. of *mHássin*)
Final:	li-9yáal	'the children'
	yið̣Hačúun	'they are laughing'
	maryamóo	'diminutive of Maryam (girl's name)'
	ð̣aHHáčč	'he made you laugh'

B. Examples of more than one long syllable:

ma9aazíibhum	'those responsible for them, their elders'
garaaṭíis	'pieces of paper' (pl. of *girṭáas*)
šuwaahíinhum	'their falcons' (pl. of *šaahíin*)
yšuufúun	'they see'
mithaawšíin	'having quarreled with each other'
maayṣíir	'(it's) impossible, it cannot happen'

Of all the long syllables only CVVC occurs in all three positions: initially, medially, and finally. CVCC (or CVC$_1$C$_2$) occurs only independently and finally as one of the doubled consonants is elided when followed by another consonant (see 4.3.2 above) and a medial three-consonant cluster is very rare in GA. Perfect tense forms with the first or second person singular suffix *-t* may have a CVCC (or CVC$_1$C$_2$) syllable finally:

'aana sikátt	'I was silent'
'inta sikátt	'you were silent'
'aana xarbáṭṭ	'I threw s.th. into disorder'
'inta xarbáṭṭ	'you threw s.th. into disorder'
fannášt	'I (you) resigned'
ṭarrášt	'I (you) sent s.th. to s.o.'
nijáHt	'I (you) succeeded'

Also perfect tense forms or nouns with the *-č* suffixed pronoun may occur finally with this syllable:

xaabaráčč	'she telephoned you'
kallamáčč	'she talked to you'
ḏaHHakáčč	'she (he) made you laugh'
simáčč	'your fish'

Similarly CCVC (or $C_1 C_2$ VC) occurs only initially as in *ṭṭárraš* 'it was sent,' *ḏḏáHHak* 'he smiled, laughed,' *tlá9waz* 'he was bothered,' etc. CCVVC (or $C_1 C_2$ VVC) occurs only initially and independently:

initially:	dduúxha	'you smoke it (f.); she smokes it (f.)'
	θθíirha	'you bring it (f.) up; she brings it (f.) up'
	gmáašhum	'their pearl'
	9yáalha	'her children'
	wláadna	'our sons'
independently:	bláaš	'free of charge'
	nzéen	'fine, O.K.'
	tmuút	'you die; she dies'

C. Examples of medium and short syllables:

yitráyyag	'he eats breakfast'
mustášfa	'hospital'
ma gaṣṣártaw	'you did your best'
máHHad	'nobody, no one'
'íklaw	'(imp.) eat (m.p.)!'
ḏrábat	'she hit'
drísan	'they studied'
waládhum	'their son'
gáḷbič	'your heart'
maktábkin	'your office'
nwáxaḏ	'it was taken'
nwákal	'it was eaten'

In forms of medium and long syllables, stress falls on the long syllable, e.g., *yitraygóon* 'they eat breakfast,' *mustašfaáy* 'my hospital,' *θneénhum* 'the two of them,' *9yaálhum* 'their children,' etc.

The syllable CVV

The syllable CVV is neither short, nor medium, nor long. As far as stress is concerned, it is treated as a long syllable. Examples:

daráahim	'money' (lit., "dirhams," p. of *dírhim*)
9alée	'on him'
9ayáayiz	'old ladies'
baáyig	'thief' (lit., "having stolen")
9aṭáa	'he gave him'
karráani	'clerk'
xallóoha	'they left her'
laġáati	'my language'
kandóora	'men's long dress, *dishdash*'

D. Examples of two CVV syllables:

gaaḷóo	'they said it (var. *gaalúu*)'
xaašúuga	'spoon'
ṣaaróo	'(dim. of *ṣaára*) Sara'
nuuróo	'(dim. of *núura*) Nora'
baa9óo	'they sold it (var. *baa9úu*)'

E. Examples of long and CVV syllables:

xaaṣmóo	'they quarreled with him (var. *xaaṣmúu*)'
saamHóoha	'they pardoned, forgave, her'
syeeyíira	'(dim. of *sayyáara*) car'
xḷeeḷíiṭa	'(dim. of *xaḷḷáaṭa*) mixer'
ṭyeeyíira	'(dim. of *ṭayyáara*) airplane'

F. Examples of CVV and long syllables:

xaabárč	'he telephoned you'
raadóoč	'they wanted you (var. *raadúuč*)'
saamáHk	'he forgave you'
Haačáač	'he spoke with you'

A short syllable is one of the structure CV. Three consecutive short syllables do not normally occur in GA (i.e., *CVCVCV).

Examples of this sequence, i.e., CVCVCV in MSA and in the speech of Arab emigrants change into CCVCV.[10] Examples:

šyára	'tree'
fHáma	'piece of coal, charcoal'
bġáḷa	'female mule'
Hmǐsa	'turtle; tortoise'
n9áya	'ewe'
ð̣rába	'he hit him'
ktába	'he wrote it'
9ráfa	'he knew him'
wrúga	'piece of paper'

G. Other examples:

maktába	'library; bookstore'
madrása	'school'
nkísar	'it was broken'
minkísir	'broken, having been broken'
9abídhum	'their slave'
nooxáða	'ship captain'
ð̣arabítta	'I hit her'

H. Note the following shift in stress:

gáabḷaw	'they met s.o.'	but	gaabḷóo	'they met him'
yitráyyag	'he eats breakfast'	but	yitrayguún	'they eat breakfast'
wálad	'boy; son'	but	waládhum	'their boy, son'
la9wázat	'she bothered'	but	la9wazáttum	'she bothered them'
9ráfaw	'they knew'	but	9rafoóni	'they knew me'
'ásim	'name'	but	'asímha	'her name'
símač	'fish'	but	simáčč	'your fish'
'úxut	'sister'	but	'uxútta	'her sister'
ṣxáḷa	'young goat'	but	ṣxaḷátta	'her young goat'

10. Except in neologisms, probably because of the influence of other speakers, e.g., *wâlada* (or *waláda*) 'his son' and *šájara* (or *šajára*) 'tree.'

Forms with the sequence CVCCVCVC, in which CC is a double consonant, have stress on the penultimate syllable:

killáhum (var. *kulláhum*)	'all of them'
gaṣṣáhum	'he cut them'

But in normal speech such forms are reduced to $CVC_1 C_2 VC$: *kílhum* (var. *kúlhum*) and *gáṣhum* (see 4.3.2 above).

PART TWO

THE MORPHOLOGY OF GULF ARABIC

6. VERBS-DERIVATION

As far as derivational systems are concerned, Gulf Arabic verbs are based on either *triliteral* roots, i.e., having three radical consonants, or *quadriliteral* roots, i.e., having four radical consonants.

6.1 Simple Verbs

A simple verb, usually referred to as *Class I* or *Form I,* is the base-form from which all the other classes or forms of the triliteral verbs are derived. The other classes of the triliteral verb, i.e., Classes II through X are derived from Class I and they are sometimes referred to as Derived Verbs or Derived Themes.[1]

6.1.1 Sound Verbs

Sound verbs are of three patterns, depending upon their stem vowels as will be explained later on: *fa9al, fi9al,* and *fi9il.*[2] Examples:

fa9al:	la9ab	'he played'	9araf	'he came to know'
	baraz	'he was ready'	ragaṣ	'he danced'
	šarad	'he ran away'	tafal	'he spat'
fi9al:	tirak	'he left'	tiras	'he filled'
	9ibar	'he crossed'	fitaH	'he opened'
	difa9	'he paid'	ṭibax	'he cooked'

---

1. See, for example, T.M. Johnstone, *Eastern Arabian Dialect Studies,* O.U.P., London, U.K., 1967, p. 45.

2. *f, 9,* and *l* throughout this study refer to the first, second, and third radicals of the verb, respectively.

It should be pointed out that the *fa9al* and *fi9al* patterns are used almost interchangeably. Examples: *la9ab* or *li9ab* 'he played,' *ragaṣ* or *rigaṣ* 'he danced,' *9abar* or *9ibar* 'he crossed,' . . . etc.

fi9il:	simi9	'he heard'	širib	'he drank'
	riji9	'he returned'	9imil	'he made'
	9irif	'he knew'	wiṣil	'he arrived'

Verbs of the *fi9il* type are unstable in most dialects of the Arabian Gulf area; they are sometimes replaced by the *fa9al* type, e.g., *wiṣil* or *wiṣal* 'he arrived.'

6.1.2 Weak Verbs

Weak verbs have one or more unstable or weak radicals. Weak radicals in Gulf Arabic are the glottal stop ' and the semivowels *w* and *y*. Weak verbs are either *defective* or *hollow*. A defective verb is here defined as one with a final weak radical. Examples:

baġa	'he wanted'	9aṭa	'he gave'
dara	'he came to know'	nasa	'he forgot'
Hača	'he spoke'	baga	'he stayed'
miša	'he walked'	šawa	'he roasted'

Hollow verbs are characterized by a medial long vowel *aa*, with no radical *9:*

gaaḷ	'he said'	baag	'he stole'
ḍ̄aaj	'he became bored'	čaan	'he was'
raaH	'he went'	šaaf	'he saw'
saar	'he left; he walked'	ṭaaH	'he fell down'
ṣaad	'he hunted'	šaal	'he lifted'
raad	'he wanted'	jaab	'he brought'
9aaf	'he loathed'	naal	'he obtained'
naam	'he slept'	xaaf	'he became afraid'

Hamzated verbs have the glottal stop (Arabic "hamza") as their first radical.[3] They are rare in GA, and most often occur without the initial syllable *'a-*. Following are the most common ones:

'akal or kal	'he ate'
'aja (var. *'aya*) or ja (var. *ya*)	'he came'
'axađ or xađ	'he took'

The occurrence of the less frequent variant *'akal* 'he ate' is due to the influence of MSA and the speech of Arab immigrants in the Gulf. The second example above, i.e., *ja* (var. *ya*) 'he came' is a doubly weak verb.[4]

6.1.3 Doubled Verbs

Simple doubled verbs are characterized by a final double consonant in the stem, i.e., the second and third radicals are identical.

daš̌š̌	'he entered'	gaṭṭ	'he threw away'
naš̌š̌	'he woke up'	ṣakk	'he closed (the door)'
gaṣṣ	'he cut'	Habb	'he kissed; he loved'
laff	'he turned'	9aḍḍ	'he bit'

6.2 Derived Verbs

6.2.1 Class II

Class II verbs are characterized by a double middle radical. They are generally transitive and derived from Class I verbs, nouns and adjectives. If they are derived from Class I verbs, they express the general meaning of 'to cause s.o. or s.th. to do s.th.' or undergo "an action expressed by the Class I verb." Examples:

---

3. MSA verbs with medial or final hamza are borrowed into GA as hollow or weak verbs, respectively, e.g., MSA *sa'al* 'he asked' and *qara'* 'he read' → GA *saal* and *qara*. MSA nouns, for example, with medial or final hamza undergo other changes in GA: *ra'iis* 'head, boss,' *ra's* 'head,' and *šay'* 'thing; s.th.' → GA *rayyis, raaṣ*, and *šayy*.

4. A doubly weak verb is one that has only one radical; the *9* and *l* radicals are missing.

Class I		*Class II*	
ð̣aHak	'he laughed'	ð̣aHHak	'he made s.o. laugh'
daras	'he studied'	darras	'he taught'
xaḷaṣ	'it finished'	xaḷḷaṣ	'he finished s.th.'
9araf	'he knew'	9arraf	'he made s.o. acquainted with s.th.'
naam	'he slept'	nawwam	'he put s.o. to sleep'
9ilim	'he knew'	9allam	'he let s.o. know s.th.'

If the Class I verb is transitive, then the corresponding Class II verb may be doubly transitive, i.e., with two objects:

darras*hum 'ingiliizi*	'he taught *them English*'
rawwaa*ni* l-*yaryuur*	'he showed *me* the *shark*'

Some Class II verbs denote intensity or frequency of action:

kasar	'he broke'	kassar	'he smashed'
qatal	'he killed'	qattal	'he massacred'
taras	'he filled'	tarras	'he filled to the brim'

A few Class II verbs are derived from foreign words, e.g., *čayyak* 'he checked' from the English verb 'to check.'

Examples of Class II verbs derived from nouns:

9awaar	'pain'	9awwar	'he inflicted pain'
fanaš	'termination (of service)'	fannaš	'he terminated s.o.'s or his own services'
qina	'singing'	qanna	'he sang'
xeema	'tent'	xayyam	'he camped'
fašal	'disappointment'	faššal	'he disappointed s.o.'
geeð̣	'summer'	gayyað̣	'he spent the summer'

Class II verbs derived from adjectives express the general meaning of 'to cause s.th. or s.o. to acquire the quality expressed by the adjective':

nað̣iif	'clean'	nað̣ð̣af	'he cleaned'
gaṣiir	'short'	gaṣṣar	'he shortened'[5]
waṣix	'dirty'	waṣṣax	'he made s.th. dirty'
jadiid	'new'	jaddad	'he renewed'

5. The phrase *ma gaṣṣar* means 'he did his best' or 'he did not let anybody down.'

Examples of defective Class II verbs are:

ṣaḷḷa	'he prayed'	rawwa	'he showed'
xaḷḷa	'he left s.th.'	Hayya	'he greeted s.o.'

6.2.2 Class III

Class III verbs are derived mainly from Class I verbs by inserting the long vowel *aa*[6] between the first and the second radicals.

xaabar	'he telephoned'	saafar	'he traveled'
baarak	'he blessed'	waafaj	'he agreed'
xaaṣam	'he quarreled with s.o.'	Haawal	'he tried'
saamaH	'he forgave s.o.'	jaawab	'he answered'
maaša	'he walked with s.o.'	Haača	'he spoke with s.o.'

Most Class III verbs are transitive:

xaabarni	'he telephoned me, engaged me on the phone'
Haačaahum	'he spoke with them (m.), engaged them in conversation'

A few are intransitive: *saafar* 'he traveled,' *Haawal* 'he tried,' etc.

Class III verbs as a class do not have one meaning or closely related meanings associated with Class I verbs. A good number of them are "associative," i.e., they express the meaning of engaging or associating s.o. in an activity. Thus:

Class I		*Class III*	
maša	'he walked'	maaša	'he engaged s.o. in walking'
Hača	'he talked'	Haača	'he engaged s.o. in conversation'

6.2.3 Class IV

This class of verbs is characterized by the prefix *'a-*, which is either rarely used or unstable in GA (see Hamzated Verbs above). The few Class IV verbs that are used in GA are either borrowings from MSA or emulation of the speech of other Arabs.

---

6. A few verbs are formed by inserting the long vowels *oo* or *ee: soolaf* 'he talked, chattered,' *reewas* 'he reversed, went backwards,' etc. These verbs are treated as quadriliterals (see 6.3 below).

'a9jab	'he pleased'	'alqa	'he delivered (a speech)'
'axbar	'he informed'	'a9lan	'he announced'
'a9ṭa	'he gave'	'a9lam	'he told'

Instead of Class IV verbs, Gulf Arabs use either Class I or Class II verbs. Examples: *9ajab, 9aṭa* (Class I), *9allam, xabbar* (Class II).

6.2.4 Class V

Almost all Class V verbs are derived from Class II verbs or by the prefixing of *t-*. They are usually reflexive of Class II; they denote the state of an object as the result of the action of the Class II verb, i.e., the subject does something to himself. Examples:

Class II		*Class V*	
9allam	'he taught'	t9allam	'he learned'
zawwaj	'he married s.o. to s.o. else'	zzawwaj[7]	'he got married'
qayyar	'he changed s.th.'	tqayyar	'it changed'
wannas	'he showed s.o. a good time'	twannas	'he had a good time'
qadda	'he gave lunch to s.o.'	tqadda	'he had lunch'
faṣṣax	'he tore s.th. apart'	tfaṣṣax	'he took off his clothes'

Some Class V verbs are passive in meaning:

Class II		*Class V*	
bannad	'he shut'	tbannad	'it was shut'
θamman	'he priced s.th.'	θθamman[8]	'it was priced'
wahhag	'he involved s.o.'	twahhag	'he was involved'
9awwar	'he inflicted pain'	t9awwar	'he was injured'
ṭarraš	'he sent s.th. or s.o.'	ṭṭarraš[9]	'he, it, was sent'

7. See 4.2 above.

8. *Ibid.*

9. *Ibid.*

Note that the last three examples of Class II verbs are transitive and the corresponding Class V verbs are intransitive. A few Class V verbs are transitive:

zzawwaj bint jamiila.	'He married a beautiful girl.'
ssallaf[10] 'alf diinaar.	'He borrowed 1000 dinars.'

The imperfect tense of these verbs denotes a passive-potential meaning:

haaða ma yitbannad.	'This cannot be shut, closed.'
l-waġt yitqayyar.	'The time is changeable, i.e., it is subject to change.'
haaða ṣ-ṣanduug yitbaṭṭaḷ.	'This box can be opened.'

6.2.5 Class VI

Most Class VI verbs are formed from Class III verbs by prefixing *t(a)-*:

Class III		*Class VI*	
šaawar	'he consulted s.o.'	tšaawar	'he consulted (deliberated) with s.o.'
gaabal	'he met s.o.'	tgaabal	'he met with s.o.' 'he had an interview with s.o.'
Haača	'he talked to s.o.'	tHaačaw	'they (m.) talked with each other'

A few Class VI verbs are formed from adjectives:

mariið̣	'sick'	tmaarað̣	'he pretended to be sick'
jaahil	'ignorant'	jjaahal[11]	'he ignored s.o.'

Class VI verbs denote the following meanings:

1. reciprocity:

txaabaraw	'they (m.) telephoned each other'
jjaawabaw[12]	'they (m.) responded to each other'

---

10. *Ibid.*
11. *Ibid.*
12. *Ibid.*

tšaawaran	'they (f.) consulted with each other'
txaaṣaman	'they (f.) quarreled with each other'

2. pretense:

jjaahal	'he ignored s.o. or s.th.; he pretended to be ignorant of s.th.'
tmaarað̣	'he pretended to be sick'
ð̣ð̣aahar	'he feigned, pretended'

This meaning usually obtains with verbs derived from adjectives.

3. Other meanings:

tabaarak[13] aḷḷa	'God, the blessed and the exalted'
tgaa9ad	'he retired'

Almost all Class VI verbs are derived from transitive Class III verbs as in the above examples and they have plural subjects except in a few cases as cited above: *tgaa9ad, tmaarað̣,* and *jjaahal.* The subjects of all the Class VI verbs cited above are animate. In a few cases there may be inanimate subjects:

s-sayaayiir ssaabagaw.	'The cars had a race.'
l-kanapaat twaafajaw.	'The sofas matched.'

6.2.6 Class VII

Class VII verbs are formed from transitive Class I verbs by prefixing *n-*. Examples:

Class I		*Class VII*	
tiras	'he filled'	ntiras	'it (he) was filled'
9araf	'he came to know'	n9araf	'it (he) became known'
tirak	'he left'	ntirak	'it (he) was left'
simi9	'he heard'	nsimi9	'it was heard'
dara	'he knew'	ndara	'it was known'
Hača	'he talked'	nHača	'it was said, talked about'
baag	'he stole'	nbaag	'it was stolen'
šaal	'he lifted'	nšaal	'it (he) was lifted'
dašš	'he entered'	ndašš	'it was entered'
gaṭṭ	'he threw away'	ngaṭṭ	'it was discarded, thrown away'

13. *tabaarak,* rather than *tbaarak,* is literary.

The irregular initial-hamzated verbs *kal* (var. *'akal*) 'he ate' and *xað* (var. *'axað*) 'he took' have the following Class VII forms: *nwakal* 'it was eaten' and *nwaxað* 'it was taken.'

Class VII verbs denote the passive of Class I verbs. The object of a Class I verb becomes the subject of the corresponding Class VII verb: *tiras t-taanki* 'He filled the tank.': *t-taanki ntiras* 'The tank was filled.' Another grammatical meaning of a Class VII verb is that its imperfect denotes a passive-potential sense:

haaða mawḍuu9 ma yinHača	'This is a subject that cannot, shouldn't, be told, talked about.'
haaða l-karš ma yintiris	'This belly cannot be filled.' (i.e., It is bottomless.)
ṣ-ṣagir ma yinšiwi	'Falcons are not to be roasted.' (i.e., It has better uses, e.g., in falconry.)

6.2.7 Class VIII

Most Class VIII verbs are formed from Class I verbs by infixing *-t-* after the first radical, i.e., between the first and the second radicals. Examples:

štaġal	'he worked'	Htifal	'he celebrated'
jtima9	'he had a meeting'	ntibah	'he paid attention'
Htaaj	'he needed'	rtaaH	'he rested'
xtaar	'he chose, selected'	Htaaj	'he needed s.th. or s.o.'
htamm	'he became concerned'	ftarr	'he turned around'
štara	'he bought'	štika	'he complained'
btida	'he began'	ktifa	'he was content (with s.t.)'
stiwa	'it became'	9tiraf	'he confessed'
ntiḍar	'he waited for s.o., s.th.'	xtilaf	'it differed'
ftaham	'he understood'	ftikar	'he thought'
rtabaš	'he got into trouble'	Htarag	'it, he, got burned'

As a class, Class VIII verbs have a reflexive or middle meaning; they are reflexive of Class I verbs, i.e., they have the meaning of doing s.th. to or for oneself:

Class I		*Class VIII*	
sima9	'he heard'	stima9	'he listened to s.th.'
jima9	'he collected'	jtima9	'he had a meeting'

In a few cases Class I and Class VIII verbs have similar meanings:

šara	'he bought'	štara	'he bought'

A few Class VIII verbs have a passive meaning:

rabaṭ	'he tied s.th.'	rtabaṭ	'it was tied'
nasa	'he forgot s.th.'	ntasa	'it was forgotten'

6.2.8 Class IX

Class IX verbs are characterized by a doubled last radical. Almost all of these verbs are derived from adjectives of color or (physical) characteristic. Examples:

Adjective		*Class IX*	
Hamar	'red'	Hmarr	'it turned red'
xað̣ar	'green'	xð̣arr	'it turned green'
'abyað̣	'white'	byað̣ð̣	'it turned white'
'aswad	'black'	swadd	'it turned black'
'amlaH	'grey'	mlaHH	'it turned grey'
9awar	'one-eyed'	9warr	'he grew blind in one eye'
9away	'crooked'	9wayy	'it turned crooked, twisted'

6.2.9 Class X

Class X verbs are characterized by a prefixed *sta-*. They are derived mainly from verbs and adjectives; a few are derived from nouns.

Underlying Verb		*Class X*	
9amal	'he made, did'	sta9mal	'he used'
qafar	'he pardoned, forgave (a sin)'	staqfar	'he sought forgiveness'
naam	'he slept'	stanwam	'he sought sleep'
jaawab (var. *yaawab*)	'he answered'	stajaab (var. *stayaab*)	'he responded (to a request)'

9aṭa	'he gave'	sta9ṭa	'he sought'
Habb	'he liked; he kissed'	staHabb	'he found s.th. or s.o. nice, good'
Underlying Adjective		*Class X*	
ṣa9b	'difficult'	staṣ9ab	'he found s.th. difficult'
zeen	'good, fine'	stazyan	'he found s.th. good'
qani	'rich'	staqna(9an)	'he did without'
Underlying Noun		*Class X*	
ruxṣa	'permission'	starxaṣ	'he had permission; he sought permission'
winsa	'good time'	staanas	'he had a good time; he enjoyed himself'
Hagg	'right, one's due'	staHagg	'he deserved s.th.'
yinn	'craziness'	stayann	'he turned crazy'

Most Class X verbs derived from Class I verbs denote the general meaning of seeking, asking, or demanding for oneself what is expressed by the Class I verb: *staqfar* 'he sought forgiveness,' *staradd* 'he got s.th. back,' etc. From adjectives Class X verbs express the general meaning of finding or considering s.th. as what is expressed by the underlying adjective: *staṣ9ab* 'he found s.th. difficult,' *stazyan* 'he found s.th. good, fine,' etc.

6.3 Quadriliteral Verbs

Quadriliteral verbs, sometimes referred to as quadriradical verbs, have four radicals. They can be simple (sound, weak, or reduplicated[14] from Class I doubled verbs) or derived. The derived ones are formed by prefixing *t(a)-* to the quadriliteral simple verb. Examples of simple quadriliteral verbs:

Sound:	la9waz	'he bothered'
	ġašmar	'he played a prank on s.o.'
	xarbaṭ	'he mixed, messed, s.th. or s.o. up'
	sandar	'he irritated'

14. A reduplicated quadriliteral verb is one in which the first two radicals are repeated, e.g., *gaṣgaṣ* 'he cut up s.th.'

Weak:	reewas	'he went in reverse'
	soogar	'he insured s.th.'
	soolaf	'he talked, chattered'
	gahwa	'he welcomed s.o. with coffee'

Reduplicated:

Class I		*Quadriliteral*	
gaṣṣ	'he cut off s.th.'	gaṣgaṣ	'he cut up s.th.'
ṭagg	'he beat; he flogged s.o.'	ṭagṭag	'he tapped s.th.; it tapped'

A few quadriliteral verbs are derived from nouns as in some of the examples given above:

Noun		*Redup. Quadriliteral*	
ġašmara	'joking, kidding'	ġašmar	'he played a prank on s.o.'
gahwa (var. *ghawa*)	'coffee'	gahwa	'he welcomed s.o. with coffee'
rwees	'reverse'	reewas	'he went in reverse'

Examples of derived quadriliteral verbs:

Quadriliterals		*Derived Quadriliterals*	
la9waz	'he bothered'	tla9waz	'he was bothered'
xarbaṭ	'he mixed, messed up'	txarbaṭ	'he was mixed up; it was messed up'
ġašmar	'he tricked s.o.'	tġašmar	'he was tricked'
gaṣgaṣ	'he cut up s.th.'	tgaṣgaṣ	'it was cut up'
gahwa	'he welcomed s.o. with coffee'	tgahwa	'he had coffee; he was given coffee'

Derived quadriliteral verbs, as far as derivation is concerned, are similar to Class V verbs: both verbs have the prefix *t-;* the structure of a Class V verb is of the pattern $tC_1aC_2C_2aC_3$; that of a derived quadriliteral verb is of the pattern $tC_1aC_2C_3aC_4$. As for meaning, most derived quadriliteral verbs are related to quadriliteral verbs in the same way as Class I verbs are related to Class VII verbs: both derived quadriliteral and Class VII verbs denote the passive meaning of transitive simple quadriliteral and Class I verbs, respectively. Examples: *la9waz* 'he bothered' and *tla9waz* 'he was bothered'; *tiras* 'he filled s.th.' and *ntiras* 's.th. was filled.' Note that the last example above, under derived quadriliterals, has the meaning of 'he had (i.e., *drank*) coffee' in addition to the passive meaning.

It has already been pointed out in 6.2.4 and 6.2.6 that most of the negative imperfect tenses of Class V and Class VII verbs denote a passive-potential meaning. The negative imperfect of derived quadriliteral verbs has a similar meaning:

haaᵭa r-rayyaal ma yitġašmar.	'This man cannot be tricked, played a prank on.'
haaᵭa l-xaṭṭ ma yitsoogar.	'This letter cannot be certified, registered.'

7. VERBS-INFLECTION

Gulf Arabic verbs are inflected for tense (perfect and imperfect), person (first, second, and third), gender (masculine and feminine), number (singular and plural), and mood (indicative and imperative). A perfect tense verb is not inflected for mood, i.e., a perfect tense verb does not have a mood. The first person singular form of the verb is not inflected for gender, i.e., there is only one form for the person speaking, regardless of sex. Similarly there is one form for the first person plural. Unlike some other dialects of Arabic, e.g., Lebanese, Jordanian, Egyptian, etc., GA has separate verb forms for the second and third person feminine or plural.

7.1 Perfect Tense

The perfect tense in GA corresponds to the following English tenses: simple past, e.g., *he came;* present perfect, e.g., *he has come;* and past perfect, e.g., *he had come.*

7.1.1 Sound Verbs

The inflections of the perfect tense, usually known as the *inflectional affixes,* are all suffixes. They are the same for all verbs in the language, and are listed in the following chart in the right-hand column. The complete perfect tense conjugation of *díras* 'he studied' is given as a model for all sound verbs. There are some variations in the conjugation of weak verbs, which are given in 7.1.2 below.

	Pronoun	Verb	Meaning	Suffix
3rd p.	huwa	díras	'he studied'	-∅
	hum	drísaw	'they (m.) studied'	-aw
	hiya	drísat	'she studied'	-at
	hin	drísan	'they (f.) studied'	-an
2nd p.	'inta	dirást	'you (m.s.) studied'	-t
	'intum	dirástu	'you (m.p.) studied'	-tu
	'inti	dirásti	'you (f.s.) studied'	-ti
	'intin	dirástin	'you (f.p.) studied'	-tin
1st p.	'aana	dirást	'I studied'	-t
	niHin	dirásna	'we studied'	-na

Note the following comments on the above perfect-tense forms:

a. The forms are built on and derived from the 3rd person singular form of the verb, which is referred to as the *stem: díras* 'he studied.' This stem is used to refer to the verb as a whole, in the same way as the infinitive is used in English. Thus, when we say the verb *díras,* which literally means 'he studied,' we refer to what corresponds to the English infinitive 'to study.'[15]

b. Note that the stem vowel *-i-* and the second radical *-r-* are switched before adding suffixes beginning with a vowel: *drísaw* 'they (m.) studied,' *drísat* 'she studied,' and *drísan* 'they (f.) studied,' although the forms *dírsaw, dírsat,* and *dírsan* are also heard.

c. The first syllable of the first four forms is stressed, while the second syllable of the other forms is stressed because of the CVCC sequence: díras → dirást 'he studied' → 'I studied' (see 5H).

All the verbs cited in 7.1.1 are regular, and thus are conjugated like *díras.*

15. From now on the third person masculine singular form of the perfect tense will be used as the citation form of the verb, i.e., the gloss will always be 'to . . . ' rather than 'he . . . .'

Classes II, III, IV, V, IX, X

The conjugation of sound Class II verbs is regular; there are no stem changes, e.g., the verb *dárras* 'to teach' has the following forms with the inflected suffixes in parentheses. Note the stress marks.

dárras	(-∅)
darrásaw	(-aw)
darrásat	(-at)
darrásan	(-an)
darrást	(-t)
darrástu	(-tu)
darrásti	(-ti)
darrástin	(-tin)
darrást	(-t)
darrásna	(-na)

Classes III, IV, V, and X are also regular and thus conjugated in the same way as Class II verbs.

Classes VI, VII, and VIII have two forms for the third person: the first one is the regular forms; the other one requires an elision of the last stem vowel (see 4.3.1). The latter forms are less commonly used; their occurrence is due to dialect overlap. Note the stress marks.

Class VI: tšaáwar 'to consult with each other'

tšaawáraw	tšaawárat	tšaawáran
tšaáwraw	tšaáwrat	tšaáwran

Class VII: *ntiras* 'to be filled (e.g., with water)'

ntirásaw	ntirásat	ntirásan
ntírsaw	ntírsat	ntírsan

Class VIII: *štaġal* 'to work'

štaġálaw	štaġálat	štaġálan
štáġlaw	štáġlat	štáġlan

Sound quadriliteral and derived quadriliteral verbs are regular and thus conjugated with no stem changes.

7.1.2 Weak Verbs[16]

A. Defective

Defective verbs have two stems: one is used before the third person suffixes and the other is used before the other suffixes, e.g., the verb *baġa* 'to want' has the two stems *baġ-* before *-a, -aw, -at, -an* and *baġee-* before the rest of the suffixes. Below is the full conjugation of the verb *baġa* 'to want':

Pronoun	Verb	Meaning	Suffix
huwa	baġa	'he wanted'	-a
hum	baġaw	'they (m.p.) wanted'	-aw
hiya	baġat	'she wanted'	-at
hin	baġan	'they (f.p.) wanted'	-an
'inta	baġeet	'you (m.s.) wanted'	-t
'intu	baġeetu	'you (m.p.) wanted'	-tu
'inti	baġeeti	'you (f.s.) wanted'	-ti
'intin	baġeetin	'you (f.p.) wanted'	-tin
'aana	baġeet	'I wanted'	-t
'niHin	baġeena	'we wanted'	-na

Defective verbs of Classes II through VIII and Class X[17] and the quadriliterals are conjugated in the same way as *baġa* above. Examples of such verbs are:

Class II

rawwa	'to show s.o. s.th.'	Hayya	'to greet s.o.'
xaḷḷa	'to leave s.o. or s.th.' 'to let s.o. do s.th.'	ṣaḷḷa	'to pray'

16. For the definition of *Weak Verbs,* see 6.1.2 above.

17. See 7.1.3 Class IX verbs below.

Class III			
maaša	'to walk with s.o.'	Haača	'to talk with s.o.'
Class IV			
'a9ṭa	'to give'	'alqa	'to deliver (a speech)'
Class V			
tqadda	'to have lunch'	t9aššša	'to have supper'
Class VI			
tHaača	'to talk with each other'	tlaaga	'to meet with each other'
Class VII			
ndara	'to be known'	nHača	'to be said, talked about'
Class VIII			
štara	'to buy'	ntisa	'to be forgotten'
Class X			
sta9ṭa	'to seek, beg s.th.'	staqna(9an)	'to do without'

Quadriliterals

gahwa	'to welcome s.o. with coffee'
tgahwa	'he had coffee; he was given coffee'

The verb 'aja (var. *'aya*) → ja (var. *ya*) 'to come' is a hamzated weak verb. Hamzated verbs in GA are rare; their variants (see 6.1.2 above) are more commonly used. Like any other doubly weak verb, *ja/ya* has two stems, *j-/y-* and *jee-/yee-*. Below is the full conjugation of *ja/ya:*[18]

Pronoun	Verb	Meaning	Suffix
huwa	ya	'he came'	-a
hum	yaw	'they (m.p.) came'	-aw
hiya	yat	'she came'	-at
hin	yan	'they (f.p.) came'	-an

18. *ya*, rather than *ja*, is more typical of GA.

Pronoun	Verb	Meaning	Suffix
’inta	yeet	‘you (m.s.) came’	-t
’intum	—tu	‘you (m.p.) came’	-tu
’inti	—ti	‘you (f.s.) came’	-ti
’intin	—tin	‘you (f.p.) came’	-tin
’aana	yeet	‘I came’	-t
niHin	—na	‘we came’	-na

This verb has another set of forms in the perfect tense. These forms are used before the first and second person inflectional suffixes: *yiit, yiitu, yiiti, yiitin, yiit,* and *yiina.* These forms are in free variation with *yeet, yeetu,* etc.

B. Hollow

Hollow verbs are based on roots whose second radical is *w* or *y*, e.g., GWL ‘to say,’ SYR ‘to leave,’ etc. In GA there are hollow verbs in Classes I, VII, VIII, and X.

Classes I and VII

Like defective verbs, hollow verbs have two perfect tense stems. For one such class of hollow verbs, the two perfect stem patterns are CaaC- for the third person endings and CiC-/CuC- for the other persons. Below are the full perfect-tense forms of the verb *gaal* ‘to say.’

gaaḷ	gaaḷaw	gaaḷat	gaaḷan
giḷt/guḷt	giḷtu/guḷtu	giḷti/guḷti	
giḷtin/guḷtin	giḷt/guḷt	giḷna/guḷna	

The alternate pattern, i.e., CuC-, is less commonly used. Other verbs that conform to this pattern are: *šaaf* (var. *čaaf*) ‘to see,’ *kaan* (var. *čaan*) ‘to be,’ *ð̣aaj* ‘to get bored,’ and *raaH* ‘to go.’

The other subclass of hollow verbs have the perfect stem patterns CaaC- and CiC- only. Examples:

ṭaaH ‘to fall down’

ṭaaH	ṭaaHaw	ṭaaHat	ṭaaHan		
ṭiHt	ṭiHtu	ṭiHti	ṭiHtin	ṭiHt	ṭiHna

Other verbs that belong to this category are: *raad* 'to want,' *saar* 'to walk; to leave,' *naam* 'to sleep,' *xaaf* 'to be afraid, scared,' and *9aaf* 'to loathe.'

Class VII hollow verbs also have the same perfect stem patterns as this subclass of hollow verbs, i.e., nCaaC- and nCiC-. Example: *nṣaab* 'to be hit.' Other examples are: *nbaag* 'to be stolen,' *nšaal* 'to be lifted, carried,' *ngaal* 'to be said, mentioned,' and *nraad* 'to be wanted, desired.'

Classes VIII and X

Classes VIII and X hollow verbs have the perfect stems CtaaC- CtaC-, and staCaaC- staCaC-, respectively. Examples:

Class VIII: *Htaaj* 'to need, be in need of s.th. or s.o.'

Htaaj	Htaajaw	Htaajat	Htaajan		
Htajt	Htajtu	Htajti	Htajtin	Htajt	Htajna

Class X: *staraaH* 'to rest'

staraaH	staraaHaw	staraaHat	staraaHan		
staraHt	staraHtu	staraHti	staraHtin	staraHat	staraHna

7.1.3 Doubled Verbs

The perfect-tense stems of doubled verbs end with two identical consonants. The stems of these verbs remain unchanged before the third person suffixes; before the other suffixes the long vowel *ee* is added, e.g., *Haṭṭeet* 'I put.' In this category there are verbs of Class I, VII, VIII, IX, and X. Below are the perfect-tense forms of the verb *dašš* 'to enter.'

dašš	daššaw	daššat	daššan		
daššeet	daššeetu	daššeeti	daššeetin	daššeet	daššeena

Other examples of Class I doubled verbs like *dašš* are: *laff* 'to make a turn,' *ṭagg* 'to hit s.o.; to flog s.o.,' *ṣakk* 'to close, shut,' *našš* 'to wake up,' and *gaṭṭ* 'to throw away, discard s.th.'

Classes II and III verbs are conjugated like sound verbs, e.g., Class II *dallal* 'to auction' has the forms *dallal, dallalaw, dallalat,* etc. and Class III *Haajaj* 'to argue' has the forms *Haajaj, Haajajaw, Haajajat,* etc.

Class VII

ndašš	'to be entered'	nHabb	'to be liked, loved'
ngaṭṭ	'to be thrown away'	nṣakk	'to be shut, closed'

Class VIII

ftarr	'to turn around'	mtadd	'to stretch out'
htamm	'to be concerned'	Htayy	'to protest'

Class IX

Hmarr	'to turn red'	9wayy	'to turn crooked, twisted'
zragg	'to turn blue'	byað̣ð̣	'to turn white'

Class X

staHagg	'to deserve'	staHabb	'to like'
sta9add	'to be ready'	stamarr	'to continue'

7.2 Imperfect Tense

The inflectional affixes of the imperfect tense are either prefixes or a combination of prefixes and suffices. Each imperfect tense verb is made up of a subject marker and a stem.

7.2.1 Sound Verbs

Below is a model conjugation of the imperfect verb *diras*[19] 'to study.'

Pronoun	Verb	Meaning	Affixes
huwa	yádris	'he studies'	ya-
hiya	tádris	'she studies'	ta-
'inta	tádris	'you (m.s.) study'	ta-
'inti	tadrisíin	'you (f.s.) study'	ta–iin
'aana	'ádris	'I study'	'a-
hum	yadrisúun	'they (m.) study'	ya–uun

19. From now on imperfect stems are cited between hyphens, e.g., *-dris-* 'to study' as opposed to the perfect stem *diras* 'to study,' which is the third person masculine singular form.

Pronoun	Verb	Meaning	Affixes
hin	yadrísin	'they (f.) study'	ya–in
'intum	tadrisúun	'you (m.p.) study'	ta–uun
'intin	tadrísin	'you (f.p.) study'	ta–in
niHin	nádris	'we study'	na-

Note the following comments on the above imperfect-tense forms:

a. The third person masculine prefix is *ya-;* for the second person it is *ta-;* for the first person singular it is *'a-;* for the first person plural it is *na-*.

b. The third person feminine singular and second person masculine singular prefixes are identical, i.e., *ta-;* the second and third person masculine plural suffixes are identical *(-uun)* and in addition the feminine plural suffixes are also identical *(-in)*.

c. The prefixes *ya-* and *ta-* have two other corresponding free variants, namely, *yi-* and *ti-*. The second person feminine singular suffix *-iin* is in free variation with *-een* and similarly *-uun* with *-oon* in the second and third person masculine plural forms. *-een* and *-oon* are preserved in the speech of older and uneducated Gulf Arabs.

d. The imperfect tense in GA expresses one or more of the following meanings:

(i) habitual: 'adris 9arabi kill yoom.
'I study Arabic every day.'

(ii) general truth value ("generic," "dispositional," etc.):
yitkallam 9arabi zeen. 'He speaks Arabic well.'

(iii) progressive: yadris 9arabi halHiin.
'He is studying Arabic now.'

(iv) future: yadris baačir?
'Will he, is he going to, study tomorrow?'

Some verbs in GA express in the imperfect tense not an action or activity but a state, condition or quality; these are called stative verbs, the imperfect tense of which may have either of the two meanings of (ii) and (iv), e.g., *yHasdak* 'he envies you' and *yHasdak biduun šakk* 'he will without doubt envy you.'

Stem Vowels

Both perfect and imperfect tenses have stem vowels. The stem vowel of a triradical verb, whether in the perfect or imperfect tense, is the vowel preceding the last radical. In MSA and most dialects of Arabic the stem vowel of the imperfect tense is predictable from the perfect tense stem vowel. In GA the predictability of the imperfect tense stem vowels is more difficult due to the past tense alternate patterns or variants, e.g., the *fa9al* and *fi9il* patterns are used almost interchangeably (see 6.1.1). However, some general remarks can be made about the formation of the imperfect tense forms. Note the following:

a. Perfect tense verbs of the *fa9al* or *fi9al* type (see 6.1.1) form their imperfect tense verbs according to the pattern *yaf9il* or *yif9al.* Examples:

Perfect	*Imperfect*	*Meaning*
diras	yadris	'to study'
tirak	yatrik	'to leave s.o. or s.th.'
baraz	yabriz	'to be ready'
šarad	yašrid	'to flee; to go away'
ragaṣ	yargiṣ	'to dance'
tiras	yatris	'to fill s.th. or s.o. with s.th.'
la9ab	yal9ab/yil9ab	'to play'
difa9	yadfa9/yidfa9	'to pay'
fitaH	yaftaH/yiftaH	'to open'
ṭibax	yaṭbax/yiṭbax	'to cook'

b. Some of the perfect tense verbs cited above also have the *fi9al* pattern as was pointed out in 6.1.1.

c. Perfect tense verbs of the *fi9il* type form their imperfect tense according to the pattern *yif9al* or *yaf9al.* Examples:

Perfect	*Imperfect*	*Meaning*
širib	yišrab/yašrab	'to drink'
riji9	yirja9/yarja9	'to return'
simi9	yisma9/yasma9	'to hear; to listen to'

It has already been pointed out in 6.1.1 that verbs of the *fi9il* type are usually replaced by the *fa9al* type. It should be pointed out that their imperfect tense forms are of the *yif9al/yaf9al* pattern and never the *yaf9il* pattern.

d. If the initial radical of a perfect tense verb is a velar, a pharyngeal, or the glottal fricative (i.e., *x, ġ; H, 9;* or *h*), then the imperfect tense form is of the pattern *yfa9il* (see APPENDIX IV). Examples:

Perfect	*Imperfect*	*Meaning*
xaṭaf	yxaṭif	'to make off with s.th.'
xaṭab	yxaṭib	'to give a speech'
ġalat	yġalit	'to make a mistake'
ġasal	yġasil	'to wash'
Halaf	yHalif	'to take an oath'
Hasad	yHasid	'to envy s.o.'
9amal	y9amil	'to make, do, s.th.'
9iraf	y9arif	'to know'
hidam	yhadim	'to destroy, demolish'
haƌar	yhaƌir	'to waste s.th.'

e. Past tense verbs with initial *w-* have the pattern *yoo9al* for their imperfect tense verbs:

wiṣal	yooṣal	'to reach (a place)'
wagaf	yoogaf	'to stop; to stand up'
wizan	yoozan/yaazin[20]	'to weigh'

Those with initial *y-* have the pattern *yee9al* for their imperfect tense verbs:

yibis	yeebas	'to get dry'
yitim	yeetam	'to be orphaned'

f. Hamzated verbs (see 6.1.2) have the pattern *yaa9il* for their imperfect tense forms:

'akal/kal	yaakil	'to eat'
'axaƌ/xaƌ	yaaxiƌ	'to take'

---

20. The alternate form *yaazin* is more commonly heard than *yoozan.*

The Imperative

The imperative is used in giving commands, i.e., in telling or asking someone or a group of people to do something, e.g., *'iktib* 'write! (m.s.)' and 'ixðaw! 'take! (m.p.).' All imperatives in GA have four different forms, reflecting differences in gender and number: masculine singular, masculine plural, feminine singular, and feminine plural. Nearly all the imperative forms are formed from the imperfect stems of verbs. The masculine singular form of the imperative is the base of all the other forms which are formed by suffixing *-i* (f.s.), *-u*/*-aw* (m.p.), and *-an* (f.p.). Below are the forms of the imperative of the verb 'to study.' The imperfect stem is *-dris-:*

'idris	'study (m.s.)!'
'idirsi	'study (f.s.)!'
'idirsu	'study (m.p.)!'
'idirsan	'study (f.p.)!'

Note that *'idris* 'study (m.s.)!' becomes *'idirsi* rather than *idrisi* due to vowel elision and anaptyxis (see 4.1 and 4.3.1). The helping vowel *-i-* is inserted after the first consonant. It should be pointed out that the forms *'idrisi, 'idrisu,* and *'idrisan* are also heard. In the speech of Bedouins and nomadic tribes, the prefix *'i-* tends to be dropped: *dris, dirsi* (var. *dirsay*), *dirsu* (var. *dirsaw*), and *dirsan.* (See 6.1.2 and (d) below.)

The following rules pertain to the formation of the masculine singular imperatives of sound verbs of Class I.

a. *'i-* is usually prefixed to the imperfect stems of the patterns *-f9il-* and *-f9al-*.

Imperfect Stem	*Imperative*	*Meaning*
-dris-	'idris	'study (m.s.)!'
-trik-	'itrik	'leave (m.s.)!'
-tris-	'itris	'fill up s.th. (m.s.)!'
-ṭbax-	'iṭbax	'cook (m.s.)!'
-l9ab-	'il9ab	'play (m.s.)!'
-šrid-	'išrid/'ušrud[21]	'run away (m.s.)!'
-rguṣ-	'irgiṣ/'urguṣ[22]	'dance (m.s.)!'

21. The alternate forms *'ušrud* and *'urguṣ* are also heard, especially among educated young Abu Dhabians.

22. *Ibid.*

-šrab-	'išrab	'drink (m.s.)!'
-rja9-	'irja9	'come back (m.s.)!'

b. Perfect tense verbs whose initial radical is a velar, a pharyngeal, or the glottal fricative *h* usually have the patterns *-f9il-* and *-f9al-* as above or *-fi9l-*, especially with suffixed pronouns: *'i9rif* 'know,' *ixdim* 'serve!', *iġsil* 'wash!', *'ihdim* 'destroy!', *'i9mal* 'make; do!', *'ixsar* 'lose!', *'ixlaṣ* 'finish!'. Note the following forms with suffixed pronouns:

'iHlib 'milk (m.s.)!' →	Hilba[23]	'milk (m.s.) it (m.)!'
	Hilbii	'milk (f.s.) it (m.) or him!'
	Hilbuu (var. *Hilboo*)	'milk (m.p.) it (m.) or him!'

All forms usually lose initial *'i-* when a suffixed pronoun is added.

c. Past tense verbs with initial *w-* (which have the imperfect tense pattern as *yoo9al*) have the imperative pattern *'oo9al:*

yooṣal 'he reaches (a place)' → 'ooṣal 'reach (m.s.)!'

yoogaf 'he stops; he stands up' → 'oogaf 'stop: stand up (m.s.)!'

wizan 'to weigh' has two imperative forms, namely, *'oozan* and *'aazin.* The latter is more commonly used, however.

d. The imperative of hamzated verbs has two patterns, one with the prefix *'i-* and the other without it. This latter pattern is more commonly used:

xað 'to take' → 'ixið/xið 'take (m.s.)!'

kal 'to eat' → 'ikil/kil 'eat (m.s.)!'

Classes II-X and Quadriliterals

The imperfect stem vowel of sound verbs of Classes II-IV, VIII, and X is *-i-*. That of the other Classes, i.e., Classes V, VI, VII, and IX is *-a-*. In most dialects the imperfect prefixes are *y(i)-* and *t(i)-*, although *y(a)-* and *t(a)-* are also heard. The vowels (a) and (i) in the imperfect prefixes are obligatory if they precede a consonant cluster; if they precede one consonant their use is usually optional.

Examples of imperfect tense verbs with *-i-* as a stem vowel:

---

23. As in the proverbial phrase: *nguul θoor yguul Hilba* 'We say "bull" and he says "milk it!",' i.e., he is being completely unreasonable.

	Perfect		*Imperfect*
Class II			
	9awwar	'to injure s.o.'	y9awwir
	fannaš	'to terminate one's services'	yfanniš
Class III			
	xaaṣam	'to quarrel with s.o.'	yxaaṣim
	waafag	'to agree'	ywaafig
Class IV			
	'a9jab	'to please s.o.'	yi9jib
	'axbar	'to inform s.o.'	yixbir
Class VIII			
	štaġaḷ	'to work'	yištaġiḷ
	Htifal	'to celebrate'	yiHtafil
Class X			
	staqfar	'to seek foregiveness'	yistaqfir
	starxaṣ	'to ask permission'	yistarxiṣ

Examples of imperfect tense verbs with *-a-* as a stem vowel:

Class V			
	twannas	'to have a good time'	yitwannas
	twahhag	'to be involved'	yitwahhag
Class VI			
	tšaawar	'to consult with each other'	yitšaawar
	twaafag	'to match each other'	yitwaafag
Class VII			
	ntiras	'to be filled'	yintaras/yintiris
	nwakal	'to be eaten'	yinwakal/yinwikil
Class IX			
	Hmarr	'to turn red'	yiHmarr
	byaḏ̣ḏ̣	'to turn white'	yibyaḏ̣ḏ̣

Note that in an example like *y9awwir* 'he injures s.o.' the double consonant *-ww-* is reduced to one consonant and the vowel *-i-* is elided when a suffix beginning with a vowel is added.[24] Examples:

24. See 4.3.2.

y9awwir → y9awruun		'they injure s.o.'
yfanniš → tfanšiin		'you (f.s.) terminate your own, s.o. else's, services'
yitwaafag → yitwaafgan		'they (f.p.) are, will be, successful'

Sound quadriliterals have the stem vowel *-i-* after the third radical. Examples:

ġašmar	'to trick s.o.'	→	yġašmir	'he tricks s.o.'
la9waz	'to bother s.o.'	→	yla9wiz	'he bothers s.o.'

Sound derived quadriliterals have the stem vowel *-a-* after the third radical. Examples:

tġašmar	'to be tricked'	→	yitġašmar	'he is tricked'
tla9waz	'to be bothered'	→	yitla9waz	'he is bothered'

The Imperative

The imperative forms of sound verbs of Classes II, III, V, VI, VIII, X and of quadriliterals are the same as the imperfect stems of those verbs. The imperatives of verbs of Classes VII, IX, and of the derived quadriliterals are not usually used. Verbs of Class IV [25] have *'i-* prefixed to the imperfect stem.

Class	Perfect	Imperfect Stem	Imperative
II	9awwar	'to injure s.o.' -9awwir-	9awwir! 'injure s.o. (m.s.)!'
III	saafar	'to travel' -saafir-	saafir! 'travel (m.s.)!'
IV	'a9lan	'to announce' -9lin-	'i9lin! 'announce (m.s.)!'
V	twannas	'to enjoy oneself' -twannas-	('i)twannas! 'enjoy yourself (m.s.)!'
VI	tšaawar	'to consult with s.o.' -tašaawar-	tšaawar! 'consult s.o.!'
VII			not usually used

25. See 6.2.3.

Class	Perfect	Imperfect Stem	Imperative
VIII	štaġaḷ	'to work' -štaġiḷ-	('i-)štaġiḷ! 'work (m.s.)!'
IX			not usually used
X	starxaṣ	'to ask for permission (to go)' -starxiṣ-	('i)starxiṣ 'ask for permission (to go) (m.s.)!'
Quad.	ġarbaḷ	'to irritate s.o.' -ġarbiḷ-	ġarbiḷ! 'irritate (m.s.) s.o.!'
Der. Quad.			not usually used

7.2.2 Weak Verbs[26]

A. Defective

Class I

Class I defective verbs have two imperfect stems: *-f9a-* and *-f9i-*. The imperfect prefix is either *ya-* or *yi-*. The paradigm below gives the inflection of the imperfect of both kinds of defective verbs.

Perfect	*Imperfect*	*Meaning*
baga	yabga	'he stays'
bagaw	yabguun	'they (m.) stay'
bagat	tabga	'she stays'
bagan	yabgin	'they (f.) stay'
bageet	tabga	'you (m.s.) stay'
bageetu	tabguun	'you (m.p.) stay'
bageeti	tabgiin	'you (f.s.) stay'
bageetin	tabgin	'you (f.p.) stay'
bageet	'abga	'I stay'
bageena	nabga	'we stay'
dara	yadri	'he knows'
daraw	yadruun	'they (m.) know'

26. For the definition of Weak Verbs, see 6.1.2 above.

darat	tadri	'she knows'
daran	yadrin	'they (f.) know'
dareet	tadri	'you (m.s.) know'
dareetu	tadruun	'you (m.p.) know'
dareeti	tadriin	'you (f.s.) know'
dareetin	tadrin	'you (f.p.) know'
dareet	'adri	'I know'
dareena	nadri	'we know'

Note that the third person plural suffixes are identical in both stem types. Similarly the second person plural and the second person feminine singular are also identical. This is due to vowel elision:

yabga 'he stays' + -uun → yabguun 'they (m.) stay'

yadri 'he knows' + -uun → yadruun 'they (m.) know'

tabgiin 'you (f.s.) stay' + -in → tabgin 'you (f.p.) stay'

tadriin 'you (f.s.) know' + -in → tadrin 'you (f.p.) know'

The verb *baġa* 'to want' is an interesting verb. With its two variant imperfect forms *yabġa* and *yabġi/yabi,* it behaves inflectionally like *yabga* 'he stays' and *yadri* 'he knows.' Note that *yabi* is in free variation with *yabġi.* **yaba* is ungrammatical.

The imperfect of the verb *ja/ya* 'to come' is *yaji* and is conjugated like *yadri* 'he knows.'

The imperative forms of Class I defective verbs have the prefix *'i-:*

'ibga	'stay (m.s.)!'	'ibgu/'ibgaw	'stay (m.p.)!'
'ibgi	'stay (f.s.)!'	'ibgin	'stay (f.p.)!'
'iHči	'talk (m.s.)!'	'iHču/'iHčaw	'talk (m.p.)!'
'iHči	'talk (f.s.)!'	'iHčin	'talk (f.p.)!'

The imperative form *ta9aal* of the verb *ja/ya* 'to come' is irregular:

ta9aal	'come (m.s.)!'	ta9aalu/ta9aalaw	'come (m.p.)!'
ta9aali	'come (f.s.)!'	ta9aalin	'come (f.p.)!'

The imperfect of verbs of Classes II-IV, VIII, and X[27] have the stem vowel *-i.* Examples:

27. Defective verbs of Class IX do not occur in GA.

Class II			
rawwa	'to show'	yrawwi	'he shows'
Hayya	'to greet'	yHayyi	'he greets'
Class III			
Haača	'to talk to s.o.'	yHaači	'he talks to s.o.'
naada	'to call to s.o.'	ynaadi	'he calls to s.o.'
Class IV			
'alqa	'to deliver (a speech)'	yilqi	'he delivers (a speech)'
'axḷa	'to vacate (a place)'	yixḷi	'he vacates (a place)'
Class VIII			
štika	'to complain'	yištiki	'he complains'
ktasa	'to get dressed'	yiktasi	'he gets dressed'
Class X			
sta9ṭa	'to beg s.th.'	yista9ṭi	'he begs s.th.'
staqna 9an	'to do without'	yistaqni	'he does without'

The other classes, i.e., V, VI, and VII have the stem vowel *-a* for their imperfect forms. Examples:

Class V			
tmašša	'to stroll'	yitmášša	'he strolls'
t9ašša	'to have dinner'	yit9ašša	'he has dinner'
Class VI			
tlaaga	'to meet each other'	yitlaaga	'he meets with s.o.'
twaaza	'to be in difficulties'	yitwaaza	'he is, will be, in difficulties'
Class VII			
ndara	'to be known'	yindara	'it is, will be, known'
nHača	'to be talked about, mentioned'	yinHača	'it is, will be, talked about, mentioned'

Note the following:

a. The final vowel of all defective verbs in the imperfect tense is dropped before suffixes.

b. The imperfect stems and the perfect stems of derived defective verbs are identical except for the final vowel.

c. *'a-* is dropped from hamzated Class IV verbs before the derivational prefix *yi-*.

The imperative forms of derived defective verbs have no prefixes except for verbs of Class IV, which usually have the prefix *'i-*. No imperative forms are derived from defective verbs of Class VII. Examples:

rawwi! (Class II)	'show (m.s.)!'
naadi! (Class III)	'call to s.o. (m.s.)!'
'ilqi! (Class IV)	'deliver (a speech) (m.s.)!'
tmašša! (Class V)	'stroll (m.s.)!'
tlaaga! (Class VI)	'meet with s.o. (m.s.)!'
štiki! (Class VIII)	'complain (m.s.)!'
sta9ṭi! (Class X)	'beg (m.s.)!'

B. Hollow

Class I

Class I hollow verbs have three imperfect stem patterns: *-fuul-*, *-fiil-*, and *-faal-*. Examples:

Pattern I: -fuul-: gaal 'to say' → yguul 'he says'

yguul	'he says'	yguuluun	'they (m.) say'
tguul	'she says'	yguulin	'they (f.) say'
tguul	'you (m.s.) say'	tguuluun	'you (m.p.) say'
tguuliin	'you (f.s.) say'	tguulin	'you (f.p.) say'
'aguul	'I say'	nguul	'we say'

Other verbs that belong to this category are: *-ruuH-* 'to go,' *-ð̣uuj-* 'to get bored,' *-buug-* 'to steal,' *-šuuf-* 'to see,' and *-kuun-* 'to be.' The perfect tense *kaan* (var. *čaan*) 'to be' has only one imperfect stem: *-kuun-*, not **-čuun-*.

Pattern II: -fiil-: ṭaaH 'to fall down' → yṭiiH 'he falls down'

yṭiiH	'he falls down'	yṭiiHuun	'they (m.) fall down'
ṭṭiiH	'she falls down'	yṭiiHin	'they (f.) fall down'
ṭṭiiH	'you (m.s.) fall down'	ṭṭiiHuun	'you (m.p.) fall down'

ṭṭiiHiin	'you (f.s.) fall down'	ṭṭiiHin	'you (f.p.) fall down'
'aṭiiH	'I fall down'	nṭiiH	'we fall down'

Other verbs that belong to this category are: *-bii9-* 'to sell,' *-ṣiir-* 'to become,' *-riid-* 'to want,' *-šiil-* 'to lift, carry s.th.,' and *-siir-* 'to leave; to go to a place.'

Pattern III: -faal-: naam 'to sleep' → ynaam 'he sleeps'

ynaam	'he sleeps'	ynaamuun	'they (m.) sleep'
tnaam	'she sleeps'	ynaamin	'they (f.) sleep'
tnaam	'you (m.s.) sleep'	tnaamuun	'you (m.p.) sleep'
tnaamiin	'you (f.s.) sleep'	tnaamin	'you (f.p.) sleep'
'anaam	'I sleep'	nnaam	'we sleep'

Other verbs that belong to this category are: *-xaaf-* 'to fear s.o., s.th.; to be afraid,' *-baat-* 'to spend the night,' and *-y9aaf-* 'to loathe.'

The imperative forms of Class I hollow verbs are the same as their imperfect stems. Examples:

guul	'say (m.s.)!'	guulu/guulaw	'say (m.p.)!'
guuli	'say (f.s.)!'	guulin	'say (f.p.)!'
šiil	'carry, lift (m.s.)!'	šiilu/šiilaw	'carry, lift (m.p.)!'
šiili	'carry, lift (f.s.)!'	šiilin	'carry, lift (f.p.)!'
naam	'sleep (m.s.)!'	naamu/naamaw	'sleep (m.p.)!'
naami	'sleep (f.s.)!'	naamin	'sleep (f.p.)!'

Derived hollow verbs that occur in GA are those of Classes VII, VIII, and X only.[28] Examples:

Class VII

nšaal	yinšaal	'to be lifted, carried'
ngaal	yingaal	'to be said, mentioned'
nšaaf	yinšaaf	'to be seen'

Class VIII

rtaaH	yirtaaH	'to rest'
Htaaj	yiHtaaj	'to need s.th.'

28. Hollow verbs of Class IV are rare in GA; they are mainly borrowings from MSA or 'pan-Arabic' *koine* forms.

xtaar	yixtaar	'to choose, select'

The perfect and imperfect stems of hollow verbs of Classes VII and VIII are identical. The inflectional prefix is usually *yi-* as in the above cited examples. The imperative form of verbs of Class VIII is the same as their imperfect stems:

rtaaH	'rest (m.s.)!'	rtaaHu/rtaaHaw	'rest (m.p.)!'
rtaaHi	'rest (f.s.)!'	rtaaHin	'rest (f.p.)!'

Class X

Class X hollow verbs have *-stafiil-* as their imperfect stem pattern. The derivational prefix is either *yi-* or *ya-*. Examples:

yistariiH	'he rests'	yistariiHuun	'they (m.) rest'
tistariiH	'she rests'	yistariiHin	'they (f.) rest'
tistariiH	'you (m.s.) rest'	tistariiHuun	'you (m.p.) rest'
tistariiHiin	'you (f.s.) rest'	tistariiHin	'you (f.p.) rest'
'astariiH	'I rest'	nistariiH	'we rest'

The imperative form of Class X hollow verbs is the same as its imperfect stem. Examples: *stariiH, stariiHi, stariiHu/stariiHaw,* and *stariiHin.*

7.2.3 Doubled Verbs

Class I

Doubled verbs of Class I have two imperfect stem vowels: *-i-* or *-u-*.[29] Below are the imperfect forms of the verbs *dašš ydišš*, 'to enter' and *Haṭṭ yHuṭṭ* 'to put, place.'

ydišš	ydiššuun	yHuṭṭ	yHuṭṭuun
ddišš	ydiššin	tHuṭṭ	yHuṭṭin
ddišš	ddiššuun	tHuṭṭ	tHuṭṭuun
ddiššiin	ddiššin	tHuṭṭiin	tHuṭṭin
'adišš	ndišš	'aHuṭṭ	nHuṭṭ

Other verbs that have the same imperfect stem as *dašš* are:

ṣakk	yṣikk	'to shut, close (the door)'
laff	yliff	'to turn (e.g., left)'

29. In rare cases the stem vowel *-a-* is heard, e.g., *ṭagg-yṭagg* 'to flog, beat s.o.,' *9aḏ̣ḏ̣-y9aḏ̣ḏ̣* 'to bite.'

xamm	yximm	'to sweep (e.g., the floor)'
9add	y9idd	'to count'
našš	ynišš	'to wake up'
gaṭṭ	ygiṭṭ	'to throw away'
Habb	yHibb	'to kiss; to like'
dagg	ydigg	'to knock'
šall	yšill	'to steal, take away, s.th.'
9agg	y9igg	'to throw away s.th.'

Other verbs that have the same imperfect stem as *Haṭṭ* are:

ṭagg	yṭugg	'to flog, beat'
9að̣ð̣	y9uð̣ð̣	'to bite'
jarr	yjurr	'to pull, drag'

The imperative forms of doubled verbs of Class I are the same as their imperfect stem:

dišš	'enter (m.s.)!'	daššu/diššaw	'enter (m.p.)!'
dišši	'enter (f.s.)!'	diššin	'enter (f.p.)!'
jurr	'pull, drag (m.s.)!'	jurru/jurraw	'pull, drag (m.p.)!'
jurri	'pull, drag (f.s.)!'	jurrin	'pull, drag (f.p.)!'

The imperfect stem of doubled verbs of Classes VII, VIII, and IX are identical with their perfect stems. Below are imperfect stems of some Class VII doubled verbs:

-ndašš-	'to be entered'
-nṣakk-	'to be shut, closed'
-n9add-	'to be counted'
-nHabb-	'to be kissed, to be liked'
-ngaṭṭ-	'to be thrown away'
-nxamm-	'to be swept'

Examples of imperfect stems of Class VIII doubled verbs are:

-ftarr-	'to turn around'
-htamm-	'to be concerned; to be interested'
-Htall-	'to conquer, occupy'

Examples of imperfect stems of Class IX doubled verbs are:

-zragg-	'to turn blue'
-Hmarr-	'to turn red'

-ṣfarr-	'to turn yellow'
-9wayy-	'to grow crooked'
-9warr-	'to grow blind in one eye'

The imperative forms of these verbs are the same as their perfect stems:

ngaṭṭ	'beat it, go away (m.s.)!'
ftarr	'turn around (m.s.)!'

Class X doubled verbs have the imperfect stem vowel *-i-* for their imperfect forms. Below are the imperfect forms of the verb *staHagg* 'to deserve.'

yistaHigg	'he deserves'	yistaHigguun	'they (m.p.) deserve'
tistaHigg	'she deserves'	yistaHiggin	'they (f.p.) deserve'
tistaHigg	'you (m.s.) deserve'	tistaHigguun	'you (m.p.) deserve'
tistaHiggiin	'you (f.s.) deserve'	tistaHiggin	'you (f.p.) deserve'
'astaHigg	'I deserve'	nistaHigg	'we deserve'

Other examples:

staHabb	yistaHibb	'to like s.th.'
sta9add	yista9idd	'to be, get ready'
staradd	yistaridd	'to regain, get back s.th.'
stamarr	yistamirr	'to continue to do s.th.'

The imperative form of these verbs is the same as its imperfect stem:

sta9idd	'get ready (m.s.)!'
staridd	'get s.th. back (m.s.)!'
stamirr	'go on (doing s.th.) (m.s.)!'

No doubled quadriliterals or derived quadriliterals have been recorded. However, borrowings from MSA and the speech of Arab immigrants in the Gulf have been heard on formal occasions: *šma'azz* (imperfect *yišma'izz*) 'to feel, be disgusted,' *ṭma'ann* (imperfect *yiṭma'inn*) 'to be reassured,' etc.

8. NOUNS-DERIVATION

The majority of nouns in GA are derived from verbs, adjectives, and other nouns. Examples:

saag	'to drive'	→	swaaga	'driving'
'amiin	'honest'	→	'amaana	'honesty'
rayyaal	'man'	→	rujuula	'manliness'

Below are the kinds of nouns:

8.1 Verbal Nouns

Verbal Nouns are nouns, the great majority of which are derived from verbs, which express or name the underlying notion of the verb, as opposed to concrete nouns, e.g., the verbal noun *swaaga* 'driving' denotes the act of driving as opposed to *saayig* 'driver,' which denotes the person whose job is driving. Verbal nouns may indicate an event, a function, a state, or a quality of the underlying verb, as will be shown below.

8.1.1 Class I

The derivation of verbal nouns from Class I verbs is irregular. There are many patterns of the verbal noun, which might be of use to the student, but it is best to learn the verbal noun along with its root verb. The following are the most common patterns[30] for Class I triradical verbs:

1. fu9uul/f9uul

Verb		*Verbal Noun*	
harab	'to break away'	h(u)ruub	'breaking away'
riji9	'to return'	r(u)juu9	'going back, returning'
šarad	'to run away'	š(u)ruud	'running away'
wiṣal	'to arrive'	w(u)ṣuul	'arrival, arriving'
9ibar	'to cross'	9(u)buur	'crossing; a crossing'
baraz	'to be ready'	b(u)ruuz	'being ready'

30. The order in which the patterns appear is not proportional to their frequency.

2. fa91

Verb		*Verbal Noun*	
ð̣arab	'to hit, beat'	ð̣arb	'beating, striking'
tirak	'to leave'	tark	'leaving'
ragaṣ	'to dance'	ragṣ	'dancing'
tiras	'to fill'	tars	'filling'
fitaH	'to open'	fatH	'opening; conquering (a city)'
čaðab	'to tell lies'	čaðb	'telling lies; lies'

fa9l is also a common pattern for triradical doubled verbs:

zaxx	'to catch, get hold of s.o. or s.th.'	zaxx	'getting hold of s.o. or s.th.'
gaṭṭ	'to throw away'	gaṭṭ	'throwing away'
ṣakk	'to close (the door)'	ṣakk	'closing (the door)'
dašš	'to enter'	dašš	'entering; entry'
zagg	'to deficate'	zagg	'deficating'
našš	'to wake up'	našš	'waking up'
ṭagg	'to flog, beat'	ṭagg	'flogging, beating'

3. fa9al

ganaṣ	'to hunt'	ganaṣ	'hunting'
simi9	'to hear'	sama9	'hearing'
9imil	'to make, do'	9amal	'making; work, job'
harab	'to run away'	harab	'running away'

4. f9aala

zaar	'to visit'	zyaara	'visiting; visit'
saag	'to drive'	swaaga	'driving'
zaad	'to increase'	zyaada	'excess; increment'
diras	'to study'	d(i)raasa	'studying; studies'

5. maf9ila

9irif	'to know'	ma9rifa	'knowledge'
nazal	'to dwell'	manzila	'rank, status'

6. fa9i

This is a common pattern for verbal nouns derived from defective verbs:

Verb		*Verbal Noun*	
baġa	'to want'	baġi	'wanting, desiring'
miša	'to walk'	maši	'walking'
Hača	'to speak'	Hači	'talking; talk'
šawa	'to roast'	šawi	'roasting'

7. fool/feel

Most hollow verbs of Class I with the imperfect stem patterns *-fuul-* or *-faal-* have their verbal nouns according to the pattern *fool:*

gaal	'to say'	gool	'saying'
ð̣aaj	'to be bored'	ð̣ooj	'being bored'
baag	'to steal'	boog	'stealing; theft'
šaaf	'to see'	šoof	'seeing'
naam	'to sleep'	noom	'sleeping'
xaaf	'to be afraid'	xoof	'being afriad; fear'

Those with the imperfect stem pattern *-fiil-* usually have *feel* as their verbal noun pattern:

saar	'to leave; to walk'	seer	'leaving; walking'
ṣaad	'to hunt; to catch'	ṣeed	'hunting; catching'
šaal	'to lift'	šeel	'lifting, carrying'

8. fi9l

9alam	'to come to know'	9ilm	'knowing; science'
ṣadag	'to tell the truth'	ṣidg/ṣidj	'telling the truth; truth'
ribaH	'to gain'	ribH	'gaining'

9. fu9l

širib	'to drink'	šurb	'drinking'
ṭaal	'to last long'	ṭuul	'length'

10. fi9la

ðakar	'to mention'	ðikra	'remembrance'
9aaš	'to live'	9iiša	'act of living: life'

8.1.2 Class II

The verbal nouns of verbs of Classes II-X follow predictable patterns. The patterns for verbal nouns of Class II verbs are *taf9iil* for sound verbs and *taf9ila* or *taf9i9a* for defective verbs:

Verb		*Verbal Noun*	
fannaš	'to terminate s.o.'s (or his own) services'	tafniiš	'terminating; termination'
darras	'to teach'	tadriis	'teaching, instructing'
9awwar	'to inflict pain'	ta9wiir	'(attack of) illness; injury'
čayyak	'to check'	tačyiik	'checking'
Hayya	'to greet s.o.'	taHiyya	'greeting s.o.; a greeting'
rabba	'to bring up; to educate'	tarbiya	'bring up; education'

The verbal noun associated with *ṣaḷḷa* 'to pray' is *ṣaḷaa* 'praying; prayer.'

8.1.3 Class III

Verbal nouns of Class III verbs have two patterns: *mfaa9ala* for sound verbs and *mfaa9aa* for defective verbs:

saa9ad	'to help s.o.'	msaa9ada	'help, assistance'
waafag	'to agree'	mwaafaga	'agreement'
Haawal	'to try'	mHaawala	'trial, act of trying'
xaabar	'to telephone'	mxaabara	'telephone conversation'
Haača	'to talk to s.o.'	mHaačaa	'talking to s.o.'
saawa	'to be equal to; to level s.th. (to the ground)'	msaawaa	'equality; leveling'

The verbal noun for *saafar* 'to travel' is *safar* 'travel(ing).'

8.1.4 Class IV

It has already been pointed out in 6.2.3 above, that Class IV verbs in GA are rare and that they are usually replaced by either Class I or Class II verbs. The few verbal nouns of Class IV verbs which are used are literary forms or borrowings from other speakers of Arabic. Examples:

Verb		*Verbal Noun*	
'a9lan	'to announce'	'i9laan	'announcement'
'a9lam	'to tell, inform'	'i9laam	'information'

Verbal nouns of Class IV hollow verbs have the pattern *'ifaala.*

'aðaa9	'to broadcast'	'iðaa9a	'broadcasting'

8.1.5 Class V

There is no verbal noun pattern peculiar to Class V verbs. Some Class V verbal nouns take Class I patterns; some others follow the pattern of Class II verbs, sometimes with changes. Examples:

t9allam	'to learn'	ta9luum	'learning' (instead of *ta9liim*)
zzawwaj	'to get married'	zuwaaj	'marriage'
tqayyar	'to change'	taqyiir	'change'
tqadda	'to have lunch'	qada	'lunching (with s.o.); lunch'
twannas	'to have a good time'	winsa	'having a good time; good time, pleasure'

8.1.6 Class VI

Class VI verbal nouns have two patterns: *tafaa9ul* for sound verbs and *tafaa9i* for defective verbs. Examples:

twaafaj	'to agree with each other'	tawaafuj	'agreement (with each other'
t9aawan	'to cooperate'	ta9aawun	'cooperation'
txaaṣam	'to quarrel with each other'	taxaaṣum	'quarreling together'
tšaawar	'to consult together'	tašaawur	'consultation (with each other)'
ddaa9am	'to collide'	tadaa9um	'collision'
tHaača	'to talk together'	taHaači	'talking together'
tnaasa	'to pretend to have forgotten s.th.'	tanaasi	'pretense of having forgotten s.th.'

8.1.7 Class VII

Verbal nouns of Class VII verbs are not common. The patterns are *nfi9aal* and *nfi9a* for sound and defective verbs, respectively.

Examples:

Verb		*Verbal Noun*	
nṣaraf	'to leave, go away'	nṣiraaf	'going away, departure'
nkisar	'to be broken, defeated'	nkisaar	'defeat'
nfajar	'to explode'	nfijaar	'explosion; exploding'
njalab	'to be turned over'	njilaab	'state of being turned over'
nkafa	'to be satisfied (e.g., with food, drink, etc.)'	nkifa	'state of being satisfied'

Doubled and hollow verbs have the patterns *nfi9aal* and *nfiyaal,* respectively, for their verbal nouns:

ngaṭṭ	'to be thrown away'	ngiṭaaṭ	'state of being thrown away'
nHall	'to be solved; to be morally degenerated'	nHilaal	'dissolution; moral degeneration'
ndaar	'to turn to one side'	ndiyaar	'turning to one side'

8.1.8 Class VIII

Most verbal nouns of Class VIII verbs are of the *ftiyaal* pattern. Examples:

Htifal	'to celebrate'	Htifaal	'celebration'
rtabaṭ	'to be tied up with s.o. or s.th.'	rtibaaṭ	'state of being tied up with s.o. or s.th.'
jtima9	'to have a meeting'	jtimaa9	'meeting'
htamm	'to be concerned with s.o. or s.th.'	htimaam	'concern'
rtaaH	'to rest; to be at ease'	rtiyaaH	'state of being at ease'

Some Class VIII verbs have verbal nouns derived from their corresponding Class I verbs: [31]

štika	'to complain'	šakwa	'complaint'
štara	'to buy'	mištara	'buying'
Htaaj	'to need s.o. or s.th., lack s.th.'	Haaja	'need; necessity'

31. See 6.2.7 for the similarity in meaning of Class I and Class VIII verbs.

8.1.9 Class IX

Verbal nouns of Class IX are very uncommon. The pattern is *f9ilaal.* Examples:

Verb		*Verbal Noun*	
ṣfarr	'to turn yellow'	ṣfiraar	'act of turning yellow'
9wayy	'to turn crooked'	9wiyaay	'act of turning crooked'

8.1.10 Class X

Verbal nouns associated with Class X verbs have three patterns: *stif9aal* for sound verbs and doubled verbs, *stif9a* for defective verbs, and *stifaala* for hollow verbs. Examples:

1. Sound and doubled: *stif9aal*

starxaṣ	'to seek permission'	stirxaaṣ	'state of seeking permission'
stakšaf	'to discover, explore'	stikšaaf	'discovery, exploration'
staHmag	'to be angry'	stiHmaag	'state of being angry'
staslaf	'to borrow (money)'	stislaaf	'borrowing (money)'
sta9mal	'to use, utilize'	sti9maal	'use, utilization'
stajwab	'to interrogate'	stijwaab	'interrogation'
staradd	'to regain'	stirdaad	'regaining'
staHagg	'to deserve, be worthy of'	stiHgaag	'worthiness, one's due'
staHabb	'to like, desire'	stiHbaab	'liking, desire'

2. Defective: *stif9a*

staqna 9an	'to do without s.th.'	stiqna	'state of doing without s.th.'
sta9fa	'to resign'	sti9fa	'resignation'
sta9ṭa	'to seek, beg'	sti9ṭa	'begging'

3. Hollow: *stifaala*

sta9aan	'to seek help, assistance'	sti9aana	'assistance, help'
staraaH	'to rest, relax'	stiraaHa	'rest, relaxation'
stafaad	'to benefit'	stifaada	'benefit'

8.1.11 Quadriliterals

The pattern for quadriliteral verbs is $C_1aC_2C_3aC_4a$. Note the shift in stress. Examples:

Verb		*Verbal Noun*	
lá9waz	'to bother'	la9wáza	'bothering'
gášmar	'to play a prank on s.o.'	gašmára	'joking, kidding'
xárbaṭ	'to mix, mess, s.th. or s.o. up'	xarbáṭa	'chaos, confusion'

Reduplicated quadriliteral verbs also have the same pattern for their verbal nouns:

gáṣgaṣ	'to cut up s.th.'	gaṣgáṣa	'act of cutting up s.th.'
ṭágṭag	'to tap s.th.'	ṭagṭága	'tapping'

Weak quadriliterals have the pattern $C_1eeC_3aC_4a$ for their verbal nouns:

réewas	'to go in reverse'	reewása	'going in reverse'
sóogar	'to insure s.th.'	soogára	'insuring, insurance'

Derived quadriliterals do not have verbal nouns associated with them; usually they have the same pattern as for simple quadriliterals:

tlá9waz	→	la9wáza
tġášmar	→	ġašmára
tgáṣgaṣ	→	gaṣgáṣa

8.2 Instance Nouns

Instance nouns, also known as nouns of single occurrence, are derived from verbal nouns or other kinds of nouns by suffixing *-a,* sometimes with appropriate stem changes. They are usually of the patterns *fa9la, fi9la,* and *fu9la.* Instance nouns express the meaning of a single occurrence (or a particular instance) of the underlying word, or a period or "spell" of such a state. Examples of instance nouns derived from verbal nouns:

Verb		*Verbal Noun*		*Instance Noun*	
ragaṣ	'to dance'	ragṣ	'dancing'	ragṣa	'a dance'
širib	'to drink'	šurb	'drinking'	šurba	'a drink'
yiġam	'to gulp'	–	–	yiġma	'a gulp'

Verb		*Verbal Noun*		*Instance Noun*	
naam	'to sleep'	noom	'sleep(ing)'	nooma	'a nap'
maat	'to die'	moot	'death'	moota	'a particular kind of death'
Harag	'to burn'	Hariij	'burning'	Hariija	'a fire'
daax	'to smoke; to feel dizzy'	doox	'smoking'	dooxa	'a puff of smoke; a confusing state of affairs'

Some instance nouns have patterns different from those of the corresponding verbal nouns:

tkallam	'to speak'	čalaam	'talk, speech'	čilma	'a word'
štaġaḷ	'to work'	šuġuḷ	'work'	šuġla	'a piece of work'
Habb	'to kiss; to like'	Hubb	'love; kissing'	Habba	'a kiss'

Examples of instance nouns derived from other nouns:

Underlying Word		*Instance Noun*	
leel	'night (time)'	leela	'a night'
Harr	'hot weather; heat'	Harra	'jealosy, envy'
'akil	'food; eating'	'akla	'a meal'

Instance nouns, unlike verbal nouns, are inflected for number.[32] Their dual and sound feminine plural are formed by suffixing *-teen* and *-aat,* respectively:

yiġma	'a gulp'	Habba	'a kiss'
yiġmateen	'two gulps'	Habbateen	'two kisses'
yiġmaat	'(more than two) gulps'	Habbaat	'(more than two) kisses'

Derived verbs (Classes II-X) and quadriliterals do not usually have instance nouns.

32. See 9.2.2 and 9.2.3.1B2.

8.3 Unit Nouns

Unit nouns indicate an individual unit or an individual item of the underlying noun. They are derived from collective nouns by suffixing *-a,* sometimes with appropriate stem changes. Note that most instance nouns are derived from verbal nouns by suffixing *-a.* Where an instance noun designates a single *occurrence* of the underlying verbal noun, a unit noun designates an individual *unit* of the underlying collective noun. Thus the instance noun *ragṣa* 'a dance' is derived from the verbal noun *ragṣ* 'dancing,' and the unit noun *beeð̣a* 'an egg' is derived from the collective noun *beeð̣* 'eggs.' Almost all kinds of vegetables, fruits, grains, flowers, fruit trees, grasses, etc., are collective nouns. Examples of unit nouns:

A. -CC or -VVC → -CCa or -VVCa

Collective Noun		*Unit Noun*	
yiHH	'watermelons'	yiHHa	'a watermelon'
Habb	'grains (e.g., of wheat)'	Habba	'a grain'
baṭṭiix	'cantaloupes'	baṭṭiixa	'a cantaloupe'
gmaaš	'pearl'	gmaaša	'a pearl'
rweed	'radishes'	rweeda	'a radish'
xaḷaaḷ	'unripe (green) dates'	xaḷaaḷa	'an unripe (green) date'
beeð̣	'eggs'	beeð̣a	'an egg'
jaam	'(sheets of) glass'	jaama	'a sheet of glass'
diyaay	'chicken; hens'	diyaaya	'a chicken, a hen'
tiffaaH	'apples'	tiffaaHa	'an apple'
burtaġaaḷ	'oranges'	burtaġaaḷa	'an orange'

B. $-C_1 VC_2 \rightarrow C_1 C_2 a$

Examples involving vowel elision are:

jibin	'cheese'	jibna	'a piece of cheese'
xubiz	'bread'	xubza	'a piece of bread'
ramiḷ	'sand'	ramḷa	'a handful of sand'
dihin	'shortening'	dihna	'a cupful of shortening'

C. fa9al → f9ala

Most collective nouns of the pattern *fa9al* have their corresponding unit nouns according to the pattern *f9ala,* or *f9ila* in a few cases. Examples:

Collective Noun		*Unit Noun*	
ša9ar	'hair'	š9ara	'a hair'
faHam	'coal, charcoal'	fHama	'a piece of coal'
naxaḷ	'palm trees'	nxaḷa	'a palm tree'
bagar	'cows'	bgara	'a cow'
baṣal	'onions'	bṣala	'an onion'
šiyar	'trees'	šyara	'a tree'
qanam	'goats, sheep'	qnama	'a goat, a sheep'

A few have the pattern *f9ula:*

warag	'paper'	wruga	'a piece of paper'
Haṭab	'wood'	Hṭuba	'a piece of wood'

D. fa9il → fa9la

Collective nouns of the pattern *fa9il* have *fa9la* as their pattern for unit nouns:

ramil (var. *ramul*)	'sand'	ramla	'a handful of sand'
šami9	'wax'	šam9a	'a candle'
tamir (var. *tamur*)	'dates'	tamra	'a date'

E. -a → -aa

Collective nouns with an *-a* ending form their unit nouns by lengthening the *-a.* Examples:

ṭamaaṭa	'tomatoes'	ṭamaaṭaa	'a tomato'
gaṭa	'sand grouse'	gaṭaa	'a sand grouse'
puteeta [33]	'potatoes'	puteetaa	'a potato'

F. With small grains, such as rice, wheat, barley, etc., the word *Habbat* 'a piece' is used before the collective noun to indicate an individual unit; with other kinds of nouns, words such as *ġiṭ9a* 'piece,' *ṣilb* 'stick,' etc., are used.

---

33. This word, a corruption of the English loan *baṭaaṭa,* has replaced the old GA *9ali willam,* the singular of which is *9ali willama* 'a potato.'

Collective Noun		*Unit Noun*	
burr	'wheat'	Habbat burr	'a grain of wheat'
ši9iir	'barley'	Habbat ši9iir	'a grain of barley'
9eeš	'rice'	Habbat 9eeš	'a grain of rice'
xaḷag	'cloth'	ġiṭ9at xaḷag	'a piece of cloth'
ðira	'corn'	Habbat ðira	'a kernel of corn'
čabriit	'matches'	ṣilb čabriit	'a match stick'

G. -i → -iyya

luumi	'(Omani) limes'	luumiyya	'a lime'
naxxi(y)	'chick peas'	naxxiyya	'a chick pea'

Unit nouns are feminine singular and, like instance nouns, have a dual form, e.g., *beeḍateen* 'two eggs' and a sound feminine plural form, e.g., *beeḍaat* '(individual) eggs.'

8.4 Feminine Nouns

In this section we are concerned with those feminine nouns that refer to female human beings and some animals, which are formed from their corresponding masculine nouns by suffixing *-a,* sometimes with appropriate stem changes.

A. In this group belong those feminine nouns that are formed from their corresponding masculine nouns by the addition of *-a* (known as the feminine morpheme) without additional changes. These are masculine nouns that end with a doubled consonant, a consonant cluster, or a consonant preceded by a long vowel. Examples:

yadd	'grandfather'	yadda	'grandmother'
9amm	'(paternal) uncle'	9amma	'(paternal) aunt'
čalb	'dog'	čalba	'bitch'
9abd	'slave'	9abda	'slave girl'
šeex	'Shaikh'	šeexa	'wife of a Shaikh'
sbaal	'ape; monkey'	sbaala	'ape; monkey (f.)'
rifiij	'friend; companion'	rifiija	'companion (f.); mistress'
zooj	'husband'	zooja	'wife'

B. This group of nouns requires vowel elision (see 4.3.1 above) before suffixing the feminine morpheme:

yaahil	'child (m.)'	yaahla	'child (f.)'
9aagil	'wise person (m.)'	9aagla	'wise person (f.)'
xaadim	'servant (m.)'	xaadma	'servant (f.)'

C. This group of nouns requires both consonant elision and vowel elision (see 4.3 above) before suffixing the feminine morpheme. Examples:

mxabbaḷ	'crazy man'	mxabḷa	'crazy woman'
m9azzib	'(house) host'	m9azba	'(house) hostess'
Hbayyib	'honey, dear one (m.)'	Hbayba	'honey, dear one (f.)'
mHassin	'barber, hair dresser (m.)'	mHasna	'barber, hair dresser (f.)'
rayyis	'boss, chief (m.)'	raysa	'boss, chief (f.)'

D. Masculine nouns ending in *-u* change *-u* into *-w* for their corresponding feminine forms:

gaṭu	'cat (m.)'	gaṭwa	'cat (f.)'
9uḍ̱u	'member (m.)'	9uḍ̱wa	'member (f.)'
luulu	'pearl'	luulwa	'a pearl'

Some others keep the *-u* and add *-ww,* as in *9adu* 'enemy (m.)' → *9aduwwa* 'enemy (f.).'

E. To this group belong those masculine nouns that end with *-i.* Most of these nouns are masculine nisba[34] (i.e., "relative") nouns. The corresponding feminine nisba nouns are formed by suffixing *-yya.*

gṭári	'Qatari (m.)'	gṭaríyya	'Qatari (f.)'
šaárji	'belonging to Sharja (m.)'	šaarjíyya	'belonging to Sharja (f.)'
bdíwi	'Bedouin (m.)'	bdiwíyya	'Bedouin (f.)'
'ardúni	'Jordanian (m.)'	'arduníyya	'Jordanian (f.)'
qáni	'rich person (m.)'	qaníyya	'rich person (f.)'
láġwi	'talkative person (m.)'	laġwíyya	'talkative person (f.)'
karráani	'clerk (m.)'	karraaníyya	'clerk (f.)'

34. See 10.5.1.3.

8.5 Participles as Nouns

Active and passive participles as nouns and adjectives will be dealth with under participles and adjectives below (see 10.4 and 10.5).

8.6 Occupational Nouns

Nouns that indicate people who have certain occupations or vocations are called occupational nouns. Most of the corresponding feminine nouns are formed by suffixing *-a,* the feminine morpheme. Occupational nouns are of certain patterns, the most frequent of which are the following:

A. faa9il

Occupational nouns of the *faa9il* pattern are derived from Class I verbs:

Verb	*Occupational Masc. Noun*	*Occupational Fem. Noun*
katab 'to write'	kaatib 'clerk (m.)'	kaatba 'clerk (f.)'
xadam 'to serve'	xaadim 'servant (m.)'	xaadma 'servant (f.)'
gaḍ̱a 'to pronounce judgment'	gaaḍ̱i 'judge (m.)'	gaaḍ̱ya 'judge (f.)'
ra9a 'to take care of'	raa9i 'shepherd; owner'	raa9ya 'shepherdess; owner (f.)'

B. fa99aal

Occupational nouns of the *fa99aal* pattern are derived from verbs and nouns.

Underlying Word	*Occupational Masc. Noun*	*Occupational Fem. Noun*
gaṣṣab 'to cut meat'	gaṣṣaab 'butcher (m.)'	gaṣṣaaba 'butcher (f.)'
ni9iiš 'kind of dance'	yawwaal 'male dancer'	na99aaša 'female dancer'
xaaṭ 'to sew'	xayyaaṭ 'tailor'	xayyaaṭa 'seamstress'
Hadag 'to catch fish'	Haddaag 'line-fisherman'	Haddaaga 'line-fisherman (f.)'

Underlying Word	*Occupational Masc. Noun*	*Occupational Fem. Noun*
xabaz 'to bake'	xabbaaz 'baker (m.)'	xabbaaza 'baker (f.)'
čaðab 'to tell lies'	čaððaab 'liar (m.)'	čaððaaba 'liar (f.)'
simač 'fish'	sammaač 'fisherman; fish dealer (m.)'	sammaača 'fisherwoman; fish dealer (f.)'
9aks 'photograph'	9akkaas 'photographer (m.)'	9akkaasa photographer (f.)'

C. mfa99il

Almost all the masculine occupational nouns of the *mfa99il* (in one or two cases, *mfa99al*) type are derived from Class II verbs. Examples:

Verb	*Occupational Masc. Noun*	*Occupational Fem. Noun*
Hassan 'to cut hair'	mHassin 'barber (m.)'	mHasna 'barber (f.)'
9azzab (no meaning)	m9azzib 'host'	m9azba 'hostess'
darras 'to teach'	m(u)darris 'instructor (m.)'	m(u)darsa 'instructor (f.)'
ṭarraš 'to send (a letter or s.o.'	mṭarriš 'sender (m.)'	mṭarša 'sender (f.)'
ṭawwa9 'to break in (a horse)'	mṭawwa9 'religious teacher (m.)'	mṭaw9a 'religious teacher (f.)'

8.7 Instrumental Nouns

An instrumental noun, or a noun of instrument, indicates the instrument or object with which the act described by the underlying word can be performed. Most instrumental nouns in GA are derived from verbs. The following are the most commonly used patterns.

A. mif9aal

Verb		*Instrumental Noun*	
fitaH	'to open'	miftaaH	'key'
nigar	'to peck'	mingaar	'beak'
daax	'to smoke'	midwaax	'pipe (smoking)'
nafax	'to inflate; to puff'	mimfaax	'bellows; air pump'
Hafar	'to dig a hole'	miHfaar	'hole digger'
yaddaf	'to row (a boat)'	miidaaf	'oar'

B. mif9al/mif9ila

sanad	'to support, buttress'	misnida	'cushion'
naxxal	'to sieve'	minxal	'sieve'
gaṣṣ	'to cut'	migaṣṣ	'scissors'
kanas	'to sweep'	miknisa	'broom'

C. fa99aala/fi99aala

saar	'to leave; to walk'	sayyaara/siyyaara	'car'
ṭaar	'to fly'	ṭayyaara/ṭiyyaara	'airplane'

D. fa9la

Most examples of this pattern are of foreign origin.

gafša	'spoon, ladle'	(Turkish)
banka	'fan'	(Hindi-Urdu)
ġarša	'bottle'	(Persian)

8.8 Locative Nouns

A locative noun or a noun of place designates the place where the action designated by the underlying word takes place. The following are the most frequently used locative noun patterns:

A. maf9ala

Underlying Word		*Locative Noun*	
kitab	'to write'	maktába	'library; bookstore'
diras	'to study'	madrása	'school'
ġabir	'tomb, grave'	maġbára	'cemetery'

Underlying Word		*Locative Noun*	
gaṣṣab	'to cut meat'	magṣ́aba	'butcher's shop'
Hakam	'to rule'	maHkáma	'law court'

B. maf9al/mif9al

sabaH	'to bathe'	misbaH	'swimming pool'
dafan	'to bury'	madfan	'burial place'
ġasal	'to wash'	miġsal	'sink'
ragad	'to sleep'	margad	'bed'
ṭaar	'to fly'	maṭaar	'airport'
ṭibax	'to cook'	miṭbax	'kitchen'

C. maf9il

yilas	'to sit (down)'	maylis	'living room'
siyad	'to kneel'	m(a)siid [35]	'mosque'
waϑ̣i9	'situation'	mawϑ̣i9	'location'
ϑ̣eef	'guest'	maϑ̣iif	'guest house'

D. fa9la

Most examples of this pattern are of foreign origin.

čabra	'vender's stand'	(Hindi)
xaana	'place; shop' [36]	(Persian)

8.9 Diminutive Nouns

Diminutive nouns, usually known as diminutives, are derived mainly from proper nouns and only a few are derived from adjectives used as nouns. Diminutives indicate a small or insignificant variety of that which is designated by the underlying word. They also indicate affection and endearment. The most commonly used patterns are:

---

35. Lit., "a place where you kneel down in prayer."

36. *xaana* is rarely used independently: it is usually preceded by some other kind of noun, e.g., *čaay xaana* 'a tea place' or a 'coffee house' and *baanziin xaana* 'a gas station,' especially in Bahraini and Kuwaiti.

A. faa9il → fwee9il

Underlying Word		*Diminutive*
saalim	'Salim (prop. noun)'	sweelim
ṣaaliH	'Salih (prop. noun)'	ṣweeliH
xaalid	'Khalid (prop. noun)'	xweelid
naaṣir	'Nasir (prop. noun)'	nweeṣir/naṣṣuur
kaatib	'clerk (m.)'	kweetib
xaadim	'servant (m.)'	xweedim

B. f9aal
f9iil → f9ayyil

1. f9aal → f9ayyil

Hmaar	'ass; donkey'	Hmayyir
Hṣaan	'horse'	Hṣayyin
ktaab	'book'	ktayyib

2. f9iil → f9ayyil

ṭ(a)Hiin	'flour; powder'	ṭHayyin
b(a)xiil	'stingy person (m.)'	bxayyil
k(a)biir	'big; old'	kbayyir
ṣ(a)ġiir	'young; little'	ṣġayyir
saxiif	'thin'	sxayyif
Habiib	'loved one, sweetheart (m.)'	Hbayyib
r(a)xiiṣ	'cheap; inexpensive'	rxayyiṣ
gaṣiir	'short; not long'	gṣayyir

C. feel → fwayyil

ṭeer	'bird'	ṭwayyir
xeeṭ	'thread (sewing)'	xwayyiṭ/xweeṭ
zeed	'Zaid (proper name)'	swayyid
zaayid	'Zayid (proper name)'	zwayyid

D. -oo

Only proper nouns belong to this class of diminutives. Most of these proper nouns are feminine with the feminine ending *-a*. *-a* is omitted before the diminutive *-oo* suffix. Some of these nouns have another diminutive pattern, *fa99uul,* which is used only for endearment; those with the *-oo* suffix imply lack of respect or disregard.

ṣaara	'Sara'	ṣaaroo/ṣayyuur
nuura	'Nora'	nuuroo
9aayša	'Aisha'	9eešoo/9ayyuuš
xadiija	'Khadija'	xadiijoo/xadduuy
Hiṣṣa	'Hissa'	Hiṣṣoo
šamma	'Shamma'	šammoo
faaṭma	'Fatima'	faṭmoo/faṭṭuum
šeexa	'Shaikha'	šeexoo/šayyuux

Examples of feminine nouns without the *-a* ending and masculine nouns:

maryam	'Miryam'	maryamoo/maryuum		(female)
zeenab	'Zainab'	zeenaboo		(female)
ṣabaaH	'Sabah'	---------------	ṣabbuuH	(female)
jum9a	'Juma'	--------------	jammuu9	(male)
naaṣir	'Nasir'	--------------	naṣṣuur	(male)
mHammad	'Mohammad'	mHammadoo	------------	(male)
'aHmad	'Ahmad'	'aHmadoo	--------------	(male)
9ali	'ali'	9alloo	--------------	(male)
9abdaḷḷa	'Abdalla'	--------------	9abbuud	(male)

D. fa99aala → f9eela

Nouns belonging to this group are characterized by a doubled consonant followed by the long vowel *-aa-*. Their corresponding diminutive nouns are of the pattern *f9ee9iila:*

sayyaara	'car'	syeeyiira
ṭayyaara	'airplane'	ṭyeeyiira
xaḷḷaaṭa	'(cement) mixer'	xḷeeḷiiṭa

E. f9ee9iil/m9ee9iil

To this pattern belong some place names and quadriliterals.

fHeeHiil	'Fuhaiheel (a small town in Kuwait)'
bleebiil	'(from *bulbul*) songbird; nightingale'

m9eeriis	'(from *mi9ris*) bridegroom'
msee9iid	'(from *'umm sa9iid*) (a town in Qatar)'

8.10 Foreign Nouns

Unlike many other dialects of Arabic, GA has a large foreign vocabulary, mainly Persian, Hindi-Urdu, and English. One of the main reasons for this linguistic influence is the presence of foreign communities in the Arabian Gulf area. Persian immigrants in the area are mainly laborers, clerks, and well established merchants and businessmen. Persian as a first language is spoken in many homes, especially in Kuwait, Qatar, and Dubai. Most Indians and Pakistanis are either odd job workmen or semi-skilled technicians. The presence of English linguistic items in GA is explained by the political and economic interest of the British in the area. In addition to borrowings from Persian, Hindi-Urdu, and English, there are a few borrowings from Turkish, French, Italian, and Portuguese, most of which are present in other Arabic dialects. Only a few of those borrowings remained unmodified; most of them have been modified somewhat, both in phonology and morphology.[37] In phonology the following modifications or sound changes have been observed. The examples given are from English.

A. Diphthongs

1. ai → ee/aa

The diphthong *ai* does not exist in GA.[38] It changes into a vowel, *ee* or *aa.* Examples:

war*teem*	'over*time*'	*seed*	'*side*'
*lee*san	'*li*cense'	*see*kal	'*cy*cle'
*dree*wil	'*dri*ver (m.)'	*leet*	'*light* (n.)'
*taa*yir	'(car) *tire*'	*waa*yir	'*wire* (n.)'

2. ow → uu/oo

37. Other morphological and syntactic modifications will be pointed out below, in the relevant sections.

38. See 3.1.

3. ey → ee

The dipthongs *ow* and *ey* do not exist in GA either. They change into the long vowels *uu/oo* and *ee,* respectively. Examples:

jal*buut*	'jolly-boat'	'is*beer*	'spare (tire)'
*tee*bil	'table'	*kuut*	'coat'
kab*ree*tar	'carburetor'	*noot*	'note'

B. Consonants

Consonants that do not exist in GA are replaced by consonants that share similar articulation features, e.g., point, manner, etc. Examples:

*w*ilf	'*v*alve'	'is*b*eer	's*p*are (tire)'
*w*arteem	'o*v*ertime'	si*b*ring	'(metal) s*p*ring'
si*b*ray	's*p*ray (n.)	boṭil	'bottle'
*b*laa*k*aat	'(spark) *p*lugs'	*b*aranda	'*v*eranda'

C. Consonant Clusters

The vowel *i*[39] is usually interpolated after the first consonant in a three-consonant sequence; if two consonants are word-initial, *'i-* usually precedes:

sikruu[40]	'screw'	sikraab	'scrap'
sibring	'spring'	siwič	'switch'
heerin	'(car) horn'	'isbaana	'spanner'[41]
sikriim	'ice cream'	'isbeer	'spare (tire)'

D. Metathesis[42]

A reversed order of consonants in foreign words is characteristic of GA:

balanti 'penalty'

E. Syllable Omission

Sometimes a whole syllable, especially the first syllable, in a long word is omitted:

---

39. See 4.1.

40. *sikruu* is in free variation with *sakruub.*

41. British for *wrench.*

42. Metathesis is here restricted to a reversed order of consonants.

seekal	'bicycle'	blaak	'spark plug'
kandeešin	'air conditioning'	manwar	'man-of-war'
sikriim	'ice cream'	'aayil	'(motor) oil'

In morphology, most borrowed verbs are those of Class II and they are wholly Arabized. Examples:

fannaš	(from *finish*)	'to resign; to terminate one's services'
čayyak	(from *check*)	'to check'
bannad	(from Persian *bandan*)	'to close, stop (e.g., work)'
tayyat	(from *tighten*)	'to tighten'
šawwat	(from *shoot*)	'to shoot (e.g., in soccer)'

Below are some of the commonest borrowed nouns.

English

batri	'battery'	dreewil	'driver'
Hafiiz	'office'	taanki	'(water) tank'
daxtar	'doctor'	kalač	'clutch'
dabal	'double'	tindeel	'foreman, supervisor'
'aayil	'(motor) oil'	batrool	'gasoline'
taayir	'(car) tire'	tankar	'tank-car'
gḷaaṣ	'glass (of s.th.)'	kandeešin	'air conditioning'
leet	'light'	peep	'pipe'
radeetar	'radiator'	kuub	'cup'
reewas	'to reverse'	sbaana	'spanner, wrench'

Persian

('i)stikaan	'small tea-cup'	bandar	'(sea) port'
bugša	'envelope'	guuṭi	'can (of s.th.)'
baxšiiš	'tip, gratuity'	čaay	'tea'
čingaaḷ	'fork'	xarda	'change, petty cash'
xaašuuga	'spoon'	nooxaða	'ship's captain'
dirwaaza	'gate'	dariiša	'window'
bannad	'to shut, close'	jaam	'glass'
rasta	'(paved) road'	9aks	'photograph'
šakar	'sugar'	9akkaas	'photographer'
quuri	'tea kettle'	hast	'there is'

Hindi-Urdu

banka	'fan'	juuti	'shoes'
beezaat	'money'	dabba[43]	'(car) trunk'
darzan	'dozen'	siida	'straight (adv.)'
ṣaaloona	'soup'	čatti	'note'
luumi	'lemons'	karraani	'clerk'

Turkish

naariila	'small hubble-bubble'	ṭurši	'pickles'
ṭooz[44]	'haze, thick dust'	ṭoofa	'wall'
čuula	'kerosine stove'	doorbiin	'telescope'
šiiša	'empty bottle'	gafša	'large spoon, ladle'
zangiin	'rich man'	kirfaaya	'bed'

9. NOUNS-INFLECTION

9.1 Gender

Nouns in GA have gender, either masculine or feminine, and a few nouns have both genders. Nouns, including personal names, that refer to males are masculine, and those referring to females are feminine. Thus, *yuusif* 'Joseph,' *jaasim* 'Jasim,' *karaama* 'Karama,' and *'aḷḷa* 'God' are masculine, while *šeexa* 'Shaikha' and *maryam* 'Miryam' are feminine. This distinction is important in grammar, since the choice of pronoun depends on the gender of the noun or person involved, and it is the function of noun gender that governs the gender inflection of verbs and adjectives. Nouns referring to non-living things also have gender. The following nouns and proper names are feminine in GA:

A. Nouns with the ending *-a*

Most nouns with the ending *-a* or *-aa* are feminine. These nouns do not have corresponding masculine nouns. Examples:

yaam9a	'university'	gahwa	'coffee'
jaafla	'caravan'	sayyaara	'car'

43. *šanṭa* (also 'suitcase') is more commonly used.

44. *ṭooz* is literally Kuwaiti; *ġbaar* is more commonly used in Abu Dhabi and the rest of the U.A.E.

madrasa	'school'	ṣaḷaa	'prayer'
daayra	'department'	bargiyya	'telegram'
9aṣaa	'stick'	gaṭaa	'sand grouse'

These nouns include foreign nouns:

sbaana	'spanner, wrench' (English)	bugša	'envelope' (Persian)
lampa	'light bulb'	diriiša	'window' (Persian)
banka	'fan' (Hindi-Urdu)	xaašuuga	'spoon' (Persian)
ṣaaloona	'soup' (Hindi-Urdu)	dirwaaza	'gate' (Persian)
jigaara	'cigarett' (English)	šiiša	'empty bottle' (Turkish)

It should be pointed out that a few nouns ending in *-a* are masculine. Examples:

masa	'night (m.)'	9aša	'dinner, supper (m.)'
mustašfa	'hospital (m.)'	qada	'lunch (m.)'
Hala	'rust (m.)'	hawa	'weather; atmosphere (m.)'
nooxaḏa	'ship's captain (m.)'	xaliifa	'Caliph; male's name'
šeeba	'old man (m.)'	šita	'winter (m.)'

Among the feminine nouns that belong here are those that are derived from their *corresponding masculine nouns.*[45] Examples:

Masculine		*Feminine*	
čalb	'dog'	čalba	'bitch'
rifiij	'companion, friend'	rifiija	'friend; mistress'
mumarriḏ̣	'nurse'	mumarriḏ̣a	'nurse'
mudiir	'director, manager'	mudiira	'director, manager'

Instance nouns[46] are derived from verbal nouns or other kinds of nouns by suffixing *-a,* and are feminine in gender:

Verbal Noun		*Instance Noun*	
ṭagg	'beating, flogging'	ṭagga	'a beating'
šurb	'drinking'	šurba	'a drink (of s.th.)'
'akil	'food, eating'	'akla	'a meal'

45. See 8.4A for some more examples.

46. See 8.2 for some more examples.

Unit Nouns[47] end with the suffix *-a* and are all feminine singular. Most collective nouns,[48] from which unit nouns are derived, are masculine singular, though the English translation may be plural, e.g., *yiHH* 'watermelons.' Examples:

Collective Noun		*Unit Noun*	
tiffaaH	'apples'	tiffaaHa	'an apple'
bagar	'cows'	bgara	'a cow'
Haṭab	'wood'	Hṭuba	'a piece of wood'
ṭamaaṭa	'tomatoes'	ṭamaaṭaa	'a tomato'

B. Some nouns do not have the feminine ending *-a*, but they are feminine by usage. These nouns include:

1. Double parts of the body:

'iid (var. *yad*)	'hand'	9een	'eye'
riil	'food; leg'	'iϑin	'ear'

2. Names of cities, towns, and countries:

'abu ϑ̣abi	'Abu Dhabi'	dbayy	'Dubai'
l-baHreen	'Bahrain'	9ajmaan	'Ajman'
giṭar	'Qatar'	beruut	'Beirut'
li-kweet	'Kuwait'	l-ġuds	'Jerusalem'
9umaan	'Oman'	l-9een	'Al-Ain'
labnaan	'Lebanon'	landan	'London'

3. Nouns which denote females. Such nouns have corresponding masculine nouns of different stems:

Masculine		*Feminine*	
'ubu	'father'	'umm	'mother'
'uxu	'brother'	'uxut	'sister'
'ibin	'son (of)'	bint	'daughter (of); girl'
ṣbayy	'young boy'	bnayya	'young girl'
rayyaal	'man'	mara	'woman'
mi9ris	'bridegroom'	9aruus(a)	'bride'
šeeba	'old man'	9ayuuz	'old woman'
yawwaal	'male dancer'	na99aaša	'female dancer'

---

47. See 8.3 for some more examples.

48. See 8.3 for some more examples.

4. Females of most animals:

diič	'rooster'	diyaaya	'hen'
θoor	'bull'	bgara	'cow'
ṭili	'goat (m.)'	ṣxaḷa	'goat (f.)'
xaruuf	'lamb'	n9aya	'ewe'
čabš	'ram'	yaa9da	'female sheep'
Hṣaan	'horse'	faras	'mare'
b(i)9iir	'camel'	naaga	'female camel'

Note that *ðakar* 'male' and *naθya* 'female' can be used for either a male or a female human being or an animal:

ðakar l-mara huwa r-rayyaal.	'The male of *woman* is *man.*'
d-diyaaya naθyat d-diič.	'The hen is the female of the rooster.'

5. A few common words, including many foreign nouns:

siččiin	'knife'	seekal	'bicycle'	gḷaaṣ	'(drinking) glass'
šams	'sun'	teebil	'table'	čatti	'a short note'
naar	'fire'	boṭil	'bottle'	sikriim	'ice cream'
leesan	'license'	batri	'battery'	čingaaḷ	'fork'

9.2 Number

Nouns have three numbers: singular, dual, and plural.

9.2.1 Singular

Singular nouns include both count and mass nouns. Count nouns designate countable entities and mass nouns indicate uncountable nouns. Singular nouns occur in a variety of patterns and it is difficult to predict the plural of a noun from the singular pattern except in a few cases,[49] which will be pointed out below. Examples of count and mass nouns are:

Count		*Mass*	
m(a)siid	'mosque'	laHam	'meat'
yaahil	'child'	šakar	'sugar'
šeeba	'old man'	Haṭab	'wood'

49. See 9.2.3.

Count		*Mass*	
9ayuuz	'old woman'	ðahab	'gold'
smiča	'a fish'	xmaam	'garbage'
b(i)9iir	'camel'	dihin	'shortening, butter'

9.2.2 Dual

In English, nouns are either singular or plural; in GA they are singular, dual, or plural. In general the dual is formed by adding the suffix *-een* to a masculine noun and *-teen* to a feminine noun ending with *-a.* Sometimes this siffixation of the dual ending requires appropriate stem changes, as will be shown below.

A. Masculine Nouns

A masculine noun ending with *-vc,* where *-v-* is any unstressed vowel except *-a-*, drops its *v* when the dual suffix is added.[50] Examples:

'asim	'name'	'asmeen	'two names'
ṣagir	'falcon'	ṣagreen	'two falcons'
qisim	'section'	qismeen	'two sections'
ð̣uhur	'noontime'	ð̣uhreen	'two noontimes'

If such a noun has *a* before the final consonant, *a* drops when it is preceded by a velar, a pharyngeal, or the glottal fricative (i.e., *x, g; H, 9;* or *h*):

	ṣaxaḷ	'young goat'	ṣaxḷeen	'two young goats'
	baġaḷ	'mule'	baġḷeen	'two mules'
	baHar	'sea'	baHreen	'two seas'
	ša9ab	'people, nation'	ša9been	'two nations'
	sahal	'meadow'	sahleen	'two meadows'
	šahar	'month'	šahreen	'two months'
but:	gaḷam	'pencil'	gaḷameen	'two pencils'
	walad	'boy'	waladeen	'two boys'
	xaḷag	'duster'	xaḷageen	'two dusters'
	seekal	'bicycle'	seekaleen	'two bicycles'
	waṭan	'homeland'	waṭaneen	'two homelands'

50. See 4.3.

The dual of nisba nouns and other nouns ending in *-i* takes *-yy-* before *-een* is added:

ḍ̣ibyaani	'Abu Dhabian'	ḍ̣ibyaaniyyeen	'two Abu Dhabians'
šaarji	'Sharja'	šaarjiyeen	'from Sharja'
kweeti	'Kuwaiti'	kweetiyyeen	'two Kuwaitis'
baHreeni	'Baharaini'	baHreeniyyeen	'two Bahrainis'
qani	'rich man'	qaniyyeen	'two rich men'
ṭili	'goat'	ṭiliyyeen	'two goats'

Nonhuman masculine nouns that end in *-a* form their dual by adding *-yeen:*

9aša	'dinner'	9ašayeen
mustašfa	'hospital'	mustašfayeen
qada	'lunch'	qadayeen

If such a noun has a human referent, it drops its *-a* and takes the suffix *-teen:*

šeeba	'old man'	šeebteen	'two old men'
xalifa	'Caliph; male's name'	xaliifteen	'two Caliphs'

If the masculine noun ends in *-u,* it drops its *-u* and takes *-ween:*

'ubu	'father'	'ubween	'two fathers'
gaṭu	'cat'	gaṭween	'two cats'
gadu	'hubble-bubble'	gadween	'two hubble-bubbles'
9uḍ̣u	'member'	9uḍ̣ween	'two members'
raadu	'radio'	raadween	'two radios'

Some others keep the *-u* and add *-ww,* as in *9adu* 'enemy' → *9aduwween* 'two enemies.' Otherwise no stem changes are required:

rayyaal	'man'	rayyaaleen	'two men'
'uteel	'hotel'	'uteeleen	'two hotels'
m(a)siid	'mosque'	m(a)siideen	'two mosques'
9abd	'slave'	9abdeen	'two slaves'

B. Feminine Nouns

Feminine nouns that do not end with *-a* form their dual by adding *-een:*

faras	'mare'	faraseen	'two mares'
siččiin	'knife'	siččiineen	'two knives'
seekal	'bicycle'	seekaleen	'two bicycles'
naar	'fire'	naareen	'two fires'
gḷaaṣ	'glass'	gḷaaṣeen	'two glasses'
riil	'foot; leg'	riileen	'two legs; two feet'

Otherwise *-teen* is added unless the singular ends with a *-t,* in which case only *-een* is added:

yaam9a	'university'	yaam9ateen	'two universities'
madrasa	'school'	madrasateen	'two schools'
banka	'fan'	bankateen	'two fans'
kirfaaya (var. *čirfaaya*)	'bed'	kirfaayateen (var. *čirfaayteen*)	'two beds'
bint	'girl'	binteen'	'two girls'

9.2.3 Plural

There are two kinds of plurals of nouns in GA: sound plurals and broken plurals. Sound plurals are of two kinds: sound masculine and sound feminine plurals.

9.2.3.1 Sound Plurals

A. Sound Masculine

Most sound masculine plural nouns refer to male human beings or a group in which there is at least one male. Sound masculine plurals are formed by suffixing *-iin*[51] to the singular noun, sometimes with appropriate stem changes. If the masculine singular noun ends with a *-vc,* the *-v-* is usually dropped,[52] e.g., *muhandis* 'engineer,' *muhandsiin* 'engineers.' Sound masculine plural nouns are of a variety of patterns among which the following are the most frequent:

1. Nouns of Participle Origin

Active and passive participles, derivation and meaning, are discussed in 10.4. The following are only examples:

---

51. Some of these plurals have alternative broken plurals in parentheses.

52. See 4.3.

Singular		*Plural*
kaatib	'clerk'	kaatbiin (alt. *kittaab*)
zaayir	'visitor'	zaayriin (alt. *zuwwaar*)
mudarris	'teacher'	mudarsiin
muslim	'Moslem'	musilmiin
mudiir	'director, manager'	mudiiriin

2. Nisba Nouns[53]

All nisba nouns end with *-i.* The plural of these nouns takes *-yy-* before *-iin* is added:

Singular		*Plural*
ḏ̣ibyaani	'Abu Dhabian'	ḏ̣ibyaaniyyiin
šaarji	'belonging to Sharja'	šaarjiyyiin
9umaani	'Omani'	9umaaniyyiin
baHreeni	'Bahraini'	baHreeniyyiin (alt. *baHaarna*)
gṭari	'Qatari'	gṭariyyiin
kweeti	'Kuwaiti'	kweetiyyiin
su9uudi	'Saudi'	su9uudiyyiin

3. Occupational Nouns[54]

Most occupational nouns have alternative broken plural forms, which are more commonly used than the corresponding sound masculine forms. Examples:

gaṣṣaab	'butcher'	gaṣṣaabiin (alt. *gaṣaaṣiib*)
9ayyaal	'male dancer'	9ayyaaliin (alt. *9ayyaala*)
čaḏḏaab	'lier'	čaḏḏaabiin
sammaač	'fish dealer, fisherman'	sammaačiin (alt. *samaamiič*)
m9azzib	'host'	m9azbiin (alt. *ma9aaziib*)
mudarris	'teacher'	mudarsiin
9akkaas	'photographer'	9akkaasiin

4. Diminutive Nouns[55]

Almost all sound masculine diminutive nouns are of adjective origin and of the *f9ayyil* pattern. They take the *-iin* suffix for their plural forms. Examples:

---

53. See 8.4E.
54. See 8.6 above.
55. See 8.9 above.

ṣqayyir	'little one'	sqayriin
Hbayyib	'loved one'	Hbaybiin
gṣayyir	'short one'	gṣayriin
rxayyiṣ	'cheap, inexpensive'	rxayṣiin
rfayyij	'companion, friend'	rfayjiin

B. Sound Feminine

Sound feminine plural nouns are formed by adding *-aat* to the singular; if the singular ends in *-a, -a* is omitted before adding *-aat*. It is used for the following classes of nouns:

1. Those referring to female human beings:

daxtoora	'doctor'	daxtooraat
ð̣ibyaaniyya	'Abu Dhabian'	ð̣ibyaaniyyaat
mumarrið̣a	'nurse'	mumarrið̣aat
na99aaša	'dancer'	na99aašaat
maṣriyya	'Egyptian'	maṣriyyaat

A few nouns that belong to this category are irregular, e.g.:

'uxut	'sister'	('a)xawaat
bint	'girl; daughter'	banaat

2. Most feminine singular nouns ending in *-a:*

saa9a	'hour; clock'	saa9aat
wazaara	'ministry'	wazaaraat
sayyaara	'car'	sayyaaraat (alt. *siyaayiir*)

Included here are the following classes of nouns: unit, instance, verbal, and nouns of participle origin. Examples:

yiHHa	'a watermelon'	yiHHaat[56]	'individual watermelons'
diyaaya	'a chicken; a hen'	diyaayaat	'individual chickens or hens'
bgara	'cow'	bgaraat	'individual cows'
puteetaa[57]	'a potato'	puteetaat	'individual potatoes'
Habbat 9eeš	'a grain of rice'	Habbaat 9eeš	'grains of rice'

56. As in *θalaaθ yiHHaat* 'three watermelons,' for example.

57. Note that the ending *-aa* is omitted before the plural suffix *-aat*.

ragṣa	'a dance'	ragṣaat	'dances'
Hariija	'a fire'	Hariijaat (alt. *Haraayij*)	'fires'
ġabga	'a gulp'	ġabgaat	'gulps'

The feminine nouns *madrasa* 'school,' *leela* 'night,' and *madiina* 'city, town' take broken plural forms (see 9.2.3.2). The plural of *sana* 'year' is the irregular *sanawaat* (alt. *siniin*).

3. Some masculine nouns including nouns of foreign origin:

maṭaar	'airport'	maṭaaraat
ṭalab	'application, request'	ṭalabaat
jawaaz	'passport'	jawaazaat
seekal	'bicycle'	seekalaat
'uteel	'hotel'	'uteelaat
paaṣ	'bus'	paaṣaat
peep	'pipe'	peepaat
leet	'light; light bulb'	leetaat

4. Certain masculine nouns ending in *-a* or *-u:*

-a:

mustašfa	'hospital'	mustašfayaat
qada	'lunch'	qadayaat
9aša	'dinner, supper'	9ašayaat

Note that such nouns add *-y-* before *-aat* is suffixed.

-u:

keelu	'kilogram'	keeluwaat
raadu	'radio'	raaduwaat
pyaanu	'piano'	pyaanuwaat

Note that almost all nouns of this category are of foreign origin. Their plural forms add *-w-* before *-aat* is suffixed.

9.2.3.2 Broken Plurals

Broken plurals are formed from the singular by changing the internal structure of the word, not by adding suffixes as in the case of sound plurals. There are a number of pluralizing patterns, a few of which can be predicted from the singular pattern, but in most cases it is very difficult if not impossible to deduce the plural pattern from the singular. For this reason, the plurals of nouns should be learned individually as they are encountered. The following are the most common broken plural patterns of nouns of triradical roots:

1. f9uul

This pattern has the variant *fu9uul.* Most nouns of this plural pattern have singular patterns as *fi9l* or *fa9l.*

Singular		*Plural*	*Singular*		*Plural*
fils	'fils'	fluus	xaṭṭ	'letter'	xṭuuṭ
malik	'king'	mluuk	bank	'bank'	bnuuk
hindi	'Indian'	hnuud	rigg	'drilling rig'	rguug
beet	'house'	byuut	hidim	'dress'	hduum
šeex	'Shaikh'	šyuux	ẟ̣eef	'guest'	ẟ̣yuuf
čaff	'hand palm'	čfuuf	ẟ̣irs	'tooth'	ẟ̣ruus
xašim	'nose'	xšuum	yifin	'eye lash'	yfuun

Note that the singular nouns in this category have sound radicals, e.g., *fils* 'fils' or final (identical) doubled consonants, e.g., *xaṭṭ* 'letter,' or weak middle radicals, e.g., *beet* 'house.'

2. f9aal

This pattern has the literary variant *fi9aal.* Most adjectives of the *fa9iil* pattern have this plural pattern. A less commonly used plural pattern for such adjectives is the sound masculine plural form: *fa9iiliin.*

k(a)biir	'big; old (age)'	kbaar	(alt. *kabiiriin*)
ṭawiil	'tall; long'	ṭwaal	(alt. *ṭawiiliin*)
ṣ(a)ġiir	'small; young (age)'	ṣġaar	(alt. *ṣaġiiriin*)
matiin	'fat'	mtaan	(alt. *matiiniin*)
θagiil	'heavy'	θgaal	(alt. *θagiiliin*)
gaṣiir	'short'	gṣaar	(alt. *gaṣiiriin*)

Examples of nouns that have this plural pattern:

ṭoofa	'wall'	ṭwaaf	dalla	'coffee pot'	dlaal
gafša	'spoon, ladle'	gfaaš	9ayyil	'child'	9yaal
Hooṭa	'sheep pen'	Hwaaṭ	čalb	'dog'	člaab
garṣ	'loaf of bread'	graaṣ	rooẟ̣a	'garden'	ryaaẟ̣
gaṭu	'male cat'	gṭaaw(a)	gadu	'hubble-bubble'	gdaaw(a)

Note that this pattern includes nouns and adjectives whose singular has a weak middle radical, e.g., *ṭawiil* 'tall; long' and *ṭoofa* 'wall.'

3. 'af9aal

f9aal and *('i)f9aal* are two variant patterns. The great majority of nouns with this plural pattern have singular patterns *fa9l, fu9(u)l,* or *fa9al.*

xaaḷ[58]	'maternal uncle'	xwaaḷ	yadd[59]	'grandfather'	'aydaad
9aam	'year'	'a9waam	walad	'boy'	wlaad
fuut	'foot (measure)'	'afwaat	sinn	'tooth'	'asnaan
kuub	'cup'	'akwaab	gaḷam	'pencil'	gḷaam (alt. *gḷaama*)
yoom	'day'	'ayyaam	simaač	'fish'	'asmaač
riim	'deer'	'aryaam	šuġul	'work'	'ašġaal
9iid	'holiday, festival'	'a9yaad	si9ir	'price'	'as9aar

4. fawaa9il

An alternative pattern is *fuwaa9il.* Most singulars of this plural pattern are (1) feminine nouns with the feminine ending *-a* and are characterized by the long vowel *-aa-* between the first and the second radicals, and (2) nouns with three consonants and a long vowel after the first consonant. Examples:

jaafla	'camel caravan'	jawaafil
9aayla	'family'	9awaayil
jaasim	'Qasim'	jawaasim[60]
šaahiin	'falcon'	šuwaahiin
saalfa	'story, anecdote'	suwaalif
šaamsi	'belonging to the *Shamsi* tribe'	šuwaamis[61]
Haadθa	'accident; event'	Hawaadiθ
daayra	'department'	duwaayir

58. Example with a weak middle radical.

59. Example with a final (identical) doubled consonant.

60. This means individuals—the name of each of whom is *jaasim*—or individuals who belong to the *Jawasim* tribe.

61. Individuals who belong to this tribe.

šaarib	'moustache'	šuwaarib
šaari9	'street'	šawaari9
ṭaabig	'floor, flat'	ṭuwaabig
doosari	'belonging to the *Dosari* tribe'	duwaasir[62]
ġaanim[63]	'magnanimous man'	ġawaanim
jaanib	'side'	jawaanib

5. fu99aal

This pattern has the variant patterns of *fi99aal* and *fa99aal.* Almost all nouns of this plural pattern are occupational nouns,[64] and their singular forms are of the *faa9il* pattern.

xaaṭir	'guest'	xuṭṭaar	yaahil	'child'	yahhaal
taajir	'merchant'	tijjaar	saakin	'inhabitant'	sikkaan
Haakim	'ruler'	Hukkaam	kaafir	'heathen'	kuffaar
Haajj	'pilgrim'	Hijjaaj	zaayir	'visitor'	zuwwaar
šeeba	'old man'	šuwwaab	ṭaalib	'student'	ṭullaab

6. fa9aa9iil

This pattern has the variant *fi9aa9iil.* Almost all singular occupational nouns of the *fa99aal* pattern have this plural pattern. Examples:

sammaač	'fish dealer, fisherman'	samaamiič
xabbaaz	'baker'	xabaabiiz
ṣabbaaġ	'dyer; painter'	ṣabaabiiġ
xayyaaṭ	'tailor'	xayaayiiṭ
gaṣṣaab	'butcher'	gaṣaaṣiib
Hammaal	'porter'	Hamaamiil
rayyaal	'man'	rayaayiil
ġawwaaṣ	'diver'	ġawaawiiṣ

Examples of non-occupational nouns:

siyyaada	'carpet'	siyaayiid	sayyaara	'car'	sayaayiir
barnuus	'blanket'	baraaniis	dikkaan	'shop'	dikaakiin
siččiin	'knife'	sičaačiin	diinaar	'dinar'	dinaaniir

62. *Ibid.*

63. Replacing the set phrase *liHyatin ġaanma* (lit., "a captivating beard").

64. See 8.6.

7. mafaa9iil

No variants of this pattern have been recorded. Most singular nouns of this plural pattern have patterns *mif9aal, maf9uul* or *mfa99il.* Examples:

miftaaH	'key'	mafaatiiH	mawḍuu9	'subject'	mawaaḍii9
miizaan	'scales, balance'	mawaaziin	maynuun	'crazy man'	mayaaniin
mismaar	'nail'	masaamiir	maw9id	'appoint-ment'	mawaa9iid
miilaad	'birth'	mawaaliid	m9azzib	'host'	ma9aaziib

8. fa9aayil

This pattern has the variant *fi9aayil.* Most singular nouns of this plural pattern are feminine with the *fi9iila* (or *fa9uula*) patterns. Examples:

gabiila	'tribe'	gabaayil	šahaada	'certificate'	šahaayid
jiziira	'island'	jizaayir	Hagiiga	'truth'	Hagaayig
digiiga	'minute'	digaayig	Hadiiga	'garden'	Hadaayig
kaniisa	'church'	kanaayis	9aruus(a)	'bride'	9araayis
diriiša	'window'	diraayiš	namuuna	'kind, sort'	namaayin

An example of a feminine noun that does not end with *-a* is *9ayuuz* 'old woman' is *9ayaayiz.*

9. fi9al

Most nouns with this pattern have the singular pattern *fi9la* or *f9ala.* This pattern has the plural variant *fu9al* if the singular contains *u, uu,* or *oo.*

duuba	'barge; ship'	duwab	dooHa	'tree; bay'	duwaH
bugša	'envelope'	bugaš	rukba	'knee'	rukab
ġitra	'head dress'	ġitar	l-yim9a	'Friday'	yima9
jirba	'goat skin bag'	jirab	šigga	'apartment'	šigag
šyara	'tree'	šiyar	wiiza	'visa'	wiyaz
šiiša	'empty bottle'	šiyaš[65]	Hijra	'room'	Hijar[66]
digma	'button'	digam	šanṭa	'suitcase, bag'	šinaṭ

65. This has the variant *'išyaš.*

66. This has the variant *'iHjar.*

10. fa9aalil

Nouns of this pattern have various singular patterns; some have four consonants and no long vowel (includes defective roots with three consonants); some others have three consonants and one long vowel.

daftar	'notebook'	dafaatir
darzan	'dozen'	daraazin
fundug	'hotel, inn'	fanaadig
daxtar	'doctor'	daxaatir (alt. *daxaatra*)
xanyar (var. *xanjar*)	'dagger'	xanaayir (var. *xanaajir*)
gahwa (var. *ghawa*)	'coffee; coffee shop'	gahaawi
tarjama	'a translation'	traajim
čoočab	'water spring'	čawaačib
ġunṣul	'consul'	ġanaaṣil

11. mafaa9il

No variants of this pattern have been recorded. Almost all singular nouns of this plural pattern are locative nouns of the *maf9al* (or *maf9ala*) pattern. Examples:

manṭaġa	'region, district'	manaaṭiġ	madrasa	'school'	madaaris
maġbara	'cemetery'	maġaabir	maktab	'office'	makaatib
maalad	'birthday (party)'	mawaalid	maṭbax	'kitchen'	maṭaabix
markaz	'center'	maraakiz	maHkama	'law court'	maHaakim
mablaġ	'sum of money'	mabaaliġ	maṣna9	'factory'	maṣaani9

A few singular nouns of different patterns have been recorded.

m(a)siid	'mosque'	m(a)saayid
meelas (var. *maylis*)	'living room; meeting'	mayaalis
miškila (var. *muškila*)	'problem'	mašaakil

12. fa9aali

This pattern has the two variants *fu9aali* and *fi9aali.* Most singular nouns of this plural pattern are of the pattern *fu9li* (var. *fi9li*).

quuri	'tea kettle'	qawaari	guuṭi	'(tin) can'	gawaaṭi
kirsi	'chair'	karaasi	juuti	'shoes'	jawaati[67]

Note that the four examples cited above, except for *kirsi*, have the medial long vowel *-uu*[68] in the singular, which changes into *-awaa-* in the plural. Other examples of this plural pattern:

čatti	'written note'	čataati (var. *čitaati*)
Habaara	'bustard'	Habaari (var. *Hibir*)

Some nouns of this pattern have the *-iyya* ending in the singular:

yuuniyya (var. *guuniyya*)	'cloth bag'[69]	yawaani (var. *gawaani*)
ṭaagiyya	'skull cap'	ṭawaagi
zuuliyya	'rug'	zuwaali

13. fi9laan

This has the variant pattern *fu9laan*. The singular patterns of the nouns of this plural are various. Examples:

ġamiiṣ	'shirt'	ġumṣaan	looH	'wood board'	liiHaan
9awar	'one-eyed man'	9iwraan	ġazaal	'gazelle'	ġizlaan
9amay	'blind man'	9imyaan	'uxu	'brother'	'ixwaan
ḏ̣abi	'deer, gazelle'	ḏ̣ibyaan	jaar (var. *yaar*)	'neighbor'	jiiraan (var. *yiiraan*)
baab	'door'	biibaan	xaliij	'gulf'	xiljaan
xaruuf	'lamb'	xirfaan	waadi	'valley'	widyaan

Note that the medial long vowels *-aa-* and *-oo-* in the singular nouns *baab* door,' *looH* 'wood board,' and *jaar* (var. *yaar*) 'neighbor' change into the long vowel *-ii-* in the plural forms: *biibaan*, *liiHaan*, and *jiiraan* (var. *yiiraan*).

14. fu9ul

This has the variant *fu9l.*[70] Most singular nouns of this plural are color adjectives of the pattern *'af9al* and *fa9al.*

---

67. 'Pairs of shoes.'

68. The underlying form of *quuri* is *quwri.*

69. As in *yuuniyyat 9eeš* 'a large bag of rice,' usually made of cloth, weighing about 160 lbs.

70. The second *u* in *fu9ul* is epenthetic.

'aswad	'black'	suud	'aṣfar	'yellow'	ṣufur
'asmar	'brown'	sumur	'azrag	'blue'	zurg (or *zirg*)
Hamar	'red'	Humur	xaḍ̣ar	'green'	xuḍ̣ur

Examples of singular nouns of other patterns:

daar	'house'	duur	raaṣ	'head'	ruuṣ
safiina	'ship'	sufun	ṭariig	'road'	ṭurug

15. f(i)9aala

No variant forms of this pattern have been recorded. Nouns of this pattern have singulars of various patterns. Examples:

gaṭu	'male cat'	gṭaawa	dugaḷ	'mast'	dgaaḷa
boṭiḷ	'bottle'	bṭaaḷa	gaḷam	'pen'	gḷaama
faaḷa	'light meal'	fwaaḷa	Hijj	'young camel'	Higaaga

16. fa9iil

No variant forms of this pattern have been recorded. Nouns with this pattern have various singular patterns. Examples:

9abd	'slave'	9abiid	Hmaar	'jackass'	Hamiir
Hurma	'woman, wife'	Hariim	nxaḷa	'palm tree'	naxiiḷ

The following plural patterns (17-21) are of limited membership; they have few examples.

17. fa9aaliin

b(i)9iir	'camel'	ba9aariin
xaḷag	'duster'	xaḷaagiin

18. mafaa9la

mHassin	'barber'	maHaasna (alt. *mHasniin*)
maṭaarzi	'bodyguard'	maṭaarza (alt. *maṭaarziyya*)

19. 'afaa9il

mukaan	'place'	'amaakin
'ajnabi (var. *'aynabi*)	'foreign; foreigner'	'ajaanib (var. *'ayaanib*)
'asim	'name'	'asaami

20. fi9(i)l

walad	'boy'	wild

'abyaḍ	'white'	biiḍ
Habaara	'bustard'	Hibir

21. 'af9il

ryaal	'riyaal (money)'	'aryil
šahar	'month'	'ašhir

Plural patterns of nouns of quadriliterals roots: [71]

22. fa9aaliil

A. This has the rare variant pattern *fi9aaliil* or *fu9aaliil.* Some nouns of this pattern have the singular *fi9laal.*

finyaan (var. *finjaan*)	'(coffee) cup'	fanaayiin (var. *fanaajiin*)
fustaan	'woman's dress'	fasaatiin
9inwaan	'address'	9anaawiin
sa9daan	'ape, monkey'	sa9aadiin
bistaan	'garden, orchard'	bisaatiin
čingaḷ	'fork'	činaagiiḷ

B. Some others have the singular pattern *fa9luul:*

jalbuut (var. *yalbuut*)	'boat'	jalaabiit (var. *yalaabiit*)
ṣanduug	'box'	ṣanaadiig
yaryuur	'shark'	yaraayiir
garguur	'fish trap'	garaagiir
9arguub	'sand dune'	9araagiib

C. Some others have various singular patterns:

gubgub(a)	'crab, lobster'	jabaajiib
xarbuuṭa	'chaos'	xaraabiiṭ
gaṣguuṣa	'cut up piece of paper or cloth'	gaṣaagiiṣ
šaahiin	'eagle, falcon'	šuwaahiin
duulaab	'wardrobe'	duwaaliib
xaašuuga	'spoon'	xuwaašiig
širbaaka	'entanglement'	šaraabiič

71. Some of these nouns have already been covered in previous patterns.

23. fa9aalila

This has the variant *fa9aalla.* The nouns that belong to this pattern have a human referent.

daxtar	'doctor'	daxaatra (var. *daxaatir*)
nooxaða	'ship's captain'	nawaaxða (var. *nawaaxið*)

9.2.3.3 Anomalous Plurals

Some common nouns have anomalous or unusual plural patterns. As is shown below, some of the plural patterns resemble sound or broken plural patterns or a combination of both sound and broken patterns or patterns unrelated to the singular form. Examples:

A. Some singular nouns, usually of foreign origin, form their plural by adding *-iyya* to the singular, sometimes with appropriate stem changes. Most of these nouns end in *-i* and are nisba or occupational nouns.[72] Such nouns are count nouns.

dreewil	'driver'	dreewliyya
pooliis	'policeman'	pooliisiyya
karraani	'clerk'	karraaniyya
9ibri	'passenger'	9ibriyya
ši9ri	(kind of fish)	ši9riyya
maṭaarzi	'bodyguard'	maṭaarziyya
kweeti	'Kuwaiti'	kweetiyya
'arduni	'Jordanian'	'arduniyya

B. Some parts of the body:

riil (var. *rijil*)	'foot; leg'	riileen (alt. *ryuul*) (var. *rijleen*) (alt. *rjuul*)
'iid (var. *yadd*)	'hand'	'iideen
θamm	'mouth'	θmaam (var. *'aθmaam*)
'iðin	'ear'	ði(i)neen
ṣubi9	'finger, toe'	'aṣaabi9

72. See 9.2.3.1A.2 and 9.2.3.1A.3.

Note that *riileen, 'iideen* and *ði(i)neen* are dual in form but in usage they are either dual or plural.

C. Some kinship nouns designating immediate family relationships:

'ubu	'father'	'abbahaat[73]
'umm	'mother'	'ummuhaat
'uxu	'brother'	'ixwaan
'uxut	'sister'	xawaat[74]

D. Others

mara (also *Hurma*)	'woman; wife'	Hariim
banṭaḷoon	'pants'	banaaṭḷiin
jigaara	'cigarette'	jigaayir
taksi	'taxi'	tikaasi
taanki	'water tank'	tuwaanki

9.3 Nunation

In literary Arabic indefinite nouns have three case endings *-un, -an,* and *-in* for the nominative, accusative, and genitive cases, respectively.[75] This suffix *n,* signalling indefinite nouns in the literary language, is known in Arabic grammar as *tanwiin,* which the English term "nunation" stands for. In GA, as in any other dialect of Arabic, nouns are not inflected for case. In GA, however, some indefinite nouns in a non-final position, in set or idiomatic phrases, proverbs and poetry have the ending *-in,* which is not a case inflection since it only means that the word on which it occurs is not the last word of its sentence (see also 10.6.2C for nunation in active participles).

Examples in set phrases:

rayyaalin 9ood	'an old, big man'
rayyaalin zeen	'a good man'
weehin yimiil	'a beautiful face'

---

73. There is also the rare literary form *'aabaa'.*

74. There is also the rare literary form *'axawaat.*

75. The *n* common to these three endings occurs only in indefinite nouns and adjectives.

liHyatin ġaanma — 'a good man' (lit., "a captivating, charming beard")

Examples in proverbs and idiomatic phrases:

ḏ̣ulmin b-s-sawiyya 9adlin b-r-ra9iyya.

Meaning: 'Injustice done to all people equally is preferable to justice for some and injustice for others.'

wild č-čalb čalbin miθla.[76]

Equivalent to the English saying: Like father like son.

Hissin 9aali w-yirja9 xaali.

Literally: "(It is) a high voice and it comes back empty." Equivalent to the English proverb: Much cry little wool.

Example from poetry:

z-zeen zeenin law ga9ad min manaama
w-š-šeen šeenin law ġassal b-ṣaabuun

Equivalent to: The leopard can't change his spots.
Meaning: 'A beautiful person is always beautiful even at the time he wakes up, and an ugly person is always ugly although he washes himself with soap.'

kill, meaning 'everyone, each person,' is usually used with the *-in* ending in set phrases:

killin Haliiba yjiiba.

Meaning: 'one is brought (or drawn back) by one's own milk.' Equivalent to the English saying: Like father like son.

killin yara n-naas b-9een ṭab9a.

Meaning: 'Each person sees people through his own eyes.' Literally: "Each person sees people with the eye of his nature."

10. NOUN MODIFIERS

10.1 Construct Phrases[77]

A noun construct is a construction composed of two noun phrases syntactically bound together. The first element consists of a

---

76. This proverb is always used in a pajorative sense.

77. Construct phrases in this section are restricted to *Noun* and *Elative* constructs. Numeral, Non-Numeral, and Ordinal constructs appear under Quantifiers below.

noun which must always be indefinite in form. The entire construction is definite or indefinite in accordance with the second element, which can be a single noun, or a noun phrase:

yuuniyyat 9eeš	'a rice sack' or 'a sack of rice'
yuuniyyat l-9eeš	'the rice sack' or 'the sack of rice'
yuuniyyat 9eeš čibiira	'a large rice sack'
yuuniyyat 9eeš r-rayyaal	'the man's rice sack' 'the rice sack of the man' 'the man's sack of rice'

The second noun may be another noun construct or a series of constructs:

gaṣir Haakim l-'imaara	'the palace of the ruler of the Emirate'
gaṣir Haakim 'imaarat bu ð̣abi[78]	'the palace of the ruler of the Emirate of *Abu Dhabi*'

What determines definiteness or indefiniteness in a noun construct is the second element. If the second element is definite, the first one is "treated as definite";[79] if it is indefinite, the first one is indefinite also:

siyyaadat msiid čibiira	'a big mosque carpet'
siyyaadat li-msiid č-čibiira	'the big mosque carpet'

If both elements of a noun construct have the same gender, structural ambiguity results:

suug s-simač č-čibiir	'the market of big fish' 'the big market of fish'
yaddat bint ṭawiila	'the grandmother of a tall girl' 'the tall grandmother of a girl'

This type of structural ambiguity is usually resolved by the use of *Hagg*[80] or *maal* 'belonging to, characteristic of':

---

78. *Abu ð̣abi* becomes *bu ð̣abi* in rapid speech.

79. "Treated as definite" means that if the first element has an attribute, then the attribute shows definite agreement by having the article prefix *l-*, as the above examples show.

80. *Hagg* is usually used with animate or inanimate nouns while *maal* is used with inanimate nouns, especially appliances, spare parts, etc.

s-suug Hagg s-simač č-čibiir	'the market of big fish'
s-suug č-čibiir Hagg s-simač	'the big market of fish'
t-taayir maal s-seekal ṣ-ṣaġiir	'the tire of the small bicycle'
t-taayir ṣ-ṣaġiir maal s-seekal	'the small tire of the bicycle'

Noun constructs are classified as "verb-derived" (i.e., the underlying structure contains a verb) or, simply, "derived" and "ordinary" (i.e., all others). In the following analysis the meanings of ordinary and derived noun constructs are defined in terms of their underlying structures.

10.1.1 Ordinary Noun Constructs

1. Possession

a. alienable

ġitrat r-rayyaal	'the man's head dress'

Here *r-rayyaal* 'the man' is a concrete noun semantically capable of owning *ġitra* 'head dress.' The whole phrase is related to *l-ġitra Hagg r-rayyaal* 'The head dress belongs to, is for, the man.' Other examples:

gaḷam l-walad	'the boy's pen(cil)'
beezaat l-kuuli	'the laborer's money'
juuti 'ubuuy	'my father's shoes'
9ačwat šeeba	'the cane of an old man'
ṣooġat l-9aruus	'the bride's jewelry'

b. inalienable

weeh l-bint	'the girl's face'
ϑanab č-čalb	'the tail of the dog'
čaff l-yaahil	'the child's palm'
raaṣ l-yaryuur	'the head of the shark'
warag šyara	'the leaves of a tree'

2. Naming

madiinat dbayy	'the city of Dubai'
raaṣ l-xeema	'Ras Al-khaima' (lit., "the head of the tent")
xaliij 9umaan	'the Gulf of Oman'
'aal nhayyaan	'the Nahayan Family'
waaHat li-breemi	'the Buraimi Oasis'

The first noun is usually a deletable geographical noun, and the second is a proper noun. *madiinat dbayy* is derived from *l-madiina 'asimha dbayy* 'the name of the city is Dubai.'

3. Container-Contents

finyaan gahwa	here: 'a cup of coffee' not 'a coffee cup'
quuri čaay	here: 'a kettle of tea' not 'a tea kettle'
guuṭi ṭamaaṭ	here: 'a can of tomatoes' not 'a tomato can'
. yuuniyyat 9eeš	here: 'a sack of rice' not 'a rice sack'

The first noun is a noun denoting some kind of receptable, and the second is a concrete noun of material. *finyaan gahwa* is derived from *finyaan min l-gahwa.*

4. Composition

xaatim ðahab	'a gold ring'
kirsi yild	'a leather chair'
xaašuugat fiḍḍa	'a silver spoon'
n9aal blaastiik	'plastic slippers'
barnuus ṣuuf	'a wool blanket'

The first noun is a concrete noun, and the second is a noun of material. *xaatim ðahab* is derived from: *l-xaatim min ðahab* 'the ring is made of gold.'

5. Qualification

'ayyaam l-bard	'the days of the cold, cold days'
rayyaal ṣ-ṣidg	'the man of truth, truthful man'
kalaam 9adil	'true, just talk; straight talk'

This type of construct reflects a relationship wherein the second noun describes the first. The second noun is an abstract noun with a non-specified (generic) determiner. The construct formation of *N*[81] + N can be paraphrased by N + adjective, e.g., *'ayyaam li-bruuda* 'the cold days' and *rayyaal ṣidg* 'a truthful man.'

6. Limitation

kuub čaay	'a tea cup'
šyarat burtaġaal	'an orange tree'
madrasat 'awlaad	'a boys' school'

81. *N* is the noun head.

dallat gahwa	'a coffee pot'
maay xoor	'water of a gulf, salty water'

The second noun limits or restricts the first one. The formation of *N* + N can be paraphrased by *N* is for N or is of the class (or characteristic) of N.

10.1.2 Verb-Derived Noun Constructs

Verb-derived noun constructs have as their first element a verbal noun, an active or a passive participle [82] or a locative noun, and as their second element the agent or the goal of the action. They show the following grammatical relationships:

1. Intransitive Verb and Subject

   $\text{Verb}_{\text{intra}}$-Subject

kaθrat š-šarikaat 'the great number of companies'	← š-šarikaat yakθuruun. 'Companies become many.'
gillat l-maay 'the scarcity of water'	← l-maay ygill. 'Water becomes scarce.'
ṭuul l-waġt 'all the time'	← l-waġt yṭuul. 'Time lingers (long).'
zood l-Harr 'the increase of hot weather'	← l-Harr yziid. 'Hot weather increases.'

2. Transitive Verb and Object

tafniiš l-kuuliyya	'the firing of coolies'
la9wazat n-naas	'the bothering of people'
tadriib l-junuud	'the training of soldiers'
tarbiyat li-9yaal	'the bringing up of children'

Constructs that belong to this category are ambiguous: if *tafniiš l-kuuliyya* is related to *X yfanniš l-kuuliyya* 'X terminates the services of the coolies,' then the grammatical relationship is V_{tra}—obj.; but if it is related to *l-kuuliyya yfanšuun,* 'the coolies terminate their (own) services,' then the construction is related to V_{intra}—subj.

3. Subject and Object

   a. subj.—obj.

---

82. See 10.4.

baayig s-saa9a ← l-baayig ybuug s-saa9a.
'the watch thief' 'The thief steals the watch.'

saayig s-sayyaara ← s-saayig ysuug s-sayyaara.
'the car driver' 'The driver drives the car.'

mṭarriš l-xaṭṭ ← li-mṭarriš yṭarriš l-xaṭṭ.
'the letter sender' 'The sender sends the letter.'

b. obj.—subj.

m(u)wað̣ð̣af li-Hkuuma ← li-Hkuuma twað̣ð̣if l-muwað̣ð̣af.
'the government employee' 'The government employes the employee.'

mdallal 'ubuu ← 'ubuu ydallila.
'his father's spoiled one' 'His father spoils him.'

4. Noun (loc.)—Subj.

maylis š-šyuux ← l-mukaan illi yajlis š-šyuux fii
'the Shaikhs' sitting room' 'the place where the Shaikhs sit'

msiid 9umar ← l-mukaan illi siyad 9umar fii
'Omar's mosque' 'the place where Omar knelt (for prayer)'

majra l-maay ← l-mukaan illi yajri l-maay fii
'the course of the water' 'the place where water runs'

The first, *N*, is a locative noun, which is derived from the underlying intransitive verb:

maylis (lit., "a place for sitting"): yalas 'to sit'
msiid (lit., "a place for kneeling"): sayad 'to kneel'
majra (lit., "a place for running"): jara 'to run'

5. Noun (loc.)—Obj.

ṭaffaayat jigaara ← mukaan ykubbuun fii jigaayir
'an ash tray' 'a place where they throw away cigarettes'

ma9rað̣ jawaati ← mukaan y9arð̣uun fii jawaati
'an exhibition of shoes' 'a place where they exhibit shoes'

maṣna9 ġraaš ← mukaan yiṣna9uun fii ġraaš
'a bottle factory' 'a place where they make bottles'

10.2 Elative Constructs

An elative construct is one in which the first element is an elative adjective.[83] This form, derived from the corresponding adjective, is termed in Arabic grammar an elative adjective. It is an adjective of rating, i.e., 'the best one,' 'the worst one,' 'the most beautiful one,' etc.

'aHsan rayyaal	'the best man'
'aHsan r-rayaayiil	'the best (of the) men'

An elative may be used in construct with either an indefinite singular or plural noun, or a definite plural noun:

'aHsan rayyaal	'the best man'
'aHsan rayaayiil	'the best men'
'aHsan r-rayaayiil	'the best (of the) men'

It is to be noted that an elative used in construct with an indefinite noun is rendered in English as if it were definite, as in the first phrase above. *'aHsan rayyaal* 'the best man' has the same meaning as that expressed by the attributive construction:

r-rayyaal l-'aHsan	'the best man'

The last phrase in the examples above is ambiguous with respect to the number of things being described. It means either 'the best one of the men' (partitive) or 'the best who are men.'

The gender and number of an elative construct depend upon its referent, regardless of the following term:

haaðа 'aHsan r-rayaayiil.	'This is the best man.'
haðeel 'aHsan r-rayaayiil.	'These are the best men.'

But if the following term is indefinite, gender and number concord depends upon that of the following term:

haaða 'amtan gaṣṣaab.	'This is the fattest butcher.'
haðeel 'amtan gaṣṣaabeen.	'These are the (two) fattest butchers (m.dual).'
haðeel 'amtan gaṣaaṣiib.	'These are the fattest butchers (m.p.).'

---

83. The elative form of the adjective is of the pattern *'af9al,* e.g., *'aHsan* 'better,' *'aṭwal* 'taller,' etc. See 10.5.1.4 Elative Adjectives.

10.3 The Determiner System

10.3.1 The Article Prefix

a. Proper Nouns

Proper nouns in GA include the names of any common nouns such as people, places, books, films, newspapers, etc. Proper nouns have a particular syntactic role in GA and MSA. They do not need any marking for definiteness, for they are definite by virtue of being proper nouns. There are two sub-classes of proper nouns – one that takes the article prefix *l-* and another that does not. Whether proper nouns appear with or without the article prefix is a matter of lexical etymology, and not a realization of two different states of definiteness. It is interesting to note that the article prefix which appears with some proper nouns is comparable to the *the* which forms a part of such English phrases as *The Rockies, The Mississippi, The Sudan,* etc.[84]

l- has shapes depending upon the environment in which it is used: in an initial position before nouns and adjectives beginning with one consonant it is *l-*; before nouns and adjectives with clusters of two (identical) consonants it is *li-*: *li-kweet* 'Kuwait,' *li-9raag* 'Iraq,' *li-ṣxaḷa* 'the young goat, kid (f.).' In a post consonantal position it is usually pronounced *il-* as in *min il-guuṭi* 'from the can,' *ðaak il-mukaan* 'that place,' *ma9 il-9ayuuz* 'with the old woman,' but this transcription will show it as *l-*. Before a noun or adjective beginning with *t,θ,d,ð,r,z,s,š,ṣ,ṭ,ð̣,l,n,č* in a post-vowel position, the *l-* is assimilated:

ṭ-ṭaffaaya	'the ashtray'	d-dalla	'the coffee pot'
č-čaay	'the tea'	s-sammaač	'the fisherman'
θ-θalaaθ	'Tuesday'	ð̣-ð̣abb	'the lizard'

10.3.2 Quantifiers

10.3.2.1 Numerals

10.3.2.1.1 Cardinals

Cardinals in GA constitute a subclass of nouns and modify only count nouns. They are divided into the following categories:

---

84. See the handling of this phenomenon by Verma, Manindra, "A Synchronic Comparative Study of the Noun Phrase in English and Hindi." Unpublished Ph.D. dissertation, University of Michigan, 1966.

a. Cardinals$_1$

waaHid 'one' and *θneen* 'two' have the feminine forms *waHda* and *θinteen.* They obligatorily follow the noun they modify and show full agreement with it:

rayyaal waaHid	'one man' (m.s.)
rayyaaleen θneen(a)	'two men' (m.dual)
Hurma waHda	'one woman' (f.s.)
Hurmateen θinteen	'two women' (f.dual)
r-rayyaal l-waaHid	'the one man'
r-rayyaaleen li-θneen	'the two men'
l-Hurma l-waHda	'the one woman'
l-Hurmateen θ-θinteen	'the two women'

waaHid and *θneen* are used in counting and in an answer to the question, How many? Example:

čam waaHid tabi?	'How many (ones) do you want?'
waaHid walla θneen.	'One or two.'

They are used in conjunction with a noun for emphasis, as in *rayyaal waaHid* 'one man.' *waaHid* is often used with nunation,[85] i.e., *waaHdin* in the phrase *waaHdim minhum* ← *waaHdin* minhum* 'one of them (m.).' The form *'aHad* (often *Had*) is used in a question or a negative statement meaning 'anybody, somebody':

fii Had hini?	'Is there anybody here?
ma fii Had hini.	'There isn't anybody here.'
fii Had taHat.	'There is somebody downstairs.'

When *θneen* is used with a noun for emphasis, the noun is usually plural:

čift rayaayiil θneen(a)	'I saw two men.'
Haṣṣalt Hariim θinteen.	'I found two women.'

b. Cardinals$_2$

The cardinals 3-10 have two forms: one used independently (i.e., not followed by a noun), such as in counting, and a tied form used in construct with a noun:

---

85. See 9.3.

Independent Form

θalaaθa	'three	sab9a	'seven'
'arba9a	'four'	θamaanya	'eight'
xamsa	'five'	tis9a	'nine'
sitta	'six'	9ašara	'ten'

Tied Form

If the numeral is used with a following noun, that noun must be plural; the cardinal used has the following forms:

θalaaθ (var. *θalaatt*)	'three'	sab(i)9	'seven'
'arba9	'four'	θamaan	'eight'
xam(i)s	'five'	tis(i)9	'nine'
sitt	'six'	9aš(i)r	'ten'

The long vowel *-aa-* in *θalaaθ* 'three' is often shortened to *-a-* in normal speech; final *-θ* is usually assimilated to a following dental and final *-tt* of *sitt* 'six' is assimilated to a following *t* and *d*. The transcription in this instance shows the word intact, without assimilation.

θalaθ[86] awlaad	'three boys'
θalaθ[87] daxaatir	'three doctors'
θalaθ[88] ṭabaabiix	'three cooks'
θalaθ[89] čalmaat	'three words'
sitt sanawaat	'six years'
sitt ṭalgaat	'six firings (from a gun)'
sitt daraahim	'six dirhams'
sab9 ayyaam	'seven days'
sabi9 9amaayir	'seven buildings'

The cardinals 3-10 which belong to this category are in a construct form with the noun they precede, but unlike noun constructs such numeral nouns may be definitized by the prefixation of the article *l-* and can be modified by a demonstrative pronoun, pre-posed or post-posed to the whole phrase.

---

86. (Var. *θalatt*)
87. *Ibid.*
88. *Ibid.*
89. *Ibid.*

θamaan diyaayaat	'eight chickens, hens'
θ-θamaan diyaayat	'the eight chickens, hens'
d-diyaayaat θ-θamaan	'the eight chickens, hens'
haaðì θ-θamann diyaayaat	'these eight chickens, hens'
θ-θamaan diyaayaat haaðì	'these eight chickens, hens'

c. Cardinals$_3$

The cardinals 11-19 have two forms, an independent form and a tied form:

Hda9aš	'eleven'	sitta9aš	'sixteen'
θna9aš	'twelve'	sabi9ta9aš	'seventeen'
θalatta9aš	'thirteen'	θamaanta9aš	'eighteen'
'arba9ta9aš	'fourteen'	tisi9ta9aš	'nineteen'
xamista9aš	'fifteen'		

The tied form used has a suffixed *ar* to the independent form:

Hda9šar	sitta9šar
θna9šar	sabi9ta9šar
θalatta9šar	θamanta9šar
'arba9ta9šar	tisi9ta9šar
xamista9šar	

The noun counted is singular in form and it is only the numeral that takes the article prefix:

Hda9šar b(i)9iir	'eleven camels'
θna9šar naaga	'twelve camels (f.)'
sitta9šar Hmisa	'sixteen turtles'
li-Hda9šar bi9iir	'the eleven camels'
θ-θamanta9šar Hmisa	'the eighteen turtles'

d. Cardinals$_4$

With 20, 30, 40 through 90, the noun counted is singular in form as it is after *cardinals*$_3$. These cardinals are invariable and can take the article prefix:

9išriin ga9uud	'twenty young camels (m.)'
θalaaθiin barnuus	'twenty blankets'
'arba9iin šyara	'forty trees'

xamsiin kuuli	'fifty coolies'
sittiin dirhim	'sixty dirhams'
sab9iin rubbiyya	'seventy rupees'
θamaaniin duuba	'eighty barges'
tis9iin walad	'ninety boys'
l-9išriin gubguba	'the twenty crabs, lobsters'
t-tis9iin ṭeer	'the ninety birds'

Compound numbers from 21 through 99 (except for *Cardinals*$_4$) are expressed by using the units digit first followed by the tens digit with the conjunction *w-* 'and' in between:

xamsa w-9išriin	'twenty-five'
waaHid w-xamsiin	'fifty-one'
θneen w-tis9iin	'ninety-two'
θamaanya w-sittiin	'sixty-eight'

The noun modified always follows the whole numeral in GA and is singular:

sitta w-sittiin Hijra	'sixty-six rooms'

e. Cardinals$_5$

This category comprises the hundreds 100, 200, 300, through 900. The word for 100 is *'imya* (var. *miya*) and the irregular dual form *miiteen* is 200. The cardinal is invariable (the construct form of *'imya* is *'imyat* or *miyat*) and it can take the article prefix; the noun modified is singular:

'imyat beet	'100 houses'
miiteen jindi	'200 soldiers'
θalaθimyat širṭi	'300 policemen'
'arba9imyat ġarša	'400 bottles'
xamsimyat ktaab	'500 books'
sittimyat dreewil	'600 drivers'
sab9imyat beet	'700 houses'
θamaanimyat diinaar	'800 dinars'
tis9imyat fils	'900 fils'
l-miyat naaga	'the 100 camels (f.)'
s-sittimyat banka	'the 600 fans'

Compound numbers from 101 through 199 (except for *Cardinals*$_5$) are expressed by pre-posing these cardinals followed by *w-* to compound numbers from 21 through 99 as was pointed out in *Cardinals*$_4$:

tis9imya w-xamsa w-tis9iin	'995'
miiteen w-sab9a w-θamaaniin	'287'

f. Cardinals$_6$

These are the thousands and the millions. *'alf*[90] '1000' has a dual form *'alfeen* and a plural form *'aalaaf* 'thousands.' The thousands from 1000 through 10,000 are given below with optional alternatives (with the exception of 1000 and 2000), occurring less frequently than the forms preceding them:

'alf		'1000'
'alfeen		'2000'
θalaθaalaaf	θalaattaalaaf	'3000'
'araba9aalaaf	'arba9ataalaaf	'4000'
xamsaalaaf	xamsataalaaf	'5000'
sittaalaaf	sittataalaaf	'6000'
sab9aalaaf	sabi9taalaaf	'7000'
θamaanaalaaf	θamaantaalaaf	'8000'
tis9aalaaf	tisa9taalaaf	'9000'
9ašraalaaf	9ašartaalaaf	'10,000'

Thousands 11,000 through 100,000 are expressed by using the numeral form 11-1000 plus *'alf* '1000.' Examples:

Hda9šar 'alf	'11,000'
sitta w-sab9iin 'alf	'76,000'

The word for 1,000,000 is *malyoon* and its dual form is *malyooneen* '2,000,000'; the plural is *malaayiin* 'millions,' used independently as in *malaayiin min n-naas* 'millions of people' or after one of the numerals from three through ten:

θalaθimyat malyoon	'300,000,000'
xamsimyat malyoon	'500,000,000'

---

90. Another less commonly used word is *lakk*, which is preserved in the speech of older and uneducated Gulf Arabs.

The noun after the thousands and the millions is singular:

miyat 'alf šyara	'100,000 trees'
malyooneen dirhim	'2,000,000 dirhams'

Compound numbers in which all or some of the cardinals described above are used are expressed according to the following order:

millions + thousands + hundreds + units
tens
units + tens

Each major component except the first one takes the conjunction *w-* 'and.' Examples:

xamsimyat malyoon w-θalaθimyat 'alf w-miiteen w-xamsa
500,300,205

xamsimyat malyoon w-θalaθimyat 'alf w-miiteen w-sitta9aš
500,300,216

xamsimyat malyoon w-θalaθimyat 'alf w-miiteen w-sitta w-sab9iin
500,300,276

In expressing numbers ending in *one* or *two,* the units digit, i.e., *one* or *two,* is not normally used but the noun modified is repeated:

'imyat dirhim w-dirhim	'101 dirhams'
'alf leela w-leela	'1001 nights'
θamaanimyat diinaar w-dinaareen	'802 dinars'

10.3.2.1.2 Ordinals

Ordinals are derived from cardinals according to the following formula: $C_1 aaC_2 iC_3$. In some cases the derivation is irregular:

Cardinal	*Ordinal (m.)*	*Ordinal (f.)*
waaHid	'awwal	'uula
θneen	θaani	θaanya
θalaaθa	θaaliθ	θaalθa
'arba9a	raabi9	raab9a
xamsa	xaamis	xamsa
sitta	saadis[91]	saadsa[92]

91. *saatt* is used less frequently.

92. *saatta* is used less frequently.

Cardinal	*Ordinal (m.)*	*Ordinal (f.)*
sab9a	saabi9	saab9a
θamaanya	θaamin	θaamna
tis9a	taasi9	taas9a
9ašara	9aašir	9aašra

Ordinals up to the tenth may be post-posed. From the *eleventh* upward they are obligatorily post-posed; larger ordinals than the *hundredth* are rarely used. When ordinals are post-posed, they are used attributively as adjectives, and with adjectival inflection.

Ordinals are divided into the following subclasses:

a. Ordinals$_1$

The ordinals *'awwal* 'first' and *'aaxir* 'last' stand in construct with a definite or an indefinite singular or plural noun according to the following rules:

(i) If the meaning is 'the first or last *N*,' then *N* is singular indefinite and invariable for gender:

'awwal rasta	'the first paved road'
'awwal msiid	'the first mosque'
'aaxir bint	'the last girl'
'aaxir xaṭṭ	'the last letter'

(ii) If the meaning is 'the first or last part of *N*,' then *N* is inanimate, singular, definite:

'awwal s-sana	'the first part of the year'
'awwal l-geeḍ	'the first part of the summer'
'aaxir s-saalfa	'the last part of the story'
'aaxir š-šaari9	'the last part of the street'

(iii) The plurals of *'awwal, 'awaayil,* and of *'aaxir, 'awaaxir,* may be pre-posed to inanimate, singular, definite nouns that indicate a period of time.' The meaning is 'the first, or last, part of *N*.'

'awaayil li-ṣfiri	'the first part of autumn'
'awaayil s-sana	'the first part of the year'
'awaaxir š-šahar	'the last part of the month'

(iv) The plurals, i.e., *'awaayil* and *'awaaxir* have the meaning of 'the first, the last,' if they precede a plural animate noun:

'awaayil ṭ-ṭullaab	'the first students'
'awaaxir d-dawaasir	'the last (of the) Dosaris'

b. Ordinals$_2$

For ordinals *θaani-9aašir* 'second-tenth,' the form of the ordinal is uninflected if the noun following is singular and indefinite; the entire construct is definite in meaning:

xaamis yoom	'the fifth day'
xaamis marra	'the fifth time'

If, however, the ordinal follows the noun, the entire construction is indefinite:

yoom xaamis	'a fifth day'
marra θaanya	'a second (another) time'

The members of these ordinals do not stand in construct with indefinite plural nouns. If the noun they stand in construct with is definite plural, then they are inflected for gender; the construct then has a partitive meaning:

xaamis li-9yaal	'the fifth (one) of the children'
xaamsat n-na99aašaat	'the fifth (one) of the female dancers'

c. Ordinals$_3$

This class includes ordinals from the *eleventh* upward. These ordinals are subdivided into the following subclasses:

(i) *li-Hda9aš* 'the eleventh' through *t-tisi9ta9aš* 'the nineteenth' and *l-9išriin* 'the twentieth,' *θ-θalaaθiin* 'the thirtieth,' *l-'arba9iin* 'the fiftieth'. . . etc. These ordinals do not show cardinal-ordinal distinction in form but they do in word-order: they obligatorily follow the noun-head. They do not show gender concord:

l-b(i)9iir li-Hda9aš	'the eighteenth camel (m.)'
l-walad l-9išriin	'the twentieth boy'
s-sayyaara l-xamsiin	'the fiftieth car'

10.3.2.2 Non-Numerals

10.3.2.2.1 Partitives

Partitives include nouns designating indefinite amounts and quantities. They do not show any concord with the nouns they modify, but are related to them in a partitive relationship:

'aġlab	'most of'
'akθar	'most of'
mu9ḍ̣am	'majority, most of'
(l-)qaliil min	'a few of, a little of'
kaθiir min	'a lot of'
waayid (var. *waajid*) min	'a lot of'
l-kaθiir min	'a whole lot of'

They modify a definite plural count noun, or a definite collective or a mass noun. Any of these may be specified or non-specified in meaning:

'aġlab	r-rayaayiil	'most (of the) men'
'akθar	n-naxaḷ	'most (of the) palm trees'
mu9ḍ̣am	l-mayy	'most of the water'
l-qaliil min	l-badu	'a few of (the) Bedouins'
l-kaθiir min	s-simač	'a whole lot of fish'

Each one of the partitives on the left can be pre-posed to any of the nouns on the right: *r-rayaayiil* '(the) men' (pl., count), *n-naxaḷ* '(the) palm trees' (coll.), and *l-mayy* '(the) water.' This usage is also extended to nouns indicating size, e.g., *baHar min č-čaḏib* 'an ocean of lies,' *gaṭra min l-9ilm* 'a drop of science, knowledge,' etc.

'aġlabiyya and *'akθariyya* 'majority, most' belong to this category of partitives, but they tend to modify a human noun:

'aġlabiyyat s-samaamiič	'most of the fishermen'
akθariyyat l-muwaḍ̣ḍ̣afiin	'most of the employees'

ba9ḍ̣ 'some' ṃodifies either a plural count or a definite non-count noun. In either case, the noun modified may be translated as definite or indefinite:

ba9ḍ̣ r-rayaayiil	'some (of the) men'
ba9ḍ̣ rayaayiil	'some men'
ba9ḍ̣ l-mayy	'some of the water'
ba9ḍ̣ l-yiHH	'some (of the) watermelons'

10.3.2.2.2 Fractions

Cardinals from 3-5 have fractions derived from them; the pattern is *fu9l,* except for *θilθ* 'one third.' The form corresponding to *θneen* 'two' is irregular: *nuṣṣ* 'half.'

Cardinal		*Fraction*	
θneen	'two'	nuṣṣ	'half'
θalaaθa	'three'	θilθ	'one-third'
'arba9a	'four'	rub9	'one-fourth'
xamsa	'five'	xums	'one-fifth'
sitta	'six'	suds	'one-sixth'
sab9a	'seven'	sub(u)9	'one-seventh'
θamaanya	'eight'	θum(u)n	'one-eighth'
tis9a	'nine'	tus(u)9	'one-ninth'
9ašara	'ten'	9uš(u)r	'one-tenth'

The fractions *nuṣṣ* 'half,' *θilθ* 'one-third,' *rub9* 'one-fourth' and *xums* 'one-fifth' can be made dual or plural: the dual morpheme is *-een* and their plural pattern is *'af9aal:*

θilθeen	'two-thirds'
nuṣṣeen	'two-halves'
rub9een	'two-fourths'
xumseen	'two-sixths'
θalaaθat[93] arbaa9	'three-fourths'
'arba9at axmaas	'four-fifths'

Higher fractions are usually expressed periphrastically with the cardinal numerals and the use of the preposition *min* 'of, from':

waaHid min sitta	'one-sixth'
'arba9a min sab9a	'four-sevenths'
xamsa min sitta9aš	'five-sixteenths'
θallatta9aš min miya	'thirteen-hundredths'
sitta min tis9a w-sab9iin	'six seventy-ninths'

10.3.3 Intensifiers

Intensifying quantifiers include *kill* 'all, whole, every,' *jimii9, 9umuum* 'all, whole, entire,' and *nafs* 'same (very), -self-.'

The meaning of *kill* varies, depending upon whether the following noun is definite or indefinite, singular or plural:

93. (Var. *θalaatt* or *θalatt*)

kill gaṭu	'each (every) cat'
kill li-gṭaawa	'all (the) cats'
kill madiina	'each (every) city'
kill l-madiina	'the whole city'

In GA *kill* may take nunation, especially in proverbs and set phrases:

killin ymidd riila 9ala gadd l-Haafa.

As you make your bed, you must lie in it. (lit., "Each person stretches his leg according to his quilt.")

killin Haliiba yjiiba.

Like father like son. (lit., "One is brought by one's own milk.")

The total intensifiers *jimii9, 9umuum* 'all, whole, entire' modify count and non-count nouns:

jimii9 l-karraaniyya	'all (of the) clerks'
jimii9 n-naas	'all (of the) people'
9umuum ṭ-ṭullaab	'all (of the) students'
9umuum d-duwaayir	'all (of the) departments'

nafs 'same, -self' is used with a definite common noun, and is ambiguous:

nafs r-rayyaal	'the same man' or 'the man himself'
nafs l-Hariim	'the same women' or 'the women themselves'
nafs li-hduum	'the same clothes' or 'the clothes themselves'

10.3.4 Demonstratives

In addition to the article prefix, another part of the determiner system of GA occurs in pre-modification position. It is the demonstrative pronoun. Members of this limited set of pronouns precede only specified definite nouns, and must agree with the nouns they precede in gender and number:

haaϑa l-gaṣir (cf: *haaϑa gaṣir.*)	'this palace (m.s.)' ('This is a palace.')
haaϑi d-diriiša	'this window (f.s.)'
haϑeel(a) l-gaṣreen	'these two palaces (m.dual)'
haϑeel(a) l-Hurumteen	'these two women (f.dual)'
haϑeel(a) li-wlaad	'these boys (m.p.)'
haϑeel(a) d-diraayiš	'these windows (f.p.)'

In *haaða walad.* 'This is a boy.' the demonstrative *haaða* 'this' occurs as an independent noun head of the noun phrase which is the entire subject of the sentence. On the other hand, to add emphasis to the semantic force of the demonstrative pronoun, it may follow the noun it modifies with the semantic restrictions on its concord as mentioned above:

l-mudiir haaða	'this director'
l-waladeen haðeel(a)	'these two boys'

A demonstrative pronoun as a nominal modifier never precedes a noun construct. It modifies either N_1 or N_2. If it modifies N_1, it must follow the entire construct:

biri l-madiina haaða	'this tower of the city'

If it modifies N_2, it may precede or follow it:

biri haaði l-madiina	'the tower of this city'
biri l-madiina haaði	

Of these two choices the former is the usual order in GA.

If the two elements of the construct agree in number and gender, ambiguity results:

šaahiin li-bdiwi haaða	'the falcon of this Bedouin (m.)' or 'this falcon of the Bedouin (m.)'
9ačwat l-9ayuuz haaði	'the cane of this old lady' or 'this cane of the old lady'

But *šaahiin haaða li-bdiwi* and *9ačwat haaði l-9ayuuz* only mean 'the falcon of this Bedouin (m.)' and 'the cane of this old lady,' respectively.

The other demonstratives are:

(ha)ðaak	'that (m.)'	(ha)ðiič	'that (f.)'
(ha)ðoolaak	'those (m.p.)'	(ha)ðeelaak (ha)ðilaak	'those (f.p.)'

10.4 Participles

A participle is a verbal adjective depicting its referent as being in a state as a necessary consequence of the event, process or activity designated by the underlying verb. For the purposes of this part of the study we are interested in participles as post-nominal modifiers.

10.4.1 Active Participle

10.4.1.1 Derivation

Class I

Sound: faa9il

Verb		*AP*	
da9am	'to hit (in a car accident)'	daa9im	'having hit'
la9ab	'to play'	laa9ib	'having played'
9araf	'to know'	9aarif	'knowing' or 'having known'
baraz	'to be ready'	baariz	'ready'
ragad	'to sleep'	raagid	'sleeping'
tiras	'to fill'	taaris	'having filled'
9imil	'to make'	9aamil	'having made'
wiṣil	'to arrive'	waaṣil	'arriving' or 'having arrived'

Defective: faa9i

baġa	'to want'	baaġi	'wanting' or 'having wanted'
Hača	'to speak'	Haači	'having spoken'
dara	'to know'	daari	'having known'
miša	'to walk'	maaši	'walking' or 'having walked'

Hollow: faayi9

ᶞ̣aaj	'to be bored'	ᶞ̣aayij	'bored'
gaaḷ	'to say'	gaayiḷ	'having said'
raaH	'to go'	raayiH	'going' or 'having gone'
daax	'to smoke'	daayix	'dizzy'
ṭaaH	'to fall down'	ṭaayiH	'having fallen down'
xaaf	'to be afraid'	xaayif	'afraid'

Doubled: faa99

dašš	'to enter'	daašš	'entering' or 'having entered'
našš	'to wake up'	naašš	'having waked up, awake'

Verb		*AP*	
gaṣṣ	'to cut'	gaaṣṣ	'having cut'
laff	'to make a turn'	laaff	'turning' or 'having turned'
ṭagg	'to hit, flog'	ṭaagg	'having flogged, beaten'
gaṭṭ	'to throw away'	gaaṭṭ	'having thrown away'
Hamzated: waa9il			
kal ← 'akal 'to eat'		waakil	'having eaten'
xađ ← 'axađ 'to take'		waaxiđ	'having taken'

The active participle from the verb *ya* (var. *ja*) 'to come' is irregular: *yaay* (var. *jaay*) 'coming; having come.'

Class II

Sound: mfa99il			
tarras	'to fill to the brim'	mtarris	'having filled'
faššal	'to disappoint'	mfaššil	'having disappointed'
ṭarraš	'to send'	mṭarriš	'having sent'
fannaš	'to terminate s.o.'s or one's own services'	mfanniš	'having terminated'
xayyam	'to camp'	mxayyim	'having camped'
Defective: mfa99i			
qanna	'to sing'	mqanni	'having sung'
rawwa	'to show'	mrawwi	'having shown'
Hayya	'to greet s.o.'	mHayyi	'having greeted'
ṣaḷḷa	'to pray'	mṣaḷḷi	'having prayed'

Class III

Sound: mfaa9il			
waafaj	'to agree'	mwaafij	'having agreed'
baarak	'to bless'	mbaarik	'having blessed'
xaaṣam	'to quarrel with s.o.'	mxaaṣim	'having quarreled with s.o.'
saafar	'to travel'	msaafir	'traveling' or 'having traveled'
xaabar	'to telephone'	mxaabir	'having telephoned'
saamaH	'to forgive s.o.'	msaamiH	'having forgiven'

Defective: mfaa9i

Verb		*AP*	
Haača	'to speak with s.o.'	mHaači	'having spoken with s.o.'
maaša	'to walk with s.o.'	mmaaši	'having walked with s.o.'

Class IV

Sound: muf9il[94]

'a9jab	'to please'	mu9jib	'pleasing' or 'having pleased'
'axbar	'to inform'	muxbir	'having informed'
'a9lan	'to announce'	mu9lin	'having announced'
'a9lam	'to tell, inform'	mu9lim	'having informed'

Defective: muf9i

'a9ṭa	'to give'	mu9ṭi	'giving' or 'having given'

Class V

Sound: mitfa99il

tsallaf	'to borrow money'	mitsallif	'having borrowed'
tqayyar	'to change'	mitqayyir	'changing, changeable'
twannas	'to have a good time'	mitwannis	'having a good time' or 'having had a good time'
tbannad	'to be shut'	mitbannid	'(being) shut'
twahhag	'to be involved'	mitwahhig	'(being) involved'
t9awwar	'to be injured'	mit9awwir	'having been injured'
tčayyak	'to be checked'	mitčayyik	'having been checked'

Defective: mitfa99i

tqadda	'to have lunch'	mitqaddi	'having had lunch'
tHadda	'to defy'	mitHaddi	'defying'

Class VI

Sound: mitfaa9il

tgaabal	'to meet with s.o.'	mitgaabil	'having met'
tšaawar	'to consult (deliberate) with s.o.'	mitšaawir	'having consulted'

94. See 6.2.3 Class IV verbs.

Verb		*AP*	
taxaaṣam	'to quarrel with each other'	mitxaaṣim	'having quarreled'
ḍ̣ḍ̣aahar	'to feign, pretend'	miḍ̣ḍ̣aahir	'pretending'
Defective: mitfaa9i			
tlaaga	'to meet with each other'	mitlaagi	'meeting' or 'having met'
tHaača	'to talk with each other'	mitHaači	'having talked'
Class VII			
Sound: minfi9il			
ntiras	'to be filled'	mintiris	'full'
n9araf	'to be known'	min9irif	'having been known'
nsima9	'to be heard'	minsimi9	'having been heard'
Defective: minfi9i			
nHača	'to be said'	minHiči	'having been said'
nčasa	'to be clothed'	minčisi	'(being) clothed'
ndara	'to be known'	mindiri	'having been known'
Hollow: minfaa9			
nbaag	'to be stolen'	minbaag	'having been stolen'
Doubled			
nṭagg	'to be beaten, flogged'	minṭagg	'having been flogged, beaten'
ngaṭṭ	'to be thrown away'	mingaṭṭ	'having been thrown away'
ngaṣṣ	'to be cut'	mingaṣṣ	'having been cut'
Class VIII			
Sound: mifti9il			
Htifal	'to celebrate'	miHtifil	'celebrating'
xtalaf	'to be different'	mixtilif	'different'
štaġal	'to work'	mištiġil	'having worked'
stima9	'to listen'	mistimi9	'listening'

Defective: mifti9i

Verb		*AP*	
štara	'to buy'	mištiri	'having bought'
štika	'to complain'	mištiki	'complaining' or 'having complained'
ntasa	'to be forgotten'	mintisi	'forgotten'

Hollow: miftaal

Htaaj	'to need'	miHtaaj	'in need of'
Htaar	'to be puzzled'	miHtaar	'puzzled'
rtaaH	'to rest'	mirtaaH	'comfortable'

Doubled: mifta99

htamm	'to become concerned'	mihtamm	'concerned'
ftarr	'to turn around'	miftarr	'having turned around'

Class IX

mif9all

xḏ̣arr	'to turn green'	mixḏ̣arr	'green, greenish'
Hmarr	'to turn red'	miHmarr	'red, reddish'
byaḏ̣ḏ̣	'to turn white'	mibyaḏ̣ḏ̣	'white, whitish'
zragg	'to turn blue'	mizragg	'blue, bluish'
9wayy	'to turn crooked, twisted'	mi9wayy	'having turned crooked, twisted'

Class X

Sound: mistaf9il

sta9mal	'to use'	mista9mil	'having used'
stazyan	'to find s.th. good'	mistazyin	'finding s.th. good'
starxaṣ	'to have permission, to seek permission'	mistarxiṣ	'having had permission'

Defective: mistaf9i

stabga	'to keep s.th. for oneself'	mistabgi	'keeping s.th. for oneself'
sta9ṭa	'to seek s.th.; to beg'	mista9ṭi	'begging; seeking s.th.'
staqna 9an	'to do without'	mistaqni 9an	'doing without' or 'having done without'

Verb		*AP*	
sta9fa	'to resign'	mista9fi	'having resigned'
Hollow: mista9iil			
staraaH	'to rest, be comfortable'	mistariiH	'restful; comfortable'
stajaab (var. *stayaab*)	'to respond'	mistajiib (var. *mistayiib*)	'responding'
Doubled: mistifi99/mistafi99			
staHabb	'to find s.th. or s.o. nice, good'	mistiHibb/mistaHibb	'liking s.th. or s.o.'
staHagg	'to deserve'	mistiHigg/mistaHigg	'worthy of'
staradd	'to get s.th. back'	mistiridd/mistaridd	'having gotten s.th. back'
Quadriliterals			
Sound: mfa9lil			
la9waz	'to bother s.o.'	mla9wiz	'bothering' or 'having bothered'
xarbaṭ	'to mix, mess, s.th. or s.o. up'	mxarbiṭ	'confusing'
ġašmar	'to play a prank on s.o.'	mġašmir	'having played a prank on s.o.'
Reduplicated: mfa9lil			
gaṣgaṣ	'to cut up s.th.'	mgaṣgiṣ	'having cut up s.th.'
ṭagṭag	'to tap (s.th.)'	mṭagṭig	'having tapped (s.th.)'
Derived Quadriliterals: mitfa9lil			
tla9waz	'to be bothered'	mitla9wiz	'(being) bothered' or 'having been bothered'
txarbaṭ	'to be mixed up'	mitxarbiṭ	'having been mixed up'
tgaṣgaṣ	'to be cut up'	mitgaṣgiṣ	'having been cut up'

10.4.1.2 Meanings of Active Participles

Most active participles have two dimensions of meaning: grammatical and aspectual.

a. Grammatical

bint raagṣa	'a dancing girl'
9ali mṭarriš l-xaṭṭ.	'Ali is sending, has sent, the letter.'
ṭeer mqanni	'a singing bird'
zaam mitqayyir	'a changing, changeable work schedule'

b. Aspectual

The aspect implied by a participle seems to be in many cases an individual characteristic of the participle itself, i.e., it is lexically conditioned. As will be pointed out below, there are many cases where the participle and the underlying verb do not match. Some participles seem to have a much more aspectual meaning than others, e.g., native speakers of GA often assign more specific aspectual meanings to a participle in very common use than to a less common one, e.g., in *r-rayyaal li-mla9wiz* the active participle, *li-mla9wiz,* which is not so commonly used, has the following aspectual meanings: 'the man who is bothering (somebody) (now); the bothering man (iterative); the man that (has) bothered (perfective).' In *r-rayyaal li-mṭarriš l-xaṭṭ,* on the other hand, the active participle, *l-mṭarriš*, which has a higher frequency of occurrence than *li-mla9wiz* means only 'the man who has sent the letter (perfective).'

If the underlying verb is an imperfect tense, then the active participle expresses the following aspects:

(i) Concurrent (in progress)

l-maay l-jaari	'the running water'
š-šaayil guuniyyat l-9eeš	'(the one) carrying the rice sack'
li-9yaaḷ l-maašyiin	'the children (who are) walking'
bdiwi raakib b(i)9iir	'a Bedouin riding a camel'

(ii) Iterative (customary, habitual)

ṭeer mqanni	'a song bird' (lit., "a singing bird")
rayyaalin ṣaadj	'a truthful man'

(iii) Dispositional (tending, having the ability, capacity to act)

zaam mitqayyir	'a changeable, changing work schedule'
9yaada mitHarka	'a moveable, moving clinic'

(iv) Future

r-rayyaal l-yaay baačir	'the man arriving (who is going to arrive) tomorrow'
li-msaafriin r-raayHiin d-dooHa	'the travelers going (who are going) to Doha'

If the underlying verb is a perfect tense, the corresponding active participle depicts:

(i) Completed Action

l-Hurma l-9aamla l-gahwa	'the woman who (has) made the coffee'
d-dreewil li-m9awwir raaṣa	'the driver who (has) injured his head'
l-kuuli li-mfanniš	'the coolie who (has) terminated his work'
weeh miHmarr	'a face that (has) turned red'

(ii) Resultant Condition

The active participles belonging here convey an aspect not conveyed by either the perfect or the imperfect tense of the corresponding verb. Examples: *waagif* 'standing, afoot' from *wagaf* 'he stood up; he stopped' and *yoogaf* 'he stops; he stands regularly,' *yaalis* 'sitting, seated' from *yilas* 'he sat up, down' and *yiilis* 'he sits down, or up (regularly),' *naayim* 'sleeping, asleep' from *naam* 'he slept' and *yinaam* 'he goes to sleep, sleeps (regularly).'

If the underlying verb is either a perfect or an imperfect tense, the corresponding active participle expresses either a progressive or a perfective aspect. Examples:

gaað̣i 9aadil	'a judge who is, has been, just'
r-rayyaal d-daašš	'the man (who is) entering; the man who has entered'

It was mentioned in 10.4 that a participle is a verbal adjective. Like verbs, an active participle may take a direct object (i.e., a noun, a pronoun, or a suffixed pronoun). Examples:

9ali mṭarriš l-xaṭṭ.	'Ali is sending, has sent, the letter.'
9ali mṭarriš haðeel.	'Ali is sending, has sent, these.'
9ali mṭarša.	'Ali is sending, has sent, it (him).'
9ali mṭarriš-li xaṭṭ.	'Ali is sending, has sent, me a letter.'

Like adjectives, it follows the noun it modifies and agrees with it in gender, number,[95] and definiteness, and is negated by mu(u)(b). Examples:

dreewil m9awwir raaṣa	'a driver who has injured his head'
Hurma m9awra raaṣha	'a woman who has injured her head'
d-dreewliyya li-m9awriin ruuṣhum	'the drivers who have injured their heads'
l-Hariim li-m9awraat ruuṣhin	'the women who have injured their heads'
l-kuuliyyeen li-mfanšiin	'the two coolies who have resigned'
l-Hurumteen l-mitxanninaat	'the two women who are wearing perfume'
gaaḍ̄i mu(u)(b) 9aadil	'an unjust judge'
zaam mu(u)(b) mitqayyir	'an unchanging, unchangeable work schedule'

10.4.2 Passive Participle

10.4.2.1 Derivation

Passive participles are derived only from transitive verbs. Note that *active* participle forms of verbs of Class VII (which are intransitive or passive in meaning) have a passive meaning:

taanki mintiris	'a filled, full tank'
ġarša mingaṭṭa	'a discarded, thrown away bottle'

mintiris 'filled, full' and *mingaṭṭa* 'thrown away' are active participles of the verbs *ntiras* 'to be filled' and *ngaṭṭ* 'to be thrown away, discarded' in form only, for this form is equivalent to the passive participles of the underlying triradical verbs: *matruus* 'filled, full' from *tiras* 'to fill' and *magṭuuṭ* 'thrown away, discarded' from *gaṭṭ* 'to throw away, discard.' In actual practice *matruus* and *magṭuuṭ* are usually used rather than *mintiris* and *mingaṭṭ*.

All unaugmented triradical verbs form their passive participles according to the pattern *maf9uul.* The passive participles of the transitive verbs in 10.4.1.1 are:

95. The dual form is not used; the plural form is used instead (see 14.1.1A).

mad9uum	'hit (in a car accident)'	ma9ruuf	'known'
mal9uub	'played'	ma9muul	'made'
matruus	'filled; full'	maHči	'spoken'
mabġi	'desired'	magṣuuṣ	'cut'
madšuuš	'entered'	mawkuul	'eaten'
malfuuf	'turned; round'	mawxuuð	'taken'

From augmented verbs, the passive participle is formed by the prefixation of *m-* (or *mi-* before a two-consonant cluster) before the first radical of the stem, with *a* as a stem vowel (vowel preceding the last radical). From quadriliterals, the pattern is *mfa9lal.* Examples:

mrawwa	'shown, exhibited'	mxaḷḷa	'left, deserted'
mfannaš	'terminated'	m9awwar	'injured'
mjaawab	'answered'	mHaača	'spoken to'
miftarr	'turned around'	mista9mal	'used'
mistaHabb	'liked, desired'	mistaHagg	'having been worthy of'
mla9waz	'bothered'	mxarbaṭ	'mixed up'

Passive participles derived from transitive verbs that take prepositional objects always have pronouns suffixed to the prepositions. The suffixed pronouns have as their antecedents the noun-head of the construction. The participle does not show agreement with the subject; it remains in the base form (i.e., m.s.):

rayyaal maHkuum 9alee	'a convicted man'
Hurma maHkuum 9aleeha	'a convicted woman'
gað̣iyya madri biiha	'a known case'
gað̣aaya madri biihum	'known cases'

10.4.2.2 Meanings of Passive Participles

Every passive participle has two dimensions of meaning: grammatical and aspectual.

a. Grammatical

A passive participle depicts its referent as the goal of the action:

sayyaara mad9uuma	'a hit car'
baab maṣkuuk	'a closed door'

ktaab mabyuug	'a book that has been stolen'
guuṭi mbaṭṭal	'a can that has been opened'

b. Aspectual

(i) Perfective

gaḷam maksuur	'a broken pencil'
ktaab mabyuug	'a stolen book'

The referent is the goal of the action. It is depicted as being "having been *V-ed*."

(ii) Perfective or Progressive

l-miškila l-mabHuuθ fiiha	'the problem that has been (or is being) discussed'
l-'imaaraat l-masmuu9 9anha	'the Emirates that have been (or are being) heard about'
ṭ-ṭamaaṭ l-mabyuu9	'the tomatoes sold (now or regularly)'
s-sayaayiir l-majyuuba min 'amriika	'the cars imported (lit., "brought") from America'

The referent is depicted as being "having been *V-ed*" or "being *V-ed.*"

(iii) Potential

šayyin makruuh	'a detestable, odious thing'
Haakim maHbuub	'a lovable, likable ruler'

The referent is depicted as being "capable of being *V-ed*" or "tending to be *V-ed.*"

10.5 Adjectives

10.5.1 Derivation

10.5.1.1 Positive Adjectives

Most positive adjectives in GA have verbs as their underlying forms and are of the *fa9iil* pattern.

ṭawiil	'tall; long'	←	ṭaal	'to grow, turn tall' Class I

gaṣiir	'short'	←	giṣir	'to turn short' Class I
raxiiṣ	'inexpensive'	←	rixiṣ	'to become inexpensive' Class I
k(a)biir (var. *čibiir*)	'big, large'	←	kibir	'to grow big, large' Class I
matiin	'fat'	←	mitin	'to grow fat' Class I
qadiim (var. *jadiim*)	'old, ancient'	←	qidim (var. *jidim*)	'to become ancient' Class I
yadiid (var. *jadiid*)	'new'	←	yidid (var. *jidid*)	'to turn new' Class I
yamiil (var. *jamiil*)	'beautiful'	←	yimil (var. *jimil*)	'to grow, turn beautiful' Class I
naḏ̣iif	'clean'	←	niḏ̣if	'to turn clean' Class I

One or two positive adjectives of this pattern are derived from nouns:

faġiir	'poor'	←	fiġar	'poverty'
9ajiib	'strange'	←	9ajab	'strangeness'

A few positive adjectives are of the *fayyil* pattern. They are derived from Class I hollow verbs:

ṭayyib	'good, fine'	←	ṭaab	'to be good, fine'
hayyin	'easy'	←	haan	'to be easy'
bayyin	'clear'	←	baan	'to be clear'
mayyit	'dead'	←	maat	'to die'
ḏ̣ayyig	'narrow'	←	ḏ̣aag	'to become narrow'

Those of the *fa9i* pattern have verbal nouns as their underlying forms:

qani	'rich'	←	qana	'richness'
qawi (var. *gawi*)	'strong'	←	quwwa (var. *guwwa*)	'power, strength'
ṣaxi	'bountiful, generous'	←	ṣaxaawa	'generosity'
ḏaki	'clever'	←	ḏaka	'cleverness'
šaqi	'naughty'	←	šaqaawa	'naughtiness'

hadi	'quiet'	←	hudaay	'quietness'
qabi	'stupid'	←	qabaawa	'stupidity'

A few positive adjectives are derived from other classes of verbs:

muhimm	'important'	←	htamm	'to become concerned'
maynuun (var. *majnuun*)	'crazy'	←	nyann (var. *njann*)	'to become crazy'

There are positive adjectives of some other patterns:

waṣix	'dirty'	←	waṣax	'dirt'
Haarr	'hot'	←	Haraara	'heat; temperature'
murr	'bitter'	←	maraara	'bitterness'
Hiḷu	'sweet'	←	Haḷaawa	'sweetness'
Haadd	'sharp (knife)'	←	Hadd	'edge'[96]
9ood	'big, large; old'	←	no underlying form	
dijiij	'thin; skinny'	←	no underlying form	

10.5.1.2 *fa9laan* Adjectives

fa9laan adjectives, as their name indicates, are of the *fa9laan* pattern. Almost all of them are derived from Class I verbs, e.g., *Himig* 'to get mad, angry' has the *fa9laan* adjective *Hamgaan* which describes someone, a male, as being in, or undergoing, a state of anger.

The most commonly used *fa9laan* adjectives are the following:

ta9baan	'tired'	←	ti9ib	'to get tired'
xajlaan	'embarrassed'	←	xijil	'to be embarrassed'
xasraan	'broke'	←	xisir	'to lose (e.g., in a game)'
Hamgaan	'mad'	←	Himig	'to get mad'
ġaḍ̱baan	'furious'	←	ġiḍ̱ib	'to get furious'
sakraan	'drunk'	←	sikir	'to get drunk'
šab9aan	'full (of food)'	←	šibi9	'to be full of food'
9aṭšaan	'thirsty'	←	9iṭiš	'to be thirsty'
ġalṭaan	'mistaken'	←	ġiliṭ	'to make a mistake'
farHaan	'happy'	←	firiH	'to be happy'
na9saan	'sleepy (person)'	←	ni9is	'to be sleepy'

96. Such as the edge of a sword.

kaslaan	'lazy'	←	kisil	'to be lazy'
bardaan[97]	'cold'	←	birid	'to get cold'
Harraan[98]	'hot, sweating'	←	no underlying form	
9argaan	'sweating'	←	9irij	'to sweat'
yarbaan	'inflicted with scabies'	←	yirib	'to be inflicted with scabies'
ḓamyaan	'very thirsty'	←	ḓimi	'to get thirsty'
Hamyaan	'hot, running a temperature'	←	Himi	'to get hot'
juu9aan	'hungry'	←	jaa9	'to be hungry'
naymaan	'sleepy (leg)'	←	naam	'to sleep'
talfaan	'deserted'	←	tilif	'to be deserted'
rawyaan	'well-watered'	←	riwi	'to be satiated with water'
xarbaan	'out of order'	←	xirib	'to be out of order'

10.5.1.3 Nisba Adjectives

Nisba adjectives, sometimes known as relative adjectives, indicate something characteristic of, or having to do with what the underlying word designates. Most nisba adjectives are derived from nouns, a few from adjectives, and a small number from prepositions. They are formed by suffixing *-i* to the word, sometimes with appropriate stem changes.[99]

The following are examples of nisba adjectives that require no stem changes:

'ardun	'Jordan'	→	'arduni	'Jordanian'
šarg	'east'	→	šarji	'eastern'
šaxṣ	'person'	→	šaxṣi	'personal, private'
xaliij	'gulf'	→	xaliiji	'gulf (adj.)'
9umaan	'Oman'	→	9umaani	'Omani'
ꝺahab	'gold'	→	ꝺahabi	'gold, golden'

---

97. *bardaan* 'cold' is used only with animate nouns; *baarid* is used with inanimate nouns. The same distinction in meaning applies, respectively, to *Harraan* vs. *Haarr* 'hot.'

98. *Ibid.*

99. See 4.3.1.

markaz	'center'	→ markazi	'central'
foog	'above'	→ foogi[100]	'located higher or above'

Some nisbas require *vowel elision* when *-i* is added:

9agil	'mind'	→ 9agli	'mental'
'aṣil	'origin'	→ 'aṣli	'original; genuine'
ramiḷ	'sand'	→ ramḷi	'sandy'
baHar	'sea'	→ baHri	'naval'
šahar	'month'	→ šahri	'monthly'
taHat	'below'	→ taHti[101]	'located lower or below'

Some nouns with the *-a* ending lose this ending when *-i* is added:

š-šaarja	'Sharja'	→ šaarji	'from Sharja'
Hagiiga	'fact; truth'	→ Hagiigi	'factual'
9aada	'habit; custom'	→ 9aadi	'habitual; regular'
kanada	'Canada'	→ kanadi	'Canadian'
l-baHreen	'Bahrain'	→ baHreeni[102]	'Bahraini'

Some other nouns with the *-a* ending lengthen this ending and a *-w-* is added before the *-i* ending. Most such nouns are place names and of the pattern *fa9la* or *fi9la*. Examples:

baṣra	'Basra'[103]	→ baṣraawi	'from Basra'
barbara	'Barbara'[104]	→ barbaraawi	'from Barbara'
leewa	'Liwa'[105]	→ leewaawi	'from Liwa'
dalma	'Dalma'[106]	→ dalmaawi	'from Dalma'
waθba	'Wathba'[107]	→ waθbaawi	'from Wathba'

---

100. Or the less commonly used *foogaani.*

101. Or the less commonly used *taHtaani.*

102. *baHraani,* the plural of which is *baHaarna,* is another nisba adjective. It means 'characteristic of the Shiah sect' or 'a member of the Shiah sect' anywhere, not necessarily in Bahrain.

103. A city in Iraq.

104. A place name.

105. A place name in Abu Dhabi.

106. An island in Abu Dhabi.

107. *Ibid.*

čalba	'Kalba'[108]	→ čalbaawi	'from Kalba'
zirkoo	'Zirkuh'[109]	→ zirkaawi	'from Zirkuh'

10.5.1.4 Elative Adjectives

See 10.2 Elative Constructs above.

Depending upon their root structure, elative adjectives are divided into the following:

A. Sound Roots

Elatives with sound roots are formed on the pattern *'af9al* from the corresponding positive adjective.

Positive		*Elative*	
matiin	'fat'	'amtan	'fatter'
waṣix	'dirty'	'awṣax	'dirtier'
čibiir (var. *k(a)biir*)	'big; old'	'akbar[110]	'bigger; older'
9atiij	'ancient, old'	'a9taj	'older'
ḍ̱a9iif	'skinny, weak'	'aḍ̱9af	'skinnier; weaker'
9aagil	'sane'	'a9gal	'more sane'
ṣaadj (var. *saadig*)	'truthful'	'aṣdaj (var. *'aṣdag*)	'more truthful'
naašif	'dry'	'anšaf	'drier'
naḍ̱iif	'clean'	'anḍ̱af	'cleaner'
gaṣiir	'short'	'agṣar	'shorter'

B. Weak-Middle Roots

In these elatives the *9* is either a *y* or a *w* , depending on the roots of the underlying word:

zeen	'fine, good'	'azyan[111]	'finer, better'
šeen	'bad'	'ašyan	'worse'
xaayis	'rotten'	'axyas	'more rotten'
zaayid	'excessive'	'azyad (var. *'azwad*)	'more excessive'

108. A town on the Gulf of Oman.

109. An island in Abu Dhabi.

110. For k → č see APPENDIX III.

111. Or *'aHsan.*

ẓ̱ayyig	'narrow'	'aẓ̱yag	'narrower'
ṭayyib	'good; delicious'	'aṭyab	'better; more delicious'
xaayif	'afraid'	'axwaf	'more afraid'
hayyin	'easy'	'ahwan	'easier'

C. Weak-Last Roots

The underlying adjectives in this section end in *-i.* The elatives derived from such adjectives are of the *'af9a* pattern.

ġaali	'expensive'	'aġla	'more expensive'
qawi (var. *gawi*)	'strong'	'aqwa (var. *'agwa*)	'stronger'
qani	'rich'	'aqna	'richer'
ṣaaHi	'conscious'	'aṣHa	'more conscious'
9aali	'high'	'a9la	'higher'
šaqi	'naughty'	'ašqa	'naughtier'
hadi	'quiet'	'ahda	'quieter'
ṣixi	'generous'	'aṣxa	'more generous'
qabi	'stupid'	'aqba	'more stupid'

D. Double Roots

In these elatives the second and third roots are identical. They are derived from positive adjectives in which the second and the third roots are also identical. The pattern is *'afa99.*

Haarr	'hot'	'aHarr	'hotter'
yadiid (var. *jadiid*)	'new'	'ayadd[112] (var. *'ajadd*)	'newer'
qaliil	'few; little'	'aqall	'fewer; less'
xafiif	'light, not heavy'	'axaff[113]	'lighter'
murr	'bitter'	'amarr	'more bitter'
Haaff	'dry'	'aHaff	'drier'
Haadd	'sharp'	'aHadd	'sharper'
maynuun	'crazy, mad'	'ayann	'crazier'
xasiis	'low, mean'	'axass	'meaner'

112. Or *'aydad* (var. *'ajdad*).

113. Or *'axfaf.*

A few adjectives do not have any of the above elative patterns. The elative of such adjectives is expressed by pre-posing *'akθar* 'more' (the elative of *kaθiir* 'much, a lot'):

ḏ̣amyaan	'thirsty'	ḏ̣amyaan 'akθar	'thirstier'
Hamyaan	'hot, feverish'	Hamyaan 'akθar	'more feverish'
yarbaan	'mangy; scabby'	yarbaan 'akθar	'scabbier'
ḏ̣aruuri	'necessary'	ḏ̣aruuri 'akθar	'more necessary'
mixtilif	'different'	mixtilif 'akθar	'more different'

10.5.2 Inflection

10.5.2.1 Gender

Adjectives have two genders: masculine and feminine. They differ from nouns in that nouns are either masculine or feminine; adjectives have two forms, a masculine form and a feminine form, depending upon the noun they modify. The feminine singular form of the adjective is formed from the masculine singular form by suffixing *-a,* sometimes with appropriate stem changes as described below.

1. Adjectives of the patterns *maf9uul, fa9iil* (or *fi9iil*), *fa9laan,* or other adjectives that end with either a single consonant prededed by a long vowel or a double consonant preceded by a short or a long vowel require no stem change when *-a* is suffixed. Examples:

maynuun	'crazy'	→	maynuuna
matruus	'full'	→	matruusa
maḏbuuH	'slaughtered'	→	maḏbuuHa
xasiis	'low, mean'	→	xasiisa
matiin	'fat'	→	matiina
yadiid (var. *jadiid*)	'new'	→	yadiida (var. *jadiida*)
xasraan	'broke'	→	xasraana
yarbaan	'mangy, scabby'	→	yarbaana
talfaan	'deserted'	→	talfaana
zeen	'good, fine'	→	zeena
šeen	'bad'	→	šeena
9ood	'big; old'	→	9ooda

murr	'bitter'	→	murra
Haaff	'dry'	→	Haaffa
daašš	'entering'	→	daašša

2. Feminine nisba adjectives are formed from their corresponding masculine forms by changing the suffix *-i* into *-iyya*:

'arduni	'Jordanian'	→	'arduniyya
kweeti	'Kuwaiti'	→	kweetiyya
'aṣli	'original'	→	'aṣliyya
9aadi	'habitual; regular'	→	9aadiyya
dalmaawi	'from Dalma'	→	dalmaawiyya
barbaraawi	'from Barbara'	→	barbaraawiyya

3. Adjectives with final weak roots of the *fa9i* pattern also change *-i* into *-iyya;* those of the *faa9i* pattern change *-i* into *-ya.* Examples:

ṣixi	'bountiful; generous'	→	ṣixiyya
hadi	'quiet'	→	hadiyya
qawi	'strong'	→	qawiyya
9aali	'high'	→	9aalya
ġaali	'expensive'	→	ġaalya
baagi	'remaining; remainder'	→	baagya
maaši	'walking'	→	maašya
baaġi	'oppressive; tyrant'	→	baaġya

4. Adjectives[114] of the patterns *faa9il, fayyil,* or other adjectives that end with -VC in which -V- is an unstressed vowel,[115] drop -V- when *-a* is suffixed. Those adjectives that end with -CCVC (usually participles) also drop one of the double consonants when *-a* is added (see 4.3.2).

baariz	'ready'	→	baarza
raagid	'sleeping'	→	raagda
taaris	'filling'	→	taarsa
hayyin	'easy'	→	hayna

114. A good number of these adjectives are active and passive participles.

115. See 4.3.1.

bayyin	'clear'	→	bayna
ϑ̣ayyig	'narrow'	→	ϑ̣ayga
mṣaxxan	'running a temperature'	→	mṣaxna
mfanniš	'having terminated'	→	mfanša
mṭarriš	'having sent'	→	mṭarša
mfaššil	'having disappointed'	→	mfašla
mwaafij	'having agreed'	→	mwaafja
mitwannis	'having a good time'	→	mitwansa
mixtilif	'different'	→	mixtilfa
mreewis	'have gone in reverse'	→	mreewsa

5. Feminine adjectives of color and defect are formed from their corresponding masculine forms according to the patterns *fa9la* for sound forms, *feela* for forms with a medial *-y-* and *foola* for forms with a medial *-w-*. Examples:

Hamar	'red'	→	Hamra
xaϑ̣ar	'green'	→	xaϑ̣ra
xaraš	'inflicted with smallpox'	→	xarša
9aray	'limping, lame'	→	9arya
9amay	'blind'	→	9amya
9aϑ̣ab	'having a paralyzed hand'	→	9aϑ̣ba
ġatam	'mute'	→	ġatma

'azrag	'blue'	→	zarga
'aṣfar	'yellow'	→	ṣafra
'asmar	'dark'	→	samra
'amlaH	'grey'	→	malHa
'aṣmax	'mute'	→	ṣamxa
'ašlag	'cross-eyed'	→	šalga
'aṣlay	'deaf'	→	ṣalya

'abyaϑ̣	'white'	→	beeϑ̣a

'aswad	'black'	→	sooda
9awar	'one-eyed'	→	9oora
9away	'crooked, bent'	→	9ooya

10.5.2.2 Number

Adjectives, like nouns, have dual and plural forms. In GA the dual is very rarely used; the plural form is used instead, e.g., *9ayleen ᵭ9aaf* 'two thin (weak) children' instead of *9ayleen ᵭa9iifeen* (see 14.1.1A). Most plural forms are sound masculine forms; sound feminine forms are not commonly used (see 14.1.1A). These adjectives include those of the patterns *fa9iil, fa9il, fa9i, fa99, fu99, fa9laan,* nisba adjectives, and adjectives of participle patterns. Some nisba adjectives and all adjectives of color and defect have broken plural forms. Note that the appropriate stem changes in the formation of the sound plural forms are the same as those for the formation of the feminine forms described above.

ᵭa9iif	'thin; weak'	→	ᵭa9iifiin (or *ᵭ9aaf*)
ṭawiil	'tall; long'	→	ṭawiiliin (or *ṭwaal*)
gaṣiir	'short'	→	gaṣiiriin (or *gṣaar*)
ᵭayyig	'narrow'	→	ᵭaygiin
waṣix	'dirty'	→	waṣxiin
hadi	'quiet'	→	hadiyyiin
ṣixi	'bountiful, generous'	→	sixiyyiin
Haarr	'hot'	→	Haarriin
Haadd	'sharp (knife)'	→	Haaddiin
murr	'bitter'	→	murriin
ᵭamyaan	'very thirsty'	→	ᵭamyaaniin
ġaᵭbaan	'furious'	→	ġaᵭbaaniin
9umaani	'Omani'	→	9umaaniyyiin (or *9umaaniyya*)
baHreeni	'Bahraini'	→	baHreeniyyiin (or *baHreeniyya*)
zirkaawi	'from Zirkoo'	→	zirkaawiyyiin (or *zirkaawiyya*)
baagi	'remaining'	→	baagyiin
ġaali	'expensive'	→	ġaalyiin
maaši	'walking'	→	maašyiin
9aali	'high'	→	9aalyiin

Major Broken Plural Patterns

1. f9aal

Masculine singular adjectives of the *fa9iil/fi9iil* pattern usually have two plural patterns: a sound pattern, e.g., *ḏ̣a9iifiin* 'thin; weak,' as in some of the above examples, and a broken pattern *f9aal*. Examples:

θagiil	'heavy'	→	θgaal (or *θagiiliin*)
gaṣiir	'short'	→	gṣaar (or *gaṣiiriin*)
čibiir (var. *k(a)biir*)	'big; old'	→	kbaar (or *kabiiriin*)
dijiij	'thin'	→	djaaj (or *dajiijiin*)
qaliil	'little; few'	→	qlaal (or *qaliiliin*)
matiin	'fat'	→	mtaan (or *matiiniin*)
naḏ̣iif	'clean'	→	nḏ̣aaf (or *naḏ̣iifiin*)
ṣaġiir	'small; young'	→	ṣġaar (or *ṣaġiiriin*)
yadiid (var. *jadiid*)	'new'	→	ydaad (or *yadiidiin*) (or *yiddad*)

2. fi9laan

Most adjectives of defect have this broken plural pattern. Masculine singular adjectives of defect in GA are of the patterns *fa9al* or *'af9al* (see APPENDIX V).

9amay	'blind'	→	9imyaan
9awar	'one-eyed'	→	9iwraan
9aray	'limping, lame'	→	9iryaan
9away	'crooked; not straight'	→	9iwyaan (or *9ooyaan*)
habal	'weak-minded'	→	hiblaan
ġatam	'mute'	→	ġitmaan
9aḏ̣ab	'having a paralyzed hand'	→	9iḏ̣baan
xaraš	'inflicted with smallpox'	→	xiršaan
'aṣmax	'dumb'	→	ṣimxaan
'aθram	'having a split lip'	→	θirmaan
'abḏ̣am	'toothless'	→	biḏ̣maan

'ašlag	'cross-eyed'	→	šilgaan
'aṣlay	'deaf'	→	ṣilyaan

3. fu9ul/fi9l/fuul

Adjectives of color have this broken plural pattern. The singular form of this kind of adjective is of the patterns *fa9al* or *'af9al;* it is *'af9al* unless the first radical is any of the following consonant sounds: *ġ,9,',x,H,h* (see APPENDIX V).

Hamar	'red'	→	Humur
xaḍ̄ar	'green'	→	xuḍ̄ur
'abyaḍ̄	'white'	→	biiḍ̄
'azrag	'blue'	→	zirg (or *zurg*)
'aṭlas	'dark blue'	→	ṭils
'aswad	'black'	→	suud
'asmar	'dark'	→	sumur
'amlaH	'grey'	→	milH
'aṣfar	'yellow'	→	ṣufur

4. fa9laawiyya

These are nisba adjectives that indicate a national origin or an ethnic group. Note that these adjectives have other plural patterns, as pointed above.

baṣraawi	'from Basra'	→	baṣraawiyya
baHreeni	'Bahraini'	→	baHreeniyya
čalbaawi	'from Kalba'	→	čalbaawiyya
leewaawi	'from Liwa'	→	leewaawiyya
barbaraawi	'from Barbara'	→	barbaraawiyya

5. mafaa9iil

maynuun	'crazy; insane'	→	mayaaniin
mxabbaḷ	'dismayed; foolish'	→	maxaabiiḷ

11. PRONOUNS

11.1 Independent Pronouns

Independent pronouns are free forms. They are inflected for gender and number. In GA there are ten such pronouns. The most characteristic forms of which are the following:

3rd person m.s.	*huwa*	2nd person m.s.	*'inta*
3rd person m.p.	*hum*	2nd person m.p.	*'intum*
3rd person f.s.	*hiya*	2nd person f.s.	*'inti*
3rd person f.p.	*hin*	2nd person f.p.	*'intin*
	1st person s.	*'aana*	
	1st person p.	*niHin*	

The following are the less common variants of some independent pronouns:

Personal Pronoun	*Variants*
huwa	huu,huwwa, 'uhu
hiya	hii, hiyya, 'ihi
hum	humma, 'uhum
'inta	'int, 'init
'intum	'intu
'aana	'ana, 'aani
niHin	Hinna, niHna, 'iHna

The forms under *Personal Pronouns* above are the basic forms of the dialects of GA; those on the right, i.e., the *Variants,* are also used in Bahraini and Qatari: *huwwa, humma, hiyya, 'aani,* and *'iHna* are characteristic of Bahraini, while *huwwa, hiyya, 'int,* and *'iHna* or *Hinna* are characteristic of Qatari.

Some speakers use only one form, i.e., *hum,* for both the masculine and the feminine 3rd person plural. The same speakers would also use *'intu* for both the masculine and the feminine 2nd person plural. There are no dual forms of personal pronouns in GA; the plural forms are used instead.

The independent pronoun is used:

1. As the subject or predicate of an equational sentence (see 13.1): *niHin min rab9a.* 'We are from his group (lit., "relations").' *hum waajid zeen.* 'They (m.p.) are very good.'

2. As the subject of a verbal sentence (see 13.2) for emphasis: *huwa yabi yaHči wiyyaač.* 'He wants to talk to you (f.s.).' *'aana naššeet s-saa9a xams.* 'I woke up at five.' *hin drisan wiyyaay* 'They (f.) studied with me.'

11.2 Suffixed Pronouns

Pronouns may be suffixed to verbs, nouns, active participles, and particles. When suffixed to verbs, function as the objects of those verbs, and when suffixed to nouns they indicate possession. For active participles see C below, and for particles see 12. PARTICLES below.

A. *Suffixed to Verbs*

The following table shows the personal pronouns and the corresponding verb suffixed forms:

Personal Pronoun		*Verb Suffixed Pronoun*
huwa	'he'	-a
hum	'they (m.)'	-hum
hiya	'she'	-ha
hin	'they (f.)'	-hin
'inta	'you (m.s.)'	-k/-ak
'intum	'you (m.p.)'	-ku(m)
'inti	'you (f.s.)'	-č/-ič
'intin	'you (f.p.)'	-ku, kin
'aana	'I'	-ni
niHin	'we'	-na

Example:

fannaš	'to terminate someone's services'
fannaša	'he terminated him'
fannašhum	'he terminated them (m.)'
fannašha	'he terminated her.'
fannašhin	'he terminated them (f.)'
fannašk	'he terminated you (m.s.)'
fannaškum	'he terminated you (m.p.)'
fannašč	'he terminated you (f.s.)'
fannaškin	'he terminated you (m.p.)'
fannašni	'he terminated me'
fannašna	'he terminated us'

The suffixed pronouns that indicate the second person singular have two forms each: *-k* and *-ak* for the masculine, and the corresponding

-č and -*ič* for the feminine. -*ak* and -*ič* are used after a verb form that ends with -VVC or -$VC_1 C_2$ or -VCC. Elsewhere -*k* and -*č* are used. The second person plural has two forms each: -*ku*/-*kum* for the masculine and -*ku*/-*kin* for the feminine. These forms are not phonetically conditioned but are used interchangeably.[116]

When suffixed to verbs, these bound forms sometimes require certain changes in the verbs:

1. CVCVC → CCVC

Sound verbs of Class I of the *fa9al* pattern change into *f9al*- before -*a* is suffixed:

9araf	'he knew'	→	9rafa	'he knew him'
tiras	'he filled'	→	trasa	'he filled it (m.), him'
ðabaH	'he slaughtered'	→	ðbaHa	'he slaughtered it (m.), him'

2. -f + h- → -ff-
   -t + h- → -tt-

The *h* in the suffixed pronouns -*hum*, -*ha*, and -*hin* changes into *f* or *t* if preceded by a verb form [117] that ends with *f* or *t* (see 4.2). Examples:

šaaf	'he saw'	→	šaaffum	'he saw them (m.)'
			šaaffa	'he saw her'
			šaaffin	'he saw them (f.)'

The following examples involve anaptyxis and then assimilation:

šift	'I saw'	→ *šifthum	→	šifittum	'I saw them (m.)'
		*šiftha	→	šifitta	'I saw her'
		*šifthin	→	šifittin	'I saw them (f.)'
ð̣arabt	'I hit'	→ *ð̣arabthum	→	ð̣arabittum	'I hit them (m.)'
		*ð̣arabtha	→	ð̣arabitta	'I hit her'
		*ð̣arabthin	→	ð̣arabittin	'I hit them (f.)'

3. CCVCVt → CVCCVt
   CVCVCVt → CVCCVt

A verb form of the *fa9alat* (or *f9alat*) pattern changes into *fa9lat* before the suffixed pronoun -*a* is added:

---

116. -*ku* is more commonly used (for both forms) than -*kum* or -*kin*.

117. Verb form here indicates either a verb by itself or a verb plus subject marker.

9rafat	'shc knew'	→	9arfata	'she knew it (m.), him'
ɵbaHat	'she killed'	→	ɵabHata	'she killed it (m.), him'
trasat	'she filled'	→	tirsata	'she filled it (m.), him'
tfalat	'she spit'	→	taflata	'she spit it (m.)'

If the suffixed pronoun *-č* is added, the *-t* of *f9alat* changes into *-č* and assimilates (see 4.2). This transcription, however, will show *-tč* instead of *-čč*:

9rafat	+	-č	→	9rafatč
ɵbaHat	+	-č	→	ɵbaHatč
trasat	+	-č	→	trasatč

It should be noted that the forms *9arfatč, ɵabHatč*, and *tirsatč* are also possible. The forms *9arafatič, ɵabaHatič*, . . . etc., are rare. This rule applies to any other sound form of any other class of verb. Examples:

fannašat + -č	→	fannašatč	'she terminated your (f.s.) services'
xaabarat + -č	→	xaabaratč	'she telephoned you (f.s.)'
jjaahalat + -č	→	jjaahalatč	'she ignored you (f.s.)'
staHabbat + -č	→	staHabbatč	'she liked you (f.s.)'
la9wazat + -č	→	la9wazatč	'she bothered you (f.s.)'
gahwat + -č	→	gahwatč	'she gave you (f.s.) coffee'
gaṣgaṣat + -č	→	gaṣgaṣatč	'she tore you (f.s.) up into little pieces'

The forms *xaabaratič* 'she telephoned you' (f.s.), *fannašatič* 'she terminated your (f.s.) services' . . . , etc., are also possible.

4. -an → -aw → -oo

The third person feminine form of the verb is not used if it is followed by a suffixed pronoun; the masculine form is used instead, e.g., *9rafan* 'they (f.) knew,' *ɵbaHan* 'they killed,' *šaafan* 'they (f.) saw,' etc., change into *9rafaw-, ɵbaHaw-, šaafaw-*, etc. The *-aw* of these masculine forms changes into *-oo* before suffixed pronouns:

9rafaw + -a	→	9rafoo	'they (m. or f.) knew him, it (m.)'
+ -hum	→	9rafoohum	'they (m. or f.) knew them (m.)'
+ -ha	→	9rafooha	'they (m. or f.) knew her'
+ -k	→	9rafook	'they (m. or f.) knew you (m.s.)'

+ -č	→ 9rafooč	'they (m. or f.) knew you (f.s.)'
+ -ni	→ 9rafooni	'they (m. or f.) knew me'
	etc.	etc.	etc.

The forms *9arfoo, 9arfooha, 9arfook,* etc., or the variants *9arfuu, 9arfuuha, 9arfuuk,* etc., are also used.

5. CVCV → CVCVV

If a verb form ends with a vowel, that vowel is lengthened before the suffixed pronouns are added. This rule applies to weak verbs (both perfect and imperfect) and verbs with the subject markers *-tu, -ti,* and *-na.* Examples:

baġa	'he wanted'	→ baġaa	'he wanted him'
		→ baġaač	'he wanted you (f.s.)'
baġeetu	'you (m.p. or f.p.) wanted'	→ baġeetuu	'you (m.p. or f.p.) wanted him'
baġeeti	'you (f.s.) wanted'	→ baġeetii	'you (f.s.) wanted him'
		→ baġeetiina	'you (f.s.) wanted us'
		→ baġeetiihum	'you (f.s.) wanted them (m.)'
baġeena	'we wanted'	→ baġeenaa	'we wanted him'
		→ baġeenaahum	'we wanted them (m.)'
		→ baġeenaač	'we wanted you (f.s.)'
		→ baġeenaak	'we wanted you (m.s.)'
		→ baġeenaaku(m)	'we wanted you (m.p.)'
		→ baġeenaakin	'we wanted you (f.p.)'
yabi	'he wants'	→ yabii	'he wants him, it (m.)'
		→ yabiihum	'he wants them (m.)'
		→ yabiič	'he wants you (f.s.)'
	etc.	etc.	etc.
la9wazna	'we bothered'	→ la9waznaa	'we bothered him'
		→ la9waznaahum	'we bothered them (m.)'
		→ la9waznaaha	'we bothered her'
		→ la9waznaak	'we bothered you (m.s.)'
	etc.	etc.	etc.

6. -CC → -C

If a verb form ends with a double consonant, the double consonant is reduced to one single consonant before the suffixed pronouns *-hum, -ha, -hin, -ku(m), -kin* (or *-ku*), *-ni,* and *-na* (see 4.3.2). Examples:

gaṭṭ 'he threw away'	→	gaṭhum	'he threw them (m.) away'
		gaṭha	'he threw her away'
		gaṭhin	'he threw them (f.) away'
		gaṭku(m)	'he threw you (m.p.) away'
		gaṭkin	'he threw you (f.p.) away'
		gaṭni	'he threw me away'
		gaṭna	'he threw us away'

Some speakers interpolate the epenthetic vowel *-a-* between the verb and the suffixed pronoun. Thus the forms *gaṭṭahum, gaṭṭaha, gaṭṭahin,* etc., are also possible.

B. *Suffixed to Nouns*

As mentioned above, suffixed pronouns indicate possession when added to nouns. However, in GA possession is more commonly expressed by the use of *maal* 'belonging to.' Thus, *haaði l-gahwa maali* 'this coffee is mine' is more commonly used than *haaði gahwati* 'this is my coffee.' The following are the personal pronouns and the corresponding noun suffixed forms:

Personal Pronoun		*Noun Suffixed Pronoun*
huwa	'he'	-a
hum	'they (m.)'	-hum/-ahum
hiya	'she'	-ha/-aha
hin	'they (f.)'	-hin/-ahin
'inta	'you (m.s.)'	-k/-ak
'intum	'you (m.p.)'	-kum/-akum
'inti	'you (f.s.)'	-č/-ič
'intin	'you (f.p.)'	-kin/-akin
'aana	'I'	-i/-y(a)
niHin	'we'	-na/-ana

NOTE THE FOLLOWING:

1. If a noun ends with -VCC, it takes the suffixes *-ahum, -aha, -ahin, -ak, -ič, -akin,* and *-ana,* if -CC is a consonant cluster.

Examples:

Halj	'throat; mouth'	→	Halji	'my throat'
			Haljahum	'their (m.) throat'
			Haljak	'your (m.s.) throat'
			Haljič	'your (f.s.) throat'
	etc.		etc.	etc.

It should be noted that some speakers use the forms *Halijhum, Halijha, Halijhin,* etc., interpolating the anaptyctic vowel *-i-* between the consonant cluster *-lj-* to avoid the occurrence of a three-consonant cluster. If -CC is a double consonant, then it is reduced to one consonant and takes the suffixes *-hum, -ha, -kin, -na* (see 4.3.2). Note that this rule is the same as that for verbs (as was shown above) and particles, as shown below. Examples:

yiHH	'watermelons'	→	yiHhum	'their (m.) watermelons'
			yiHha	'her watermelons'
			yiHhin	'their (f.) watermelons'
			yiHna	'our watermelons'
		but:	yiHHi	'my watermelons'
			yiHHa	'his watermelons'
			yiHHič	'your (f.s.) watermelons'

2. As with verbs, if a noun ends with *-f* or *-t* preceded by a vowel, the *h* in *-hum, -ha,* and *-hin* assimilates into *f* or *t:*

ṣeef	'summer'	→	ṣeeffum	'their (m.) summer'
			ṣeeffa	'her summer'
			ṣeeffin	'their (f.) summer'
beet	'house'	→	beettum	'their (m.) house'
			beetta	'her house'
			beettin	'their (f.) house'

The following examples involve anaptyxis and then assimilation:

bišt	'robe, dress'	→	*bišttum	→	bišittum
			*bišttin	→	bišittin
wilf	'valve'	→	*wilffum	→	wiliffum
			*wilffa	→	wiliffa
			*wilffin	→	wiliffin

3. If a noun ends with the sequence -CCVC, it takes the suffixes *-a, -hum, -ha, -hin, -k* (or *-ak*), *-ič, -kin, -i,* and *-na.*

margad	'sleeping place'	→	margada	'his sleeping place'
			margadhum	'their (m.) sleeping place'
			margadhin	'their (f.) sleeping place'
			margadkum	'your (m.p.) sleeping place'
		etc.	etc.	etc.

4. If a masculine noun ends with a vowel, the vowel is usually lengthened before the suffixes and the third person masculine suffix *-a* is ϕ and *-y(a)* is used instead of *-i.* Examples:

mustašfi[118]	'hospital'	→	mustašfii	'his hospital'
		→	mustašfiihum	'their (m.) hospital'
		→	mustašfiiha	'her hospital'
		→	mustašfiihin	'their (f.) hospital'
		etc.	etc.	etc.

The form for 'my hospital' is *mustašfaay(a).*

Similarly with *qada* 'lunch' we have the following forms: *qadaa* 'his lunch,' *qadaahum* 'their (m.) lunch,' *qadaahin* 'their (f.) lunch,' etc., and *qadaay(a)* 'my lunch.' *'uxu* 'brother' and *gadu* 'hubble-bubble' become *'uxuu-* and *gaduu-*, respectively. Examples:

'uxuu	'his brother'	gaduu	'his hubble-bubble'
'uxuuha	'her brother'	gaduuha	'her hubble-bubble'
'uxuukum	'your (m.p.) brother'	gaduukum	'your (m.p.) hubble-bubble'
'uxuuy(a)	'my brother'	gaduuy(a)	'my hubble-bubble'

5. A noun that ends with -VC drops its V when a vowel-initial suffix is added unless V is stressed in the noun stem or in the resultant form (see 4.3.1 and 9.2.2A). Examples:

xašim	'nose'	+ -a	→ xašma	'his nose'
		+ -i	→ xašmi	'my nose'
		+ -ič	→ xašmič	'your (f.s.) nose'

118. *mustašfa* is more commonly used.

		+ -ha	→ xašimha	'her nose' (or *xašmaha*)
		+ -kum	→ xašimkum	'your (m.p.) nose' (or *xašmakum*)
simač	'fish'	+ -a	→ simča	'his fish'[119]
		+ -i	→ simči	'my fish'
		+ -č	→ simačč	'your (f.s.) fish'
	but:	+ -ha	→ simačha	'her fish'
		+ -kum	→ simačkum	'your (m.p.) fish'
margad	'sleeping place'	+ -a	→ margada	'his sleeping place'
		+ -i	→ margadi	'my sleeping place'
		+ -ič	→ margadič	'your (f.s.) sleeping place'
	but:	+ -ha	→ margadha	'her sleeping place'
		+ -kum	→ margadkum	'your (m.p.) sleeping place'
'uxut	'sister'	+ -a	→ 'uxta	'his sister'
		+ -i	→ 'uxti	'my sister'
		+ -ič	→ 'uxtič	'your (f.s.) sister'
		+ -ha	→ 'uxutta	'her sister'
		+ -kum	→ 'uxutkum	'your (m.p.) sister'

6. Feminine singular nouns ending in *-a* add *-t-* before the suffixed pronoun. Before a suffix beginning with a vowel, we have two alternate forms:

šanṭa	'bag'	+ -a	→ šanṭaṭa	'his bag' (or *šaniṭṭa*)
		+ -i	→ šanṭati	'my bag' (or *šaniṭṭi*)
		+ -ič	→ šanṭatič	'your (f.s.) bag' (or *šaniṭṭič*)
		+ -ha	→ šanṭatta	'her bag'
		+ -kum	→ sanṭatkum	'your (m.p.) bag'
Hurma	'wife; woman'	+ -a	→ Hurmata	'his wife' (or *Hurumta*)

119. (cf. *smiča* 'a fish')

		+ -i	→ Hurmati	'my wife' (or *Hurumti*)
Hijra	'room'	+ -a	→ Hijrata	'his room' (or *Hijirta*)
		+ -i	→ Hijrati	'my room' (or *Hijirti*)
		+ -ič	→ Hijratič	'your (f.s.) room' (or *Hijirtič*)
		+ -ha	→ Hijratta	'her room'
		+ -kum	→ Hijratkum	'your (m.p.) room'

If the noun is of the *f9ala* pattern, the final *-a* drops before *-a, -i,* and *-ič* and only *-t-* is added:

ṣxaḷa	'young goat'	+ -a	→ ṣxaḷta	'his young goat'
		+ -i	→ ṣxaḷti	'my young goat'
		+ -ič	→ ṣxaḷtič	'your (f.s.) young goat'
	but:	+ -ha	→ ṣxaḷatta	'her young goat'

Other examples of this pattern are: *bgara* 'cow,' *šyara* 'tree,' *nxaḷa* 'palm tree,' *n9aya* 'ewe,' *ṣxara* 'rock,' *ghawa* 'coffee,' *š9ara* 'a hair,' *bġaḷa* 'female mule,' *fHama* 'piece of coal, charcoal,' etc.

C. Suffixed to Active Participles[120]

Pronouns suffixed to active participles are in some respects like those suffixed to verbs and in others like those suffixed to nouns. Below are examples of active participles with suffixed pronouns. Note that there are two forms of active participle + suffixed pronoun: one without nunation (see 9.3) and the other with nunation. The latter form has the nunation ending *-inn* before the suffixed pronoun. Both forms are used.

The verb *9araf* 'to know': active participle *9aarif.*

Without Nunation	*With Nunation*	
9aarfa	9aarfinna	'having known him'
9aariffum	9aarfinhum	'having known them (m.)'
9aariffa	9aarfinha	'having known her'

120. Note that such active participles must be used as verbs, e.g., *kaatba* here means 'having (m.s.) written it (m.s.)' and not 'its (m.s.) writer (m.s.).'

Without Nunation	*With Nunation*	
9aariffin	9aarfinhin	'having known them (f.)'
9aarfak	9aarfinnak	'having known you (m.s.)'
9aarifku(m)	9aarfinku(m)	'having known you (m.p.)'
9aarfič	9aarfinnič	'having known you (f.s.)'
9aarifkin	9aarfinkin	'having known you (f.p.)'
9aarifni	9aarfinni	'having known me'
9aarifna	9aarfinna	'having known us'

(Note the ambiguity in *9aarfinna* 'having known *us*, or *him*.')

The subjects indicated by the active participle in the examples cited above are *he*, *you* (m.s.), and *I*. The following forms have *she*, *you* (f.s.), and *I* as subjects:

9aarifta	9aariftinna	'having known him'
9aarfattum	9aariftinhum	'having known them (m.)'
9aarfatta	9aariftinha	'having known her'
9aarfattin	9aariftinhin	'having known them (f.)'
9aariftak	9aariftinnak	'having known you (m.s.)'
9aarfatku(m)	9aariftinku(m)	'having known you (m.p.)'
9aariftič	9aariftinnič	'having known you (f.s.)'
9aarfatkin	9aariftinkin	'having known you (f.p.)'
9aarfatni	9aariftinni	'having known me'
9aarfatna	9aariftinna	'having known us'

(Note the ambiguity in *9aariftinna* 'having known *us*, or *him*.')

Note the following processes for the formation of some of the forms above:

9aarifta:	9aárif	(by derivation of active participle)
	*9aarif*at*-	(feminine suffix)
	*9aarifat*a*	(third person m.s. suffix)
	*9aarifta	(vowel elision)
	9aaríifta	(stress)
9aariftinna:	9aárif	(by derivation of active participle)
	*9aarifatin	(feminine-nunation)

	*9aarifatinna	(third person m.s. suffix)
	*9aarifatínna	(stress)
	9aariftínna	(vowel elision)
9aarfattin:	9aárif	(by derivation of active participle)
	*9aarif*at*	(feminine suffix)
	*9aarfat	(vowel elision)
	*9aarfathin	(suffixed *-hin*)
	9aarfáttin	(assimilation)

Other examples of active participle + suffixed pronoun:

Without Nunation	*With Nunation*	
daašša	daaššinna	'having entered it'
waakilta	waakiltinna	'having eaten it'
mfanniš hum	mfanšinhum	'having terminated their (m.) services'
mfanšattum	mfanništinhum	'having terminated their (m.) services'
mxaaṣimhin	mxaaṣminhin	'having quarreled with them (f.)'
mxaaṣmattin	mxaaṣimtinhin	'having quarreled with them (f.)'
mHaačiina	mHaačinna	'having spoken with us'
mHaačyatna	mHaačiitinna	'having spoken with us'
mla9wizni	mla9iwzinni	'having bothered me'
mla9iwzatni	mla9wiztinni	'having bothered me'

The last two forms are derived according to the following:

mla9iwzatni:	*mla9wiz-at-ni	
	*mla9wizátni	
	*mla9wzátni	
	mla9iwzátni	
mla9wiztinni:	mlá9wiz	(base form)
	*mla9wzat	(vowel elision)
	*mla9iwzat	(anaptyxis)
	*mla9wztinni	(vowel elision)
	mla9wiztínni	(anaptyxis)

For the suffixation of pronouns to particles, see 12. PARTICLES below.

11.3 Demonstrative Pronouns

The main forms of the demonstrative pronouns that indicate near objects or persons are:

masculine singular:	*haaða*	'this (one), that (one)'
feminine singular:	*haaði*	'this (one), that (one)'
masculine plural:	*(ha)ðeel,* *(ha)ðeela*	'these, those'
feminine plural:	*(ha)ðeel,* *(ha)ðeela*	'these, those'

The main forms of the demonstrative pronouns that indicate distant objects or persons are:

masculine singular:	*(ha)ðaak*	'that (one)'
feminine singular:	*(ha)ðiič*	'that (one)'
masculine plural:	*(ha)ðoolaak*	'those'
feminine plural:	*(ha)ðeelaak,* *(ha)ðilaak*	'those'

It should be pointed out that *haa-/ha-* is a prefixed particle which has the meaning of 'Ha! Look! There!' It is used obligatorily in *haaða* and *haaði.* In the other forms there is a tendency in GA to use it with objects or persons that are pointed out or physically present; with other objects its use is optional. The following examples show the usage of demonstrative pronouns:

haaða šeebtin zeena.	'This is a good old man.'
haaða min faḍ̣l aḷḷa.	'This (thing) is from God's kindness, graciousness.'
haðiič saa9a mbaarka.	'That is a blessed time.'
haaði Hazza killiš zeena.	'This is a very good time.'
haðeel, lo jaw, čaan šifittum.	'These (people), if they had come, I would have seen them.'
ðoolaak, š-yabuun?	'Those (people), what do they want?'
š-yabin ðeelaak?	'What do those (women) want?'
ðiič 'ayyaam činna fiiha mistaansiin.	'Those were days during which we were happy.'
'itris haaða!	'Fill (m s.) this!'

ðoolaak illi 'abiihum.	'Those are the things (m.) I want.'
haaða rizg l-yoom w-rizg baačir 9ala ḷḷa (proverb).	(lit. 'This is today's bread, tomorrow's is from God.')

12. PARTICLES

12.1 Interrogatives

The main interrogative particles in GA are the following:

man, min	'who'	ween	'where'
šu(u), š-, (w)eeš	'what'	leeš	'why'
'ay(ya)	'which (one), what'	čeef, keef	'how'
čam, kam	'how much; how many'	mata, mita	'when'

Each of the interrogative particles except for *'ay(ya)* 'which (one)' can be used independently as a one-word question, and in a pre- or post-verbal position:

man?	'Who?'	ween?	'Where?'
čam?	'How much?' 'How many?'	mata?	'When?'

man tabiin? tabiin man?	'Who do you (f.s.) want?'
šu tiras? tiras šu?	'What did he fill?
čam yHaṣṣil? yHaṣṣil čam?	'How much does he make, get?'

'ay(ya) must be used in a pre-nominal position:

'ay(ya) Hazza?	'What time?'
'ay(ya) ktaab tabi?	'Which book do you (m.s.) want?'

It can be preceded by a preposition:

fi 'ay(ya) daayra tištaġluun?	'Which department do you (m.p.) work in?'

Note that **'ay(ya) daayra tištaġluun fi?* is ungrammatical.

min 'ay(ya) balad inti?	'Which country are you (f.s.) from?'

man 'who,' *šu* 'what,' *čam* 'how many; how much,' *ween* 'where' and *čeef* 'how' can be used as parts of equational sentences (see 13.1):

man 'ubuuk?	'Who is your (m.s.) father?'
šu 'asma?	'What is his, its (m.) name?'
čam ṭ-ṭamaaṭ?	'How much are the tomatoes?'
čam diriiša fiiha?	'How many windows are there in it?'
ween l-kuuli?	'Where is the coolie?'
čeef l-hawa?	'How is the weather?'

man 'who,' *šu* 'what,' *ween* 'where,' and *mata* 'when' can be preceded by a preposition:

jiddaam man ga9ad?	'Who did he sit in front of?'
wiyya šu baṭṭal l-guuṭi?	'What did he open the can with?'
min ween d-daxtar?	'Where is the doctor from?'
'ila mata yištaġil?	'Up to what (time), until when, is he working?'

Notice the use of the preposition *min* 'from' with *mata* 'when.'

min mata 'inta hini?	'Since when have you been here?'

man 'who' and *šu* 'what' can be used after the prepositions *Hagg* or *maal* to mean 'whose; for whom, to whom' and 'for what,' respectively:

Hagg man haaði s-sayyaara?	'Whose is this car?'
maal man haaða l-baanuuš?	'Whose is this canoe?'
haaða s-sikruu maal šuu?	'What is this screw (used) for?'

man preceded by a noun expresses the meaning of 'Whose . . . ?'

beet man haaða?	'Whose house is this?'
9yaal man haaðeel?	'Whose children are these?'

čam 'how many' is optionally preceded by the preposition *9ala* 'on' in the speech of some Qataris, in which case it means only 'how much is, are . . . ?', i.e., in inquiring about the price of s.th.

9ala čam l-yiHH?	'How much are the watermelons?'
9ala čam l-guuṭi?	'How much is the can?'

čam can be followed by the preposition *min* 'from' to mean 'how many':

čam min sana čint hnaak?	'How many years were you (m.s.) there?'

Note the following idiomatic uses of *čam:*

čam ṣaarlič hini?	'How long have you (f.s.) been here?'
čam min hini la-dbayy?	'How far is it from here to Dubai?'

The English phrase *how many people?* is expressed by *čam* followed by *waaHid* 'one':

čam waaHid čaan hnaak?	'How many people were there?'

š- 'what' obligatorily precedes a verb, a noun, or a particle:

š-tabi taakil?	'What do you (m.s.) want to eat?'
š-asimha?	'What is her name?'
š-fiik?	'What's wrong with you (m.s.)?'

š- may precede the noun *da9wa* 'matter; law suit' to mean 'What's the matter? . . .' or 'Why . . . ?':

š-da9wa ġaali waayid?	'What's the matter! Why is it so expensive?' 'Why is it very expensive?'
š-da9wa ykallif hal-kiθir?	'Why does it cost this much?'

In addition to *šu(u), š-,* and *(w)eeš* 'what,' the forms *šinu(w), šinhu(w),* and *šinhi(y)* also occur, especially in Bahraini. Of these *šinhu(w)* is either masculine or feminine and *šinhi(y)* is only feminine.

Of all the interrogatives, only *ween* 'where' may take suffixed pronouns:

weenhum?	'Where are they (m.)?'
weena?	'Where is he?'

Note the compound form *mneen* of *min ween* 'from where':

mneen inti?	'Where are you (f.s.) from?'

šloon 'how' is characteristic of Bahraini and Kuwaiti speech. It is rarely used in the U.A.E., usually with a suffixed pronoun to mean 'to inquire about someone's health':

šloonič?	'How are you (f.s.)?'
šloonak?	'How are you (m.s.)?'

It is *čeef,* rather than *šloon,* that is used to express other meanings, e.g., *čeef riHti?* 'How did you (f.s.) go?', *čeef yiit hini?* 'How did you (m.s.) come here?', etc. In such constructions *šloon* has the meaning of 'why?' or 'how come?'

12.2 Prepositions

All prepositions in GA can take suffixed pronouns. In most cases the suffixation of pronouns to prepositions is governed by the same rules as for nouns. Thus *minni* 'from me,' *minha* 'from her,' *wiyyaay* 'with me,' *miθli* 'like me,' *miθilhum* 'like them (m.),' *yammič* 'by you (f.s.),' *yamna* 'by us,' etc. In a few cases the base forms differ on suffixation, which involves *fi* 'in,' *9ala* 'on,' and prepositions of the pattern CVC, except for *ma9* 'with.' The suffixed pronoun that corresponds to 'I' is *-yy* after *fi* and *9ala.* The rest follow the same rules: *fiyy,* 'in me,' *fiik* 'in you (m.s.),' *fiič* 'in you (f.s.),' *fiihum* 'in them,' *fiikum* 'in you (m.p.),' etc. *9ala* 'on' changes into *9ale-: 9alee* 'on him,' *9aleeha* 'on her,' *9aleeč* 'on you (f.s.),' *9aleekum* 'on you (m.p.),' etc. Examples of prepositions of the pattern CVC are: *min* 'from,' and *9an* 'about.' Before suffixes with initial -V, *9an* changes into *9ann-.* Thus *9anna* 'about him' *9annak* or *9ank* 'about you (m.s.),' *9annič* or *9anč* 'about you (f.s.),' etc. Similarly *min* changes into *minn-.* Examples: *minna* 'from him,' *minna* or *minnana* 'from us,' *minkum* 'from you (m.p.),' *minč* or *minnič* 'from you (f.s.),' etc. *ma9* 'with' may also have the stem *ma9a-.* Thus: *ma9i* or *ma9aay* 'with me,' *ma9ič* or *ma9aač* 'with you (f.s.),' *ma9kin* or *ma9aakin* 'with you (f.p.).'

Prepositions in GA are divided into the following groups:

A. These are prepositions proper, i.e., they are used only as prepositions and are followed by a noun, a suffixed pronoun, a demonstrative pronoun, or a particle. The following are the most common:

fi: 'in; on; within, during; by, among'

čaðib fi čaðib	'lies after lies, lies among (other) lies'

The proverbial phrase *xriṭi fi xriṭi* has a similar meaning.

fi ðaak l-yoom	'(on) that day'
fi s-subuu9 l-maaḍ̣i	'during last week'
xamsa fi sitta	'five by six'

(cf. *fii* 'there is; there are,' *čaan fii* 'there was; there were,' and the negative *ma fii* 'there isn't, there aren't,' *ma čaan fii* 'there wasn't; there weren't.') See 13.3, Sentences 15-23.

min: 'from; (from) among; belonging to; of; ago'

'aana min dbayy.	'I am from Dubai.'
min faḍ̣l aḷḷa	'from God's favor, benevolence'

min r-rmeeθaat	'belonging to, from, the Rumaithi tribe'
minhum waaHid baṭṭaal.	'One of them is bad.'
min waaHid la-waaHid	'from one to another'
min yoom la-yoom	'from day to day'
š-gilt min saa9a?	'What did you (m.s.) say an hour ago?'

9ala: 'on, over, according to (one's taste, liking); against'

s-salaamu 9aleeč!	'Peace be upon you (f.s.)!'
9ala xašmi	'gladly, with pleasure'
mid riilak 9ala gadd lHaafak.	'As you make your bed, you must lie on it.' (lit., "Stretch your (m.s.) leg according to your quilt.")
9ala kulli Haal[121]	'in any case; however'
ma 9aleek!	'Never mind! Don't worry!'
wiyyaahum wiyyaahum; 9aleehum 9aleehum	'with them and against them, for their own good'

9an: 'about; away from'

xabbarni 9ank.	'He told me about you (m.s.).'
ġaab 9an hala.	'He went away from his people.'

b-: 'with; by means of; for (at the price of)'

štiraa b-fluusa.	'He bought it (m.s.) with his money.'
gṭa9a b-s-siččiin.	'He cut it (m.s.) with the knife.'
saafar b-ṭ-ṭayyaara.	'He traveled by plane.'
čint b-ruuHi.	'I was alone; I was by myself.'
d-darzan b-diinaar	'one dinar per dozen'

been: 'between; among'

beeni w-beenak	'between me and you (m.s.)'
xaðeet waHda min beenhum.	'I took one from among them.'
l-9awar been l-9imyaan baaša.	'The one-eyed in the country of the blind is king.'

121. This is a literary borrowing. *-i* in *kulli* is a case ending.

9ugub: after; in'

9ugub baačir	'after tomorrow'
9ugb ð̣-ð̣uhur	'(in the) afternoon'
9ugub saa9a	'in an hour'

wiyya: 'with, in the company of'

riHt wiyya 9abdaḷḷa.	'I went with Abdalla.'
sirt wiyyaahum.	'I went (lit., "walked") with them.'

Note the use of *wiyya ba9ð̣* 'together.'

ma9: Synonymous with *wiyya,* though less commonly used.

yamm: 'by, near; beside'

yilas yamm š-šeex.	'He sat by the Shaikh.'
l-Hafiiz yamm l-mustašfi.	'The office is near the hospital.'
čaan yammi.	'He was beside me.'

miθil: 'like, similar to; the same as'

miθil'ubuu.	'(He is) like his father.'
miθl l-yoom	'the same as today'

šarwa: Synonymous with *miθil,* but it is used with human beings only, e.g., *šarwaač* 'like you (f.s.),' *šarwaahum* 'like them (m.p.),' etc.

9ind: 'at; close by; in the possession of'

9ind li-bṭuun ð̣ð̣ii9 li-9guul.	(lit., "At the (time of) bellies minds get lost.")
tHaṣla 9ind l-gaṣṣaab.	'You (m.s.) will find it at the butcher's.'
9indič 9yaaḷ?	'Do you (f.s.) have any children?'

Hawaali: 'approximately, about'

yilast Hawaali sana.	'I stayed about a year.'
našš Hawaali s-saa9a xams.	'He got up at about five o'clock.'

Hool is sometimes used to express the same meaning.

B. These are prepositions that can also be used as adverbs and as nouns. The following are the most common:

foog: 'over, above; up'

foog n-naxaḷ	'over, above, palm trees'
xaḷḷna nruuH foog!	'Let's go up, upstairs!'
foog 'afð̣al min taHat.	'Up, upstairs, is better than down, downstairs.'

taHat: opposite of *foog*

l-karraani taHt l-mudiir.	'The clerk is under the director.'
taHat raaṣa xabar.	'He is hiding, withholding s.th.' (lit. "There is news under his head.")

wara: 'behind; after'

wara d-diriiša	'behind the window'
reewas ya9ni raaH la-wara.	'He reversed means he went backwards.'
jiddaam 'aHsan min wara.	'The front (e.g., position) is better than the back.'

The literary *xalf* is a variant of *wara.*

jiddaam: opposite of *wara*

jiddaam l-bank	'in front of the bank'
siir jiddaam!	'Go in front!'

daaxiḷ: 'inside, within'

daaxḷ l-Hijra	'inside the room'
dašš daaxiḷ.	'He went inside.'
min d-daaxiḷ	'from the inside'

xaarij: opposite of *daaxiḷ*

xaarij beetna	'outside our house'
xaarj l-jiziira	'outside the (Arabian) Peninsula'
fi l-xaarij	'abroad'

gabil: 'before, prior to; ago'

gabl ṣ-ṣalaa	'before prayer'
gabl s-saa9a sitt	'before six o'clock'

gabil saa9a	'an hour ago'
yiit hini min gabil.	'I have been here before.'
gabil 'aHsan min ba9deen.	'Before is better than later.'

Note that nisba adjectives (see 11.5.1.3) can be derived from this group of prepositions, e.g., *foogi* or *foogaani* 'upper,' *taHti* or *taHtaani* 'lower,' etc., except for *gabil.* The nisba adjective from *wara* is *warraani.*

C. This group of prepositions can be used as nouns only. Examples:

ṣoob: 'toward, in the direction of; place, direction'

ṣoob l-baHar	'toward the sea'
ta9aal ṣoobna!	'Come to our place!'
ðaak ṣ-ṣoob	'(in) that direction'

qeer: 'other than, except for; (+ article) the others, other people'

9aṭni qeer haðeel!	'Give (m.s.) me some other ones!'
killahum jaw qeer 'ibraahiim.	'They all came except for Ibrahim.'
yHibb maal l-qeer.	'He likes what belongs to others.'

Hagg: 'belonging to, for; to, for'

l-batri Hagg s-sayyaara	'the battery of the car' 'The battery belongs to the car.'
s-sayyaara Haggi (or *Haggati*)	'The car belongs to me.' 'my car'
xaðuu Hagg d-daxtar.	'They took him to the doctor.'
gilt Hagg 'ummič.	'I said to your (f.s.) mother.' 'I told your (f.s.) mother.'
ya rabb thadii Hagg nafsa w-Hagg 9yaaḷa!	'(I hope that) you, God, will lead him to the true path for (the sake of) himself and his children.'

maal: *maal* is similar in meaning and usage to *Hagg. maal,* however, cannot be used to express the meaning of to or for, as in the last three examples above. Both are often used instead of a noun construct; *maal* has a tendency to be used when the first noun indicates an appliance or is a borrowing. Examples:

*xaθuu maal d-daxtar.	'They took him to the doctor.'
meez maal ṭa9aam	'dining room table'
kanaba maal maylis	'living room sofa'
waayir maal talavizyoon	'television wire'
sikruu maal makiina	'engine screw'

When both are used as nouns, *Hagg* expresses the meaning of 'rightful possession' or 'one's due'; *maal* has the meaning of 'wealth; money; possessions.' Examples:

štaġal w-xaθ Hagga.	'He worked and took his due, what he deserved.'
xaθ maala w-saafar.	'He took his money, wealth, and traveled.'

Only *Hagg* is used by some speakers in the phrase *š-Hagga?* 'Why? What for?' or 'How much is it? What is its price?' *Hagg* and *maal* may agree with the noun they follow, especially in the speech of Kuwaitis and Bahrainis:

li-ktaab maali, Haggi.	'my book' 'The book is mine.'
s-saa9a maalti, Haggati	'my watch (clock)' 'The watch (clock) is mine.'

Many of these prepositions can be compounded with *min* or *qeer,* i.e., compound prepositions can be formed with *min* or *qeer* as the first element. Examples:

min gabiḷ	'before; ago'
min ṣoob	'from the direction of'
min 9ind	'from the place, house, of'
min taHat	'from below, under'
qeer taHat	'other than below; except for below'
qeer jiddaam	'other than in front; except for in front'

Other examples:

la-foog	'upwards'
la-wara	'backwards'
gabiḷ foog	'before above'
gabiḷ taHat	'before below'
miθil gabiḷ	'like before'
miθil foog	'like upstairs'

12.3 Conjunctions

12.3.1 Coordinating Conjunctions

The main coordinating conjunctions are the following: *w-*: 'and.' *w-* corresponds to English 'and.' It has four basic forms, depending upon its environment and the rate of speech. Either *w-* or *'u-* is used at the beginning of a sentence or a phrase: *w-jaasim?* 'And Jasim?' *w- 'inta mneen?* 'And where are you (m.s.) from?' *w-* is usually used in a pre-vowel initial position, e.g., *w-ismi* 'and my name' and medially between two vowels, e.g., *karaama w-inta* 'Karama and you (m.s.).' Otherwise *u-* is used *dbayy u-li-kweet* 'Dubai and Kuwait.' Note the use of *wa* in literary borrowings: *'ahlan wa sahlan!* 'Welcome!' (In this transcription, however, this conjunction is always shown as *w-* and prefixed to the following item.) Examples:

l-9aruus(a) w-l-mi9ris	'the bride and the bridegroom'
'asma w- 'asim 'ubuu	'his name and his father's name'
raayiH yitfaṣṣax w-yilbas d-dišdaaša.	'He is going to take off his clothes and put on the dishdash.'

walla: 'or.' *walla,* like *w-*, may join words, phrases, and rarely sentences. Examples:

'inta walla saalim?	'(Is it) you or Salim?'
gabḷ ꝺ̣-ꝺ̣uhur walla 9ugb ꝺ̣-ꝺ̣uhur	'before noon or after noon'
ya walla raaH hnaak?	'Did he come or did he go there?'
ysammuuna bu-xaliifa walla š-šeex zaayid.	'They call him Abu Khalifa or Shaikh Zayid.'

In the last example *walla* is explanatory.

'aw: 'or.' *'aw* is synonymous with *walla* and is typically used to join sentences. Example:

gaaḷ 'aw ma-gaaḷ	'(whether) he said or not'

fa-: 'and.' *fa-* is usually replaced by *w-*, but it usually implies a quick and logical or natural reaction or consequence. It approaches the meaning of 'and (my) reaction, or the reaction called for by the situation . . .' *naadaani š-šeex fa-gumt.* 'The Shaikh called me, and I got up.'

lo . . . lo: 'either . . . or'

lo hini lo hnaak	'either here or there'
lo tag9id lo tsiir.	'Either you (m.s.) stay or leave.'

la . . . wala: 'neither . . . nor, (not) either . . . or'

la la wala 9alee.	(Meaning: 'Nobody owes him anything and he does not owe anybody anything.')
la čingaal̤ wala siččiin	'neither a fork nor a knife'
la yinṭibix wala yinšiwi.	(lit., "It cannot either be cooked or roasted.")

la . . . wala sometimes has the sense of a negative command (expressed by *la* + verb) followed by a consequence or result (expressed by *wala* + verb), especially in proverbial phrases:

la tbuug wala txaaf.	(lit., "Do not steal and do not be afraid.") (Meaning: 'If you do not steal, you should not be afraid.')
la tsawwi xeer wala yjiik šarr.	(lit., "Do not do any good deeds to others and no harm, evil, comes to you.")

laakin: 'but'

čint hnaak laakin ma čifta.	'I was there but I did not see him.'
laakinna mṣaxxan	'but he is running a temperature'

12.3.2 Subordinating Conjunctions

A. Temporal

leen: 'until, till; as soon as; when'

rammasta leen gaal̤ zeen.	'I talked with him until he said, "Fine, O.K." '
leen wiṣalt riHt d-daxtar.	'As soon as I arrived, I went to the doctor.'
leen tooṣal yaaxəuunak w-yrawwuunak l-balad.	'When you arrive there, they will take you and show you the city.'

lamma: variant of *leen,* but less commonly used.

'ileen: 'till, until.' *'ileen* is a corruption of the literary *'ila 'an* with the same meaning. It shares with *leen* the meaning of 'till, until' only.

yaḷḷa: 'until, till'

ntaḏ̣arta yaḷḷa ya.	'I waited for him until he came.'

Certain prepositions and nouns are prefixed to the relative *ma* to form compound temporal conjunctions. Examples:

gabilma: 'before'

gabilma gilt 'ay šayy . . .'	'Before I said anything . . .'

9ugubma: 'after'

9ugubma 9arafta gaṭṭeeta.	'After I have known him (well), I discarded him.'

ba9dma: 'after' (variant of *9ugubma*)

yoomma: 'the day when; when'

ngahwiikum yoomma tyuuna.	'We will give you coffee (and be hospitable) when you (m.p.) come to our place.'

yoom: Synonymous with *yoomma.*

yoom ṣaxxanna l-mayy širad d-diič.	(lit., "When we heated the water, the rooster ran away.") (Meaning: 'Forewarned is forearmed.')

waġtma: 'the time when, when'

waġtma tyi 9allimna biiha.	'When you (m.s.) come, let us know about it.'

w-: 'while, when.' As a temporal conjunction, *w-* precedes an independent pronoun:

čifta w-huwa yabči.	'I saw him while he was crying.'
w-aana kint mreewis	'while I was backing up'

B. Conditional[122]

lo: 'if.' Variants of *lo* are *'iδa, 'in, (n-)čaan* or *(n-)kaan,* and *čaan.* Examples:

'iδa čift rifiijak Hilu la taakla killa.	(lit., "If you think your friend is nice, don't eat him all up at once.") (Meaning: 'Don't use up all of your credit at once.')
lo yadri 9meer čaan šagg θooba.	(lit., "If Omayr had known, he would have ripped his clothes.") (Meaning: 'Ignorance is bliss.')
čaan yabi dibs l-Hasa lHasa.	(lit., "If he wants the molasses of Al-Hasa,[123] he will lick it.") (Meaning: 'Where there is a will there is a way.')

loola: 'had or if it had not been for.' *loola* can also be used as a preposition with the meaning of 'without.'

loolaaha čaan ma yiit.	'Had it not been for her, I wouldn't have come.'
loola l-murabbi ma 9araft rabbi.	(lit., "If it had not been for the educator, I would not have known (my) God.")
loola li-bdiwi čaan maataw.	'Were it not for the Bedouin, they would have died.'

In some contexts, especially in proverbial phrases, *la* implies condition. Examples:

la-Haṣal l-maay biṭal l-9aafur.[124]	(lit., "If water is gotten, or present, cleansing is nullified.")

Also:

la Haṣal l-maal 9idd l-baagi faayda.	(lit., "If money, or wealth is gotten, count the remainder as interest.")

---

122. See 13.5 CONDITIONAL SENTENCES.

123. An Eastern Province, district, in Saudi Arabia.

124. Cleansing one's face and hands with sand, in place of water, before prayer. In Islam a sick person or a person away from water is allowed to do this in lieu of ablution with water.

C. Purpose

lajil: 'so that (. . . might), in order that (. . . might), so as to . . .'

sirt-la lajil ysaa9idni.	'I went to (see) him so that he might help me.'
'aštaġil lajl aakil.	'I work so as to eat.'

lajil can also be used as a preposition:

sawweet haaꝺa lajilha.	'I did this for her sake.'

Hatta and *Hagg* are sometimes used with the same meaning. While *Hagg* can be used as a preposition (12.1C), *Hatta* cannot in GA.

ya Hagg yšuufni. ya Hatta yšuufni.	'He came in order to see me.'

D. Others

The main conjunctions that express other meanings are:

činn-:[125] *činn-* is usually used with suffixed pronouns; it has the meaning of 'as if . . . was, were; as if . . . had.'

činna š-šeex zaayid	'as if he were Shaikh Zayid'
činha kweetiyya	'as if she were Kuwaiti'

It is usually followed by a noun or a noun phrase, as the above examples show.

li'ann: 'because'

'ariid ašrab baarid li'anni Harraan.	'I want to have a beverage because I am hot.'
s-simač ġaali l-yoom li'an ma fii simač waayid fi s-suug.	'Fish is expensive today because there isn't much fish in the market.'

linn is in free variation with *li'ann.*

laakin: 'but'

čint hnaak laakin ma čifta.	'I was there but I did not see him.'
laakinna mṣaxxan	'but he is running a temperature'

125. This is analogous to the literary *ka'anna.*

madaam: 'as long as'

madaam 'inta hni 'ašuufak baačir.	'As long as you are here, I'll see you tomorrow.'

walaw: 'although, though'

xašmak minnak walaw kaan 9away.	(lit., "Your (m.s.) nose is a part of you although it is crooked.") (Meaning: 'Do not be ashamed of your folks.')

Sometimes *lo* (or *law*) is used with the same meaning.

9ayal: 'therefore, then'

9ayal man fannaša?	'Who terminated him, then?'
huwa muub hini 9ayal.	'Therefore, he is not here.'

'inn-: This conjunction is usually used with suffixed pronouns and introduces a direct or an indirect speech clause; it has the meaning of 'that':

gaaḷ inna yabi yṭarriš xaṭṭ.	'He said that he wanted to send a letter.'
ma gilt 'inhum trikaw.	'I did not say that they had left.'

š-ma: 'whatever'

xaðat š-ma tabi.	'She took what she wanted.'

ween-ma: 'wherever'

weena-ma truuHuun wiyyaakum.	'Wherever you (m.p.) go we are with you.'

mneen-ma: 'from wherever'

š-kiθir-ma: 'however much, as much as'

'ixði š-kiθir-ma triidiin.	'Take (f.s.) as much as you want.'

'arxaṣ-ma: 'the cheapest (that)'

haaða 'arxaṣ-ma Haṣṣalt.	'This is the cheapest I could find.'

'aHsan-ma: 'the best (that)'

'aHsan-ma ykuun	'the best there is'

'awwal-ma: 'as soon as'

'awwal-ma tooṣliin	'as soon as you (f.s.) arrive'

'aaxir-ma: 'the last thing (that) . . .'

'aaxir-ma 9indi	'the last thing I have'

kil-ma: 'every time (that)'

kil-ma truuH s-suug	'every time (that) she goes to market'

miθil-ma: 'in the same manner, way, as; according to; as'

yat miθil-ma raaHat.	'She came (back) in the same way she went.' (Meaning: 'She has achieved nothing.')
miθil-ma tguul maHHad yigdar yišrab hini.	'According to what you (m.s.) say, nobody can drink here.'
miθil-ma t9arfiin, . . .	'As you (f.s.) know, . . .'

Less frequently, *zeema* is used with the same meaning.

12.4 Adverbs

Adverbs are words or phrases that modify verbs, adjectives, or other adverbs. The following are the main groups of adverbs and adverb phrases with some examples.

A. Time

'ams: 'yesterday'

wiṣil 'ams.	'He arrived yesterday.'
'ams l-xamiis.	'Yesterday was Thursday.'

l-baarHa: 'yesterday' is rarely used. In some Bedouin dialects *l-baarHa* means last night.

l-yoom: 'today'

fannaš l-yoom.	'He terminated his services today.'
l-yoom l-'aθneen.	'Today is Monday.'

baačir: 'tomorrow'

'aruuH wiyyaa baačir.	'I will go with him tomorrow.'
baačir θ-θalaaθa.	'Tomorrow is Tuesday.'

gabḷ ams: '(the day) before yesterday'

'awwal ams: in free variation with *gabḷ ams.*

9ugub baačir: 'the day after tomorrow'

halHiin: 'now,' sometimes this is reduced to *'al-Hiin* or simply *l-Hiin.*[126] *'alHiin* or *ðaHHiin* are rarely used for the same meaning.

ween tištaġliin halHiin?	'Where are you (f.s.) working now?'

halHazza: 'now, at this moment,' from *Hazza* 'time,' sometimes reduced to *'al-Hazza* or simply *l-Hazza.*

laazim aruuH halHazza.	'I have to go now.'
9indi maw9id. 'ay Hazza?	'I have an appointment. What time?'
*kam l-Hazza.	'What time is it?'

ba9deen: 'later on, later'

ba9deen fannašt min 'adma.	'Later, I left ADMA.'[127]
riHt d-daxtar ba9deen.	'I went to the doctor later on.'

taali: 'later on, afterwards,' used in free variation with *ba9deen.*

l-masa: 'at night, in the evening'

l-leela l-maẓ̌ya: 'last night'

l-'arba9a l-maaẓ̌i:[128] 'last Wednesday'

s-subuu9 l-maaẓ̌i: 'last week'

š-šahar l-maaẓ̌i: 'last month'

s-sana l-maẓ̌ya: 'last year'

min gabiḷ: 'before'

Haačeetta min gabiḷ.	'I have talked to her before.'
yiitta min gabiḷ.	'I have been to it (f.s.) before.'

---

126. *Hiin* means 'time' in literary Arabic.

127. Abu Dhabi Marine Areas, Ltd., an oil company in Abu Dhabi.

128. With all the days of the week only *l-maaẓ̌i,* regardless of gender, is used.

gabiḷ subuu9:	'a week ago'	*ba9d subuu9:*	'in a week's time'
gabiḷ šahar:	'a month ago'	*ba9d šahar:*	'in a month's time'
gabiḷ sana:	'a year ago'	*ba9d sana:*	'in a year's time'
gabiḷ saa9a:	'an hour ago'	*ba9d saa9a:*	'in an hour's time'

taww-: 'just' is always used with suffixed pronouns.

tawni yiit.[129]	'I have just come.'
tawwič kaleeti.	'You (f.s.) have just eaten.'

B. Place

hini: 'here (var. *hni,* and *'ihni*)

hini walla hnaak killa waaHid.	'Here or there is all the same.'

'ihnaak: 'there' (var. *hnaak, hunaak*)

min hini: 'from here'

min hini la-hnaak	'from here to there'

min ihnaak: 'from there'

foog 'up, over,' *taHat* 'below,' *jiddaam* 'in front,' *wara* 'behind'. . . , etc.[130]

C. Others

Among adverbs are also words or phrases that indicate manner such as quickly, slowly, straight, etc., most of which are phrases made up of particle + N; others are adverbial adjectives, and some others are adverbial nouns not included in 12.4A above. Among adverbs are also some words ending with *-an,* most of which are of literary origin or borrowings from other dialects.

b-suur9a: 'fast, quickly'

šwayy šwayy: 'slowly'

la-waHd-: 'by (one's) self'

ciði: 'like this, in this manner'

---

129. *tawwi* is grammatical, but less rarely used.

130. For these and other prepositions and prepositional phrases used as adverbs, see 12.2 Prepositions.

siida: 'straight, straight on, direct(ly)'

ṭayyib: 'well, fine'

zeen: 'well, fine'

tamaam: 'exactly, perfectly'

9adil: 'right, correctly'

siwa: 'together'

waayid: 'a lot; very' (var. *waajid*)

yitkallam waayid.	'He talks a lot.'

kaθiir: 'a lot, a great deal'

killiš: 'very,' is used only in a pre- or post-adjective or adverb position:

zeen killiš	'very good, well'
killiš zeen	'very good, well'

šwayy: 'a little'

marra: 'once, one time'

marrateen: 'twice' (var. *marteen*)

marraat: 'sometimes,' in free variation with *ba9ḏ̣ l-'aHyaan.*

saa9a 'one hour,' *saa9ateen* (var. *saa9teen*) 'two hours,' etc. *s-saa9a xams* 'at five o'clock,' *s-saa9a θinteen* 'at two o'clock,' *s-saa9a waHda* 'at one o'clock,' etc.

'awwal šayy: 'first of all'

θaani šayy: 'secondly'

daayman: 'always'

'abdan: 'never' (var. *'abadan*) used with a negative particle.

'awwalan: 'first(ly)'

'axiiran: 'lastly, at last'

12.5 Other Particles

Among particles are also words or phrases that serve other functions, such as interjections, exclamations, and polite formulas; a few belong to special grammatical categories with no English equivalents. Also included here are the negative particles.

Some of these words and phrases have already been explained in *A Basic Course in Gulf Arabic* by the same author. The reader is referred to their meanings and usages, which are usually in NOTES ON TEXT in the individual lessons.

Examples:

bass: 'enough! only'

bass! š-halHači?	'Enough! What is this talk?'
9aṭni šakar bass.	'Give (m.s.) me sugar only.'

ya: 'oh' (vocative particle)

ya mHammad!	'Mohammad!' (5VI)[131]

yareet: 'would that'

yareet agdar aHaačiiha.	'I wish I could talk to her.'

'o-: 'oh!'

'o-haaði d-dooxa ba9ad.	'Oh, this is the real problem.'

9aad: 'well now; anyhow'

waḷḷa haaði 9aad miškila.	'Well now, that's a problem.'
9aad 'aana š-darraani?	'How would I know anyway?'

haak: 'Here you are! There! Here!' *haak* has a singular referent; *haakum* has a plural referent.

haak li-fluus!	'Here is the money; take (m.s., f.s.) it!'
haakum!	'Here you (p.) are!'

9ayal:[132] 'then, therefore'

ruuH twannas 9ayal.	'Go (m.s.) have a good time, then.'
9ayal čaan ciði.	'Well, if that is so, if that is the case.'

nzeen: 'well! o.k., fine'

nzeen, š-raayak fiiha?	'Well! What do you (m.s.) think of it (f.s.), her?'
nzeen, š-asawwi biiha?	'O.K. What shall I do with it (f.s.), her?'

---

131. The numbers and Roman numerals refer to units and sections, respectively, in the *Basic Course.*

132. *9ayal,* without a previous context, is an interjection.

'illa: 'then, well; indeed'

'illa 9abdaḷḷa weena? — 'Then, where is Abdalla?'

'illa 9indahum kill šayy. — 'Indeed, they have everything.'

ha: 'well, well then,' is more emphatic than *'illa* or *nzeen,* especially in a question.

ha š-tabiin? — 'Well, what do you (f.s.) want?'

ha š-gilt? — 'Well, what do you (m.s.) think?' (lit., "Well, what did you (m.s.) say?")

labbeek: 'Here I am! At your service.! *labbeek* is from literary Arabic *labbaika* with the same meaning. It has a further use in GA, which is similar to English 'I beg your pardon! Excuse me!' in a conversation between two people.

waḷḷa: 'honestly; by golly! really!?' (Unit 12)

waḷḷaahi: This has a similar meaning to *waḷḷa,* but it is more emphatic.

bali: 'yes; right'

'ii: 'yes; right,' used in free variation with *bali.*

na9am: used in free variation with *'ii* or *bali.*

'ii na9am: 'yes, indeed,' more emphatic than *'ii.*

9adil: 'Right you are! Correct!'

la: 'no,' in an answer to a question.

la: + imperfect signals a negative command.

ma: (neg. part.) negates a verb.

muub: neg. part, negates a noun, an adjective, an adverb, or a phrase. (var. *mu(u)* and *mub*)

Hayyaak aḷḷa: 'May God preserve your (m.s.) life!' is used as a response to *marHaba* 'Hi' or *fi maan illaa* (Unit 3) 'Good-bye,' or even *čeef Haalak?* 'How are you (m.s.)?'

ya ṭawiil l-9umur: 'you, the long-lived one,' *ṭaal 9umrak* is in free variation. (Unit 34)

9iidak mbaarak: 'Happy holiday!' (Unit 36)

kil 9aam w-inta b-xeer: 'Happy New Year!' (Unit 36)

fi maan illaa: 'Good-bye! Bye!' (Unit 3)

massaak aḷḷa b-l-xeer: 'Good evening' (Unit 3)

nšaaḷḷa: 'God willing; yes (Sir)' (14 V3, Unit 19)

Haaḍ̱ir: 'Yes (Sir), certainly' (25 V2)

tfaḍ̱ḍ̱al: 'Please!' (Unit 8)

l-Hamdu lillaa: 'Praise be to God!' (Unit 12)

ma9 s-salaama: 'Bye!' and *'aḷḷa ysallimk* (Units 7 and 20)

ṣbaaH l-xeer: 'Good morning!' (Units 7 and 20)

fii: 'there is; there are' (16 V4, 29 V3)
See also 29 V3 for the perfect *kaan fii* 'there was; there were' and the negatives *ma fii* and *ma kaan fii.*

ya9ni: 'that is to say, namely' (34 V3)

š-da9wa: 'What's the matter?! What's wrong?!'

š-fiik: 'What's wrong with you (m.s.)?'

mu(ub) čiḏi: 'Isn't it so?' (34 V4)

čid: This is probably a corruption of the MSA particle *qad* 'certainly,' preceding a perfect tense verb.

PART THREE

THE SYNTAX OF GULF ARABIC

13. MAJOR SENTENCE TYPES

13.1 Nominal Sentences

A nominal sentence is one that does not have a finite verb. The subject may be a noun or a pronoun; the predicate may be a noun, an adjective, or a prepositional phrase.

1.	'ubuuy sammaač.	'My father is a fisherman, a fish dealer.'
2.	huwa gaṣṣaab min labnaan.	'He is a butcher from Lebanon.'
3.	'intum maṭaarziyya?	'Are you bodyguards?'
4.	šuġli tindeel 9ala l-9ummaaḷ.	'My job is "foreman" over the workers.'
5.	haaði ġašmara.	'This (f.) is kidding, joking.'
6.	haðeel baHaarna.	'These are (Shiite) Bahrainis.'
7.	byaat gṭari.	'Byat is Qatari.'
8.	niHin kweetiyyiin.	'We are Kuwaitis.'
9.	xašma ṭawiil.	'His nose is long.'
10.	d-draam matruus.	'The barrel is full.'
11.	haaða muub zeen.	'This is not good.'
12.	'intum zeeniin?	'Are you fine (i.e., in good health)?'

Sentences 1-8 show predicates of different kinds of nouns and 9-12 are examples of adjectival predicates.

A special kind of nominal sentence called 'equational sentence' is included in this section. An equational sentence is here defined as one in which the subject and predicate are interchangeable, or can be switched.[1] In an equational sentence the subject and the predicate are definite. Examples:

13.	šeexhum hadif. haadif šeexhum.	'Their Shaikh is Hadif.' 'Hadif is their Shaikh.'
14.	ra'iis l-'imaaraat š-šeex zaayid.	'The President of the U.A.E. is Shaikh Zayid.'
	š-šeex zaayid ra'iis l-'imaaraat.	'Shaikh Zayid is the President of the U.A.E.'
15.	'ibraahiim l-maṭaarzi Haghum.	'Ibrahim is their bodyguard.'
	l-maṭaarzi Haghum 'ibraahiim.	'Their bodyguard is Ibrahim.'

Elatives and ordinals as parts of construct phrases (see 10.2 and 10.3.2.1.2) may be found in equational sentences:

16.	haðeel 'aHsan kuuliyya 9indi.	'These are the best workmen I have.'
	'aHsan kuuliyya 9indi haðeel.	'The best workmen I have are these.'
17.	'aṭyab s-simač l-hamuur.	'The most delicious kind of fish is the hamuur.'
	l-hamuur 'aṭyab s-simač.	'The hamuur is the most delicious kind of fish.'
18.	huwa 'awwal mudiir. 'awwal mudiir huwa.	'He is the first director.' 'The first director is he.'

OTHER EXAMPLES:

19. ðaak l-yoom 'aṭwal min šahr ṣ-ṣoom.
'That day is longer than the month of fasting (i.e., *Ramadan*).'

20. 'aHṣan-ma fi l-muwaa9iin l-quuri.
'The best among the pots and pans is the kettle.'

21. 'a9taj suug fi bu ḍabi suug s-simač.
'The oldest market in Abu Dhabi is the fish market.'

22. š-šaarja θaaliθ 'imaara.
'Sharja is the third Emirate.'

23. 'aaxir bint mooza.
'The last girl is Moza.'

---

1. See Cowell, *op. cit.*, p. 405.

24. 'aHarr-ma 9indi 'abrad-ma 9indak.
 'Your hottest (i.e., most serious) matter is my coldest (i.e., least serious) matter.'

25. 9abdaḷḷa ṣadiiqi.
 'Abdalla is my friend.'

26. 9abdaḷḷa m9azbi.
 'Abdalla is the person responsible for me.'

27. 'ubuu fi l-beet.
 'His father is at home.'

28. beeta yamm s-siinama.
 'His house is by the cinema.'

29. 'aana wiyyaak.
 'I am with you.'

30. l-9irs 9ugub baačir.
 'The wedding is after tomorrow.'

31. rub9at š-ši9ri[2] b-θamaan.[3]
 '80 fils per rub'a (about 2 lbs.) of fish.'

Sentence 25 is considered here an equational sentence, though the reverse, *ṣadiiqi 9abdaḷḷa,* implies that Abdalla is my only friend, which is not normally implied by *9abdaḷḷa ṣadiiqi.* Sentence 26, on the other hand, is an equational sentence, as there is usually one person, at one time, that is responsible for someone else, i.e., a host for a guest, a car owner for a hired cab driver or chauffeur, etc. Sentence 31 is used in pricing; it literally means 'a rub'a of this kind of fish is for 800 fils.' Other examples are: *darzan l-mooz b-xamsa dirhim* 'five dirhams per dozen bananas,' *yuuniyyat l-9eeš b-miiteen dirhim* 'two-hundred dirhams per sack of rice,' *gaḷḷat s-siHH b-diinaar* 'one dinar per large basket of dates,' etc. Either the subject or the predicate of the above cited sentences can be used with modifiers:

'ubuu l-9ood sammaač.	'His big (or old) father is a fisherman, a fish dealer.'
l-qird fi 9een 'umma ġazaal.	'Beauty is in the eye of the beholder.' (lit., "A monkey in the eye of its mother is a gazelle.")
l-yaryuur Hayawaan baHri čibiir.	'The shark is a big sea animal.'

2. *š-ši9ri* is a kind of fish.

3. *θamaan* is short for *θamaanya rubbiyya* 'eight rupees' 800 fils in Bahrain, or eight dirhams in Abu Dhabi, or the equivalent of eight riyals in Qatar.

13.2 Pseudo-Verbal Sentences

A. *9ind, ma9,* and *l-*

The prepositions *9ind, ma9,* and *l-* are used with suffixed pronouns to form verb-like constructions with the general meaning of 'to have; to own.' Examples:

1.	9inda 9aayla čibiira.	'He has a big family.'
2.	9indana 9aadaat mixtilfa.	'We have different customs.'
3.	9indahum xeer waayid fi l-beet.	'They have a lot of wealth at home.'
4.	ma 9indahum yihhaal.	'They do not have (any) children.'
5.	ma 9indič ṣooġa?	'Don't you (f.s.) have (any) jewelry?'
6.	ma9ha waladeen.	'She has two children.'
7.	ma9kum šayy?	'Do you (p.) have anything?'
8.	ma ma9a fluus waayid.	'He doesn't have much money.'
9.	'ila beet qadiim.	'He has an old house.'
10.	ma lana fiiha šayy.	'We do not have anything (or any benefit) in it (f.s.).'

The noun possessed or owned is indefinite and almost always follows the prepositional pseudo-verbs as in the examples above; if the noun is definite, pseudo-verbs cease to have a verb-like quality; they form a part of an equational sentence:

11. 9inda l-9aayla. / l-9aayla 9inda.
    'The family is with him.'
12. ma9ha l-waladeen. / l-waladeen ma9ha.
    'The two boys are with her.'

A prepositional pseudo-verb is negativized by the particle *ma,* which negates verbs,[4] as in examples 4, 5, 8, and 10. Examples 11 and 12 are negativized by mu(u)(b):

13. mub 9inda l-9aayla. / l-9aayla mub 9inda.
    'The family is not with him.'
14. muu ma9ha l-waladeen. / l-waladeen muu ma9ha.
    'The two boys are not with her.'

---

4. See 18. below.

B. *fii*

The particle *fii* 'there is; there are' is also a pseudo-verb:

15. fii gahwa waayid.
'There is a lot of coffee.'

16. fii ṭamaaṭ fi li-greenhooz l-9ood.
'There are tomatoes in the big greenhouse.'

17. fii xeer waayid fi bu ḏ̣abi.
'There is a great deal of wealth in Abu Dhabi.'

18. ma fii gahwa waayid.
'There isn't much coffee.'

The perfect of *fii* is *kaan* (var. *čaan*) *fii* 'there was; there were' and the negative of the perfect *kaan fii* is *ma kaan fii. kaan* is uninflected. Examples:

19. kaan fii gahwa waayid.
'There was a lot of coffee.'

20. ma kaan fii ṭamaaṭ fi li-greenhooz l-9ood.
'There weren't any tomatoes in the big greenhouse.'

C. *hast*

In addition to *fii,* the particle *hast* (from Persian) is also used with the same meaning in Qatari:

21. hast gahwa?
'Is there (any) coffee?'

The negative is either *ma hast* 'there isn't; there aren't' or *ma miiš*,[5] usually placed before the noun:

22. ma hast gahwa.
'There is no coffee; there isn't (any) coffee.'

23. ma miiš gahwa.

The reversed order of the subject and predicate in examples 22 and 23, i.e., *gahwa ma hast* and *gahwa ma miiš* is rare.

Kuwaiti *'aku* and the negative *maaku*[6] correspond to *fii* (or *hast*) and *ma fii* (or *ma hast*) in meaning and usage. Qatari *hast* and the negative *ma hast* (or *ma miiš*) are usually *kaan fii* and *ma kaan fii; kaan hast* and *ma kaan hast* are used rarely. However, the Kuwaiti negative forms *kaan 'aku* and *kaan maaku* (or *ma kaan 'aku*) are less

5. Probably a corruption of literary *ma min šay'* 'not anything; not a single thing.'

6. *'aku* and *maaku* are also Iraqi.

commonly used in Qatar and Bahrain, and are used rarely in Abu Dhabi.

13.3 Verbal Sentences

A verbal sentence is one that contains a finite verb. There are two kinds of verbal sentences:

A. If the subject of the sentence is indefinite, it normally follows the verb. Examples:

1. čaanat 9indi mara mariiḍ̣a.
   'I had a sick wife.' (lit., "A sick wife was with me.")
2. kaan fii 'afraaH yoom waaHid.
   'There were (some) celebrations for one day.'
3. maa čaan fii ghawa.
   'There wasn't (any) coffee; there was no coffee.'
4. tiyi balaawi min taHat raaṣ l-Hariim.
   '(Some) problems are caused by women.' (lit., "(Some) problems come from under the heads of women.")
5. yaani xaṭṭ minna.
   'I had a letter from him.' (lit., "A letter came to me from him.")
6. nšaaḷḷa ma Haṣal šayy.
   'I hope nothing happened.'
7. ma baga šayy qeer guuṭi waaHid.
   'There was nothing left except one can.'
8. ṭala9 batrool fi dbayy.
   'Petroleum sprouted, came out, in Dubai.'
9. Haṣal da9ma fi s-suug.
   'An accident took place in the market.'
10. nbaag minna fluus.
    '(Some) money was stolen from him.'
11. yaahum walad sammoo miršid.
    'They had a baby boy (whom) they named Murshid.' (lit., "A baby boy came to them (whom) they named Murshid.")

Sentences 1-3 have *kaan* (var. *čaan*) 'to be' as the verb. Note that *kaan* followed by *fii* means 'there was; there were.' For stylistic purposes an indefinite subject may precede the verb, unless the verb is *kaan* (var. *čaan*) followed by *fii*, as in sentences 2 and 3. *mara mariiḏ̣a čaanat 9indi* 'I had a sick wife' is acceptable but it is very rare. In sentences 9 and 10 the verb may be inflected for gender, i.e., *Haṣalat* and *nbaagat*. If the noun precedes, however, gender agreement is compulsory: *da9ma Haṣalat* and *fluus nbaagat* only.

B. If the subject is definite, it may either precede or follow the verb, although it has a tendency to precede the verb.

Examples: *Definite Subject + Verb*

11. bu ḏ̣abi taqayyarat.
'Abu Dhabi has changed.'

12. z-zawaaj ykallif waayid.
'Marriage, getting married, costs a lot.'

13. l-mi9ris yidfa9 mablag Hagg ṣ-ṣooġa.
'The bridegroom pays a (certain) sum for the jewelry.'

14. n-naas fi 9iid l-Hiyy yilibsuun 'aHsan hduum.
'People, during the Sacrifice (lit., "Pilgrimage") Feast, wear the best clothes.'

15. 'aal-nhayyaan Hkamaw bu ḏ̣abi min zamaan.
'The Al-Nhayyan (Tribe) have ruled Abu Dhabi for a long time.'

16. 'aana ma gilit-la.
'I did not tell him.'

17. huwa ma ygaṣṣir.
'He does his best; he does not let anybody down.'

18. 'inta tabi tamši walla 9indak sayyaara?
'Do you want to walk, or do you have a car?'

Examples: *Verb + Definite Subject*

19. yiHtafluun n-naas b-l-9irs.
'The people celebrate the wedding.'

20. ba9d čam šahar ti9miik li-fluus w-titzawwaj qeeri.
'In some months money will blind you and you will marry some other one.' (lit., "other than me")

21. ṣaadni li-qruur.
'I was trapped by conceit.'

22. baššarč aḷḷa b-l-xeer.
(lit., "God brought good news of benevolence to you.")

23. sallamk aḷḷa.
'God protected you.'

24. ṣabbaaHk aḷḷa b-l-xeer!
 'Good morning!' (lit., "God bade you good morning.")

25. hadaak aḷḷa!
 'May God lead you to the true faith!'

The subject may precede the verb in sentences 19-21; sentences 22-25 are polite formulas in which the verb always precedes the subject.

13.4 Topical Sentences

A topical sentence is made up of two main parts: a *topic* which is usually a noun or a pronoun and a *comment* on the *topic;* the comment is either a nominal sentence (see 13.1) or a verbal sentence (see 13.3). The comment includes a pronoun suffixed to the noun or particle in a nominal sentence or pseudo-verbal sentence or suffixed to the verb or preposition in a verbal sentence. The referent of the suffixed pronoun is the noun or pronoun in the *topic.* In the following examples the referent and the suffixed pronoun are italicized:

1. *9ali* 'ubu*u* sammaač.
 'Ali's father is a fisherman.'

2. *niHin* ma9aaziib*na* šyuux.
 'Those responsible for us are Shaikhs.'

3. *t-tindeel* suġl*a* mub hini.
 'The forman's job is not here.'

4. *li-9yaaḷ* tarbiyat*tum* ṣa9ba.
 'Raising children is difficult.'

5. *'abu ḍ̄abi* xeer*ha* waayid.
 'The wealth of Abu Dhabi is abundant.'

6. *š-šeex* 'il*a* gaṣreen.
 'The Shaikh has two palaces.'

7. *'uhum* 9inda*hum* fluus waayid.
 'They (m.) have a lot of money.'

8. *r-rmeeθaat* 'il*hum* taariix ṭawiil.
 'The Rumaithi tribe has a long history.'

9. *giṭar* fii*ha* manaaḍ̄ir yamiila.
 'There are beautiful sights in Qatar.'

10. *l-Hariim* ma9aa*hin* li-9yaaḷ.
 'The children are with the women.'

11. *laṭiifa* raadat*ta* 'umha tzawwijha Hagg yuusif.
'Latifa's mother wanted to marry her to Yusif.'

12. *l-9ayyaal* xaðuu Hagg š-šeex.
'They (m.) took the (male) dancer to the Shaikh.'

13. *n-na99aašaat* 9aazmin*hin* l-Haakim.
'The ruler has invited the (female) dancers.'

14. *li-bdiwi* xaðu minn*a* bi9iira.
'They took the Bedouin's camel.'

15. *li-9yaaḷ* riHna wiyyaa*hum*.
'We went with the children.'

In sentences 1-5 the comment is a nominal sentence in which the pronoun is suffixed to the subject; in 6-10 the comment is a pseudo-verbal sentence with a pronoun suffixed to a preposition or *fii* 'there is; there are'; in 11 and 12 the comment is a verbal sentence with a pronoun suffixed to the verb; in 13 the pronoun is suffixed to the active participle (with nunation) *9aazmin* 'having invited,' which has the function of a verb; and in 14 and 15 the pronoun is suffixed to a preposition in the verbal sentence which is the comment.

Note that the suffixed pronouns in sentences 1-5 indicate possession; those in 11-13 function as objects either of the verbs *raadat* 'she wanted' and *xaðu* 'they (m.) took' or the active participle (with nunation) *9aazmin* 'having invited.'

Either the topic or the comment can be used with modifiers. In the following examples the modifiers are in parenthesis:

16. *9ali* (l-gaṣṣaab)(min l-baHreen) 'ubu*u* (l-9ood) sammaač.
'Ali (the butcher)(from Bahrain)—his (old) father is a fisherman.'

17. *š-šeex* (ṭawiil l-9umur) 'il*a* gaṣreen (kbaar)(fi dbayy).
'The Shaikh (the long-lived one) has two (big) palaces (in Dubai).'

13.5 Conditional Sentences

A conditional sentence in GA is one which has an *if-* clause and a result or main clause. The *if-* clause is introduced by such particles as *'iða, (n)čaan,* var. *(n) kaan, lo* (rarely *law*), and *'in* which all mean *if.* Conditionals in GA are of three types:

13.5.1 Open Conditionals

In open conditionals, the verb usually expresses possibility, i.e., a condition that may or may not be fulfilled. The verb in the *if*-clause can be perfect or imperfect, depending upon the meaning; in the result clause it can be perfect, imperfect or imperative. The particles used in open conditionals are *iđa, (n)čaan,* var. *(n)kaan,* with a following perfect or imperfect tense verb, and *lo, 'in* with a following imperfect tense verb. Examples:

1. 'iđa šift rifiijak Hilu la taakla killa.
   'Don't use up all of your credit at once.' (lit., "If you think your friend is nice, don't eat him up all at once.")
2. 'iđa čint mista9jil 'ixiđ taksi.
   'If you are in a hurry, take a taxi.'
3. 'iđa ṭaaH l-bi9iir kaθrat sičaačiina.
   'When it rains, it pours.' (lit., "If the camel falls down, its knives are plenty.")
4. 'iđa truuH l-barr tšuuffum.
   'If you go to the desert, you will see them.'
5. nčaan 9indak fluus waayid 9aṭni šayy.
   'If you have a lot of money, give me some.'
6. čaan šift šayy la tguuḷ šayy.
   'If you see anything, don't say anything.'
7. lo tabi ṣ-ṣaHiiH 'a9almak bii.
   'If you want the truth, I will tell it to you.'
8. lo 'ašuufa 'aguuḷ la.
   'If I see him, I will tell him.'
9. lo tiyi hini 'aHsan.
   'If you come here, it is better.'
10. 'in tšuufa guuḷ-la.
    'If you see him, tell him.'
11. 'in truuH hnaak tistaanis.
    'If you go there, you will have a good time.'
12. widdi 'aruuH baačir čaan čiđi.
    'I would like to go tomorrow if it is so.'

13.5.2 Unlikely Conditionals

In unlikely conditionals, the verb usually expresses a condition which presumably cannot be fulfilled now. The verbs in the *if*- clause and the main clause are in the perfect tense. Examples:

13. 'iða bağeet ṣ-ṣaHiiH 9allamtak bii.
'If you wanted the truth, I would tell you.'

14. nčaan ya riHt sallamt 9alee.
'If he came, I would go to greet him.'

15. lo gilt-lak ma ṣaddagtani.
'If I told you, you would not believe me.'

16. 'in Haṣṣalta yiit wiyyaa.
'If I found him, I would come with him.'

17. lo sawwa čiði čaan zeen.
'If he did like this, it would be fine.'

13.5.3 Unreal Conditionals

Unreal conditionals express a contrary-to-fact or rejected condition. The verb in the *if*- clause is in the perfect tense with or without the verb *čaan* (var. *kaan*) 'to be' and in the main clause it is in the perfect tense with *čaan* (var. *kaan*). *čaan* (var. *kaan*) is uninflected in such constructions. The *čaan* + perfect tense verb construction is equivalent to the English conditional perfect, i.e., *would* or *should have* + past participle. Examples:

18. 'iða yiit čaan Haṣṣalta.
'If you had come, you would have found him.'

19. 'iða kaan bağeeta kaan Haṣṣalta.
'If you had wanted it, you would have gotten it.'

20. lo čifta čaan gilt-la.
'If I had seen him, I would have told him.'

21. lo ma ṭṭa99amat čaan ṭaaHat mariiḏ̣a.
'If she had not been inoculated, she would have fallen ill.'

22. lo riHt kaan Haṣṣalta.
'If I had gone, I would have found him.'

23. lo sima9ti l-xabar čaan ṭirti min l-faraH.
'If you (f.s.) had heard the news, you would have been overjoyed.'

24. nčaan sawwa ruuHa čiði kaan maHHad 9rafa.
'If he had made himself (to look) like this, no one would have known him.'

25. lo bağeet ṣ-ṣalaa čaan Hassalitta.
'Make hay while the sun shines.' (lit., "If you had wanted prayer, you would have gotten it.")

The particle *leen* is occasionally used to mean 'if' in unreal conditionals:

26. leen Haṣṣalta čaan Habbeet 'iida.
 'If I had found him, I would have kissed his hand.'

27. leen štaġalt čaan 9aṭeetak čam dirhim.
 'If you had worked, I would have given you some money.'

If *leen* is followed by an imperfect tense verb, it tends to introduce a temporal clause (see 12.3.2.A):

leen tooṣal ruuH l-'uteel.	'When you arrive, go to the hotel.'
leen yištaġiḷ yištaġiḷ zeen.	'Whenever he works, he works well.'

In all of the above cited conditional sentences, the *if-* clause has a verb except for example 5, which has the pseudo-verbal construction *9indak* 'you have.' Examples of other pseudo-verbal constructions occur:

28. nčaan 9aleek fluus sidha.
 'If you owe money, pay it back.'

29. 'iđa minna ma 'abġaa.
 'If it is from him, I don't want it.'

30. lo fii xeer čaan ma hadda ṭ-ṭeer.
 'If it (e.g., the sparrow) had been of any use, the bird (of prey) would not have discarded it.' (It is a worthless thing.)

A participle is occasionally used in the *if-* clause:

31. lo msawwi ruuHa xunfus čaan 'afđ̣al.
 'If he turned himself into a beatle, it would be better.' 'If he had turned himself into a beatle, it would have been better.'

32. lo m9arris čaan ma ṭabb ihni.
 'If he had been married, he would not have come here.'

33. 'iđa mista9jil 'ixiđ taksi.
 'If you are in a hurry, take a taxi.'

34. 'iđa muub ṣaayir l-yoom, yṣiir baačir.
 'Whatever will be will be.' (lit., "If it does not happen today, it will happen tomorrow.")

35. nčaan 9aazminni zeen.
 'If he has invited me, fine.'

The negative particle *la* 'no; not' is sometimes used with the effect of a conditional particle. The verb in the main clause is also negated by *la* and expresses a negative command:

36. la tbuug w-la txaaf.
'If you do not steal, you won't have anything to fear.'

37. la tiftaH jeebak w-la tšuuf 9eebak.
(lit., "If you do not open your pocket, you won't see your vice.")

Sometimes *la* is used with a perfect tense verb:

38. la ġaab l-gaṭu 'il9ab ya faar.
'While the cat's away, the mice will play.' (lit., "If the cat is absent, play mouse!")

Sayings and proverbial phrases in GA abound with conditional sentences, as in examples 1, 3, 25, 30, 34, 36, 37, and 38. Other examples are:

39. 'iđa Hajjat l-bagar 9ala gruunha.
(lit., "If cows go to pilgrimage on their horns.")[7]

40. lo yadri 9meer čaan šagg θooba.
(lit., "If Omayr knew, he would rip his dress.")[8] Ignorance is bliss.

41. 'in ṭaggeet 'uuji9 w-in 9aššeet 'išbi9.
(lit., "If you beat s.o., beat him hard; and if you dine s.o., satiate him.")[9]

42. 'in đakart l-kalb wallim l-9aṣaa.
(lit., "If you mention the dog, have the stick ready.")[10]

14. CLAUSES

14.1 Noun Clauses

A noun clause has the function of a noun. It may serve as:

A. the subject of a sentence:

1. yamkin *yigdar yaji baačir.*
'It is possible that he can come tomorrow.'

2. yamkin *s-simač muub zeen.*
'It is possible that the fish is not good.'

---

7. i.e., it is an impossibility.

8. One of the Mamelukes used to have sexual intercourse with his master's (Omayr's) wife while Omayr was away. The master's wife used to say this.

9. i.e., if you do anything, do it well.

10. i.e., bad people should be treated in a manner befitting them.

3. muub ṣa9b 9aleek *truuH wiyyaahum?*
'Isn't it difficult for you to go with them?'

4. muub zeen *tla9wizhum.*
'It is not good (for you) to bother them.'

5. muub 9adil *l-baHreen winsa?*
'Isn't it true that BaHrain is fun?'

6. *riHt hnaak* mub čiđi?
'Isn't it true that you went there?' (lit., "You went there, didn't you?")

7. *li-fluus tjiib l-9aruus* mub čiđi?
'Isn't it true that money talks?' (lit., "Money brings the bride, doesn't it?")

B. the object of a verb:

9. gaaḷ *ma yigdar yruuH.*
'He said he could not go.'

10. 9araft *'inna mub yaay.*
'I knew that he was not coming.'

11. sama9t *'inhum rammasaw š-šeex.*
'I heard that they had talked to the Shaikh.'

12. rafaḓ *yiji wiyyaay.*
'He refused to come with me.'

C. the object of a preposition:

13. Haṣṣalta min *illi baaga.*
'I got it from the one who stole it.'

14. Haađi Hagg *illi ma yirHam nafsa.*
'This is for (i.e., the penalty of) the one who does not care for himself.' (lit., "This is for the one who does not have mercy upon himself.")

15. haađa 'aHsan min *illi štareenaa.*
'This is better than that which we bought.'

Noun clauses functioning as objects of prepositions are usually introduced by the relative *illi* (see 14.2) in GA.

14.2 Relative Clauses

A relative clause modifies a noun, a proper name or a pronoun (including a demonstrative pronoun). The noun, proper name, or pronoun modified by a relative clause is called the antecedent. If the antecedent is definite, the relative clause is introduced by the relative particle *'illi,* [11] less frequently *l-.* [12] *'illi* 'who(m), that, which' is invariable, i.e., it is not inflected for gender or number. If the antecedent is indefinite, *'illi* is not normally used in GA, although some speakers do rarely use it in this way. A relative clause is either verbal or nominal (see 13.1).

Examples of Definite Relative Clauses

1.	haaða r-rayyaal illi ya hni.	'This is the man who came here.'
2.	haðeel l-banaat r-raaHan.	'These are the girls who went.'
3.	haaði r-rasta lli twaddi l-9een.	'This is the road that leads to Al-Ain.'
4.	l-kuuliyya lli fannašaw	'the workers who resigned'
5.	s-saarig illi baag s-saa9a	'the thief who stole the watch'
6.	t-tiffaaH l-yiji min labnaan	'the apples that come from Lebanon'
7.	l-bint illi titzawwaj	'the girl who marries'
8.	l-binaaya lli 9ala yimiinak	'the building (which is) on your right'
9.	ṭ-ṭamaaṭ l-min s-sa9diyyaat	'the tomatoes (that are) from Sadiyat'[13]
10.	l-matHaf illi fi l-9een	'the museum (which is) in Al-Ain'

The antecedents in the above examples, *r-rayyaal* 'the man,' *l-banaat* 'the girls,' *r-rasta* 'the road,' etc., are definite and also the subjects of the relative clauses. The relative clauses in examples 1-7 are verbal, while those in examples 8-10 are nominal.

Examples of Indefinite Relative Clauses

11.	9indaha lisaan yilġi waayid.	'She has a tongue that chatters a lot.'

---

11. *'illi* has two forms: *illi* and *lli. illi* is used in a post-consonant position and *lli* is used in a post-vowel position.

12. A relative clause introduced by *'illi* is a definite relative clause; otherwise it is an indefinite relative clause. *l-* here is identical with the article prefix. *'illi* tends to be used in formal and deliberate speech, while *l-* is normally used in informal and rapid speech.

13. An island in Abu Dhabi.

12.	haađa hači ma yingaaḷ halHiin.	'This is talk which cannot, should not, be said now.'
13.	saalfa ma laha 'awwal wala taali	'a story that does not have a beginning or an end'
14.	haađa filim yḍaHHič.	'This is a film that makes one laugh.'
15.	'abġa beet gariib min l-baHar.	'I want a house (that is) by the sea.'
16.	rayyaal šeeba ma la maθiil	'an old man who has no equal'
17.	tHaṣṣil binaaya jiddaamak.	'You will find a building in front of you.'

If the antecedent is the object of the relative clause, the verb in the relative clause has a suffixed pronoun referring to the antecedent and agreeing with it in gender and number; if the relative clause has a verb + preposition, the suffixed pronoun is attached to the preposition.

Examples:

18.	*s-safiir* illi šift*a* fi beet š-šeex	'the ambassador (whom) I saw in the Shaikh's house'
19.	*l-banaat* illi šifitt*in*	'the girls (whom) I saw'
20.	*l-yiHH* illi Haṣṣalt*a*	'the watermelons (that) I found'
21.	9allimna b-*li-Hčaaya* lli gilitta.	'Tell us the story (which) you told.'
22.	*bint* tazawwaj*ha* ba9deen	'a girl (whom) he married later on'
23.	fluus mHaṣṣilh*a* min 'ubuu	'money (that) he got from his father'
24.	haađa *šayy* 'aḷḷa kaatb*a* ba9ad.	'This is something (that God has foreordained (lit., "written"), however.'
25.	'aHsan *9amal* tsawwi*i* fi Hayaatak	'the best deed, work, (that) you might do in your lifetime'
26.	*šayy* t9awwad 9al*ee*	'something (that) he got used to'
27.	*huwa* lli yiit wiyya*a*.	'He is the one (whom) I came with.'

28. *li-msaafriin* illi riHt wiyyaa*hum* — 'the passengers (that) I went, traveled, with'

29. *l-gaṣṣaab* illi štareet minn*a* l-laHam — 'the butcher (whom) I bought the meat from'

30. *l-yaam9a* lli dirast fii*ha* — 'the university (which) I studied at'

Another type of relative clause in GA is one in which a suffixed pronoun referring to the antecedent is attached to a noun. Such a relative clause is similar to an English relative clause introduced by *whose, of which,* etc., as shown in the examples below.

31. t-taksi r-raa9ii Hamad
'the taxi whose owner is Hamad'

32. l-bint illi 9yuunha jamiila
'the girl whose eyes are beautiful'
'the girl with the beautiful eyes'

33. 'aal nhayyaan illi rayaayiilhum fi kill mukaan
'Al-Nhayyan whose men are in every place'

34. l-beet illi biibaana xuḏ̣ur
'the house whose doors are green'

35. s-sayyaara t-tawaayirha qadiima
'the car with the old tires'

36. kaan waaHid rayyaal 9ood liHyita beeḏ̣a.
'There was an old man whose beard was grey (lit., "white").'

37. Hurma zeena ša9arha ṭawiil
'a beautiful woman whose hair is long'
'a beautiful woman with long hair'

38. sikant fi beet masaaHta kabiira.
'I lived in a house with a large area.'

39. 9inda sayyaara moodeelha qadiim.
'He has an old model car.'

40. kaan fii 9ayuuz 'awlaadha xamsa.
'There was an old woman who had five sons.'

Relative Clauses as Nouns

Another type of relative clause that does not modify a noun, a proper name, or a pronoun occurs in GA. Such a relative clause has the function of a noun, i.e., it may function as the subject or predicate of a sentence, or the second term of a noun construct, or the object of a verb or a preposition. *'illi,* in a relative clause functioning as the subject of a sentence, has an indefinite meaning, corresponding to 'he who,' 'the one who,' 'those who,' 'whoever,' 'that which,' etc. The verb of the relative clause is third-person masculine singular. This type of relative clause is frequently found in proverbial and idiomatic phrases. Examples:

41. 'illi ma y9arf ṣ-ṣagir yišwii.
Don't kill the goose that lays the golden egg. (lit., "He who doesn't know the falcon will roast it.")

42. 'illi ṣaar ṣaar.
Don't cry over spilled milk. (lit., "What has happened has happened.")

43. 'illi yaani kafaani.
I am satisfied. (lit., "What has come to me has been enough for me.")

44. 'illi fi l-jidir yṭal9a l-millaas.[14]
(lit., "What is in the kettle will be taken out by the ladle.")

45. 'illi ma yiṭla9 9ala 'ubuu naġaḷ.
Like father like son. (lit., "He who does not take after his father, i.e., in looks and behavior, is a bastard.")

46. 'illi ma ynuuš l-9anguud yguuḷ Haamiđ̣.[15]
(lit., "He who cannot reach the cluster of grapes says, 'It is sour.' ")

47. 'illi ma la 'awwal ma la taali.[16]
(lit., "He who has no beginning has no end.")

48. 'illi yibġa ṣ-ṣalaa ma tfuuta.
Make hay while the sun shines. (lit., "He who wants to pray won't fail to do so.")

49. 'illi ma yjiiba Haliiba ma yjiiba z-zuur.
You can lead a horse to water, but you can't make it drink. (lit., "He who is not brought by his own milk won't be brought by force.")

50. 'illi ma yiṭla9 9ala 'ubuu naġaḷ.
The child is father of the man. (lit., "He who does not take after his father is a bastard.")

---

14. It is used, for example, to describe a person who tries hard to hide or conceal a certain quality or behavior; one day it will be uncovered.

15. From the fable of the fox ascribed to Aesop. The proverb conveys the meaning of a disparagement of s.th. that has proved to be unattainable.

16. It is used, for example, to describe a person who professes loyalty and sincerity after he has proved to be disloyal and unfaithful.

The relative clauses in examples 41-50 function as subjects of the sentences.

Other examples of *relative clauses as nouns:*

51. mHammad illi raaH.
'Mohammad is the one who went.'

52. l-mudiir illi baag.
'The director is the one who has stolen.'

53. li-fluus illi tjiib l-9aruus.
Money talks. (lit., "Money is that which brings the bride.")

54. š-šeex illi sirna wiyyaa.
'The Shaikh is the one we went with.'

55. ya weel illi ma yṣuum.
'Woe unto the one who does not fast.'

56. haaði jazaat li-ybuug.
'This is the punishment of the one who steals.'

57. haaði Haal illi ybuug.
'This is the fate (lit., "condition") of the one who steals.'

58. 9aṭni lli tibġaa.
'Give me what you like.'

59. xuð illi hni.
'Take what is here.'

60. difa9 illi 9alee.
'He paid what he owed.'

61. yixtaar l-yabii.
'He chooses the one he wants.'

62. haaði Hagg l-yiji 'awwal.
'This is for the one who comes first.'

63. zoojta l-'uula yaabat-la bass darzan yahhaal!
'He had only a dozen children by his first wife!'

In examples 51-54, the relative clauses function as predicates of the sentences; in examples 55-57, they are used in construct with the nouns *weel* 'woe,' *jazaa* 'punishment,' and *Haal* 'condition.' In examples 58-61, they function as objects of the verbs *9aṭa* 'to give,' *xuð* 'take,' *difa9* 'he paid,' and *yixtaar* 'he chooses'; and in examples 62 and 63, they are governed by the prepositions *Hagg* 'belonging to' and *bass* 'except for, only.'

In the foregoing examples the relative clauses in 24, 31, and 59 have the participles *kaatib* 'having written,' *raa9i* 'having owned;

owner,' and *daašš* 'having entered.' Other examples with participles follow:

64. 'illi msawwi ruuHa xunfus
'the one who has turned himself into a beetle'

65. suug s-simač l-matruus rayayiil w-Hariim
'the fish market which is full of men and women'

66. r-raakib buṭbuṭa
'the one riding a motorcycle'
'the one on a motorcycle'

67. l-9ayyaala lli gaa9diin yargusuun b-l-bindig
'the (male) dancers who are dancing with rifles'

14.3 *Haal* Clauses

A *Haal* clause is a clause of manner or circumstance; it describes, for example, the manner in which one did something, the manner how something happened, one's condition when something happened, etc. A *Haal* clause can be:

A. a nominal sentence (see 13.1) introduced by *w-* 'and':

1. dašš *w-gaḷba ṭaayir min l-faraH.*
'He entered with an overjoyed heart.' (lit., "He entered and his heart was flying from joy.")

2. ya *w-huwa raakib b(i)9iir.*
'He came riding a camel.' (lit., "He came and (or while) he was riding a camel.")

3. Haṣṣalta *w-huwa msawwi ruuHa xunfus.*
'I found that he had turned himself into a beetle.' (lit., "I found him and he had turned himself into a beetle.")

4. ṣaarli mudda *w-aana yaalis hni yammak.*
'I have been sitting here by you for a (long) while.'

5. ṣaar-lana mudda *w-niHin naaṭriinak.*
'We have been waiting for you for a (long) while.'

6. laweeš ddišš š-šuġuḷ *w-inta mṣaxxan?*
'Why do you go to work, seeing as how you are running a temperature?'

B. a verbal sentence (see 13.3) introduced by *w-* followed by an independent pronoun followed by an imperfect-tense verb:

7. dašš *w-huwa yqanni.*
'He entered singing.'
'He entered while he was singing.'

8. Haṣṣalattin *w-hin yin9išin jiddaam š-šeex.*
'She found them dancing in front of the Shaikh.'
'She found that they (f.) were dancing in front of the Shaikh.'

C. a pseudo-verbal sentence (see 13.2) introduced by *w-* 'and':

9. saafar *w-9inda maal waayid.*
'He traveled, having acquired a lot of money.'

10. tirak *w-ma9aa 9aayala čibiira.*
'He left with a large family.'

11. yaw bu ḏabi *w-fiiha xeer waayid.*
'They came to Abu Dhabi and (i.e., at the time when) it had a lot of wealth.'

12. xaḏeet d-dalla *w-ma čaan fiiha gahwa.*
'I took the coffee pot and (i.e., at the time when) there was no coffee in it.'

D. a verbal sentence introduced by an imperfect-tense verb. The same sentences under B above can be used without *w-* with the same meaning:

13. dašš *yqanni.*

14. Haṣṣalattin *yin9išin jiddaam š-šeex.*

15. MAJOR PHRASE TYPES

15.1 Noun Phrases

A noun phrase consists of a noun and one or more modifiers. For this section of noun phrases, see 10. NOUN MODIFIERS above. Below are the major kinds of noun phrases in GA:

15.1.1 *N* + N (+ N + N . . .)

diriišat l-Hijra	'the room's window'
diriišat Hijrat l-beet	'the window of the room of the house'
diriišat Hijrat beet Saalim	'the room's window of Salim's house'

The construct phrases above can also be used with *Hagg* or *maal* 'belonging to' with the same meaning:

d-diriiša Hagg l-Hijra
diriišat l-Hijra Hagg l-beet
or: d-diriiša Hagg Hijrat l-beet
diriišat Hijrat l-beet Hagg saalim
or: diriišat l-Hijra Hagg beet saalim
or: d-diriiša Hagg Hijrat beet saalim
or: d-diriiša Hagg l-Hijra Hagg beet saalim

15.1.2 *N* (+N) + Adj. (+Adj. . . .)

msiid 9ood	'a big mosque'
li-msiid l-9ood	'the big mosque'

If two adjectives or more are used to modify the noun-head, *N*, usually there are no restrictions on the order of those adjectives:

čalb 'aswad kabiir	'a big black dog'
čalb kabiir 'aswad	

Both adjectives *'aswad* 'black' and *kabiir* 'big' modify the head, *čalb*, 'dog.'

Sometimes the last in a string of attributive adjectives may apply to the whole preceding phrase. This occurs mainly in set phrases, titles, or proper names:

d-diiwaan l-'amiiri l-qadiim	'the old Emiri Court'
l-xaliij l-9arabi l-qani	'the rich Arabian Gulf'

As has already been mentioned in Construct Phrases (see 10.1), an adjective coming after a noun construct may modify either noun depending on sense and agreement. Thus, the following three patterns of modification are established:

1. *N* N Adj. Adj.
   suug simač xaayis raxiiṣ — 'the market of cheap rotten fish'

or suug simač raxiiṣ xaayis

makaatib š-šarika l-'amriikiyya l-yadiida — 'the offices of the new American company'

or makaatib š-šarika l-yidiida l-'amriikiyya

2. *N* N Adj. Adj.

	suug s-simač l-yidiid n-naᵭiif	'the clean new fish market'
or	suug s-simač n-naᵭiif l-yadiid	
	dallat li-ghawa ṣ-ṣaġiira l-yidiida	'the small new coffee pot'
or	dallat li-ghawa l-yadiida ṣ-ṣaġiira	

3. *N* N Adj. Adj.

	makaatib š-šarika l-'amriikiyya l-yidiida	'the new offices of the American company'
	gaṣr l-Haakim l-9aadil l-ba9iid	'the distant palace of the just ruler'
but	*makaatib š-šarika l-yidiida l-'amriikiyya	
	*gaṣr l-Haakim l-ba9iid l-9aadil	

In other words, the pattern *N* N Adj. Adj. is ungrammatical. The directions of modification are parallel, i.e., either the two adjectives modify the same noun, or the first adjective modifies the second noun in the construct and the second modifies *N*, the noun-head. Of the three logical possibilities of the modification patterns above, 3. is rare.

15.1.3 Quantifier + *N*

The position of *Quantifier* can be filled by *Numeral* (cardinal[17] or ordinal), *Non-Numeral* (partitive, fraction, intensifier, or demonstrative),[18] or *Elative Adjective.* Examples:

xams Hariim	'five women'
xaamis Hurma	'the fifth woman'
ba9ᵭ l-Hariim	'some (of the) women'

---

17. Except for *waaHid* 'one' and *θneen(a)* 'two.'

18. See 10.3.2 for more examples and the rules governing the pre-posing and post-posing of these modifiers.

θilθ l-Hariim	'one-third of the women'
kill l-Hariim	'all (of the) women'
haᵭeel l-Hariim	'these women'
'aymal Hurma	'the most beautiful woman'
'aymal l-Hariim	'the most beautiful (of the) women'

The noun-head, *N*, can be the first element in a noun construct, giving the phrase *N* N, e.g., kaatib š-šarika 'the company clerk.' The plural form of this noun construct, i.e., *kuttaab š-šarika* 'the company clerks,' can be modified by a pre-nominal non-numeral. Examples:

mu9ᵭ̣am	kuttaab š-šarika	'most of the company clerks'
ba9ᵭ̣		'some of the company clerks'
nuṣṣ		'half (of) the company clerks'
kill		'all (of) the company clerks'

The non-numeral is obligatorily pre-posed, either to a noun construct, as shown above, or to an elative construct:

kill 'aHsan kuttaab š-šarika 'all (of) the best company clerks'

This last phrase can be modified only post-nominally by cardinals, ordinals, and all the subclasses of positive adjectives. There are no restrictions on the order of those post-nominal modifiers:

kill kuttaab š-šarika | l-9ašara z-zeeniin
| z-zeeniin l-9ašara

'all (of) the good ten company clerks'

The number of possible phrases can be worked out by a mathematical progression. Let M stand for a post-nominal modifier, and M_1 M_2 M_3 . . . etc., stand for the first, the second, the third modifiers . . . etc. If three modifiers are used, we can have the following six possible phrases:

M_1 M_2 M_3 M_1 M_3 M_2 M_2 M_3 M_1
M_2 M_1 M_3 M_3 M_1 M_2 M_3 M_2 M_1

If four modifiers are used, we can have 24 possible phrases; if five are used, we can have 120, etc. If *n* stands for the number of modifiers, then the number of logical possibilities is:

$$n(n-1)\,(n-2)\,(n-3), \text{etc.}$$

If coordinate modifiers are used, they behave as one unit syntactically, i.e., the coordinate modifiers as a unit can precede or follow other modifiers. The order within coordinate modifiers is free.

mašruu9	tijaari w-'iqtiṣaadi 'iqtiṣaadi w-tijaari	'amriiki

'an American commercial and economic project'

OR

mašruu9	'amriiki	tijaari w-'iqtiṣaadi 'iqtiṣaadi w-tijaari

15.1.4 *N* + Adj. + N

The construction *N* + adj. + N is not common in GA. Noun phrases of such a construction are descriptive clichés or stereotyped expressions. The whole construction functions as an adjective: the second term, which is always a definite noun, restricts or specifies the item of reference of the adjective, the first term. Such phrases are known as false *iḍaafa* constructions in literary Arabic. Examples:

ṭawiil l-lisaan	'long-tongued'
9amay l-gaḷb	'blind of heart'
'abyað̣ l-weeh	'white-faced'
9ariið̣ č-čatf	'broad-shouldered'
9að̣ab l-yadd	'paralyzed of hand'
maksuur l-gaḷb	'broken-hearted'
ṭawiil l-9umur	'long-lived'

The *N* + Adj. construction is more commonly used, e.g., *lisaana ṭawiil, gaḷba 9amay, yadda 9að̣ba,* etc.

15.1.5 *N* + Participle + N

rayyaal msawwi ruuHa xunfus	'a man who has turned himself into a beetle'
li-bdiwi r-raakib bi9iir	'the Bedouin riding a camel'
t-tindeel li-mfanniš l-kuuliyya	'the foreman who has fired the workmen'
li-ṣbayy d-daašš l-Hafiiz	'the young boy entering the office'

The *Participle* in such constructions requires a complement which functions as its object.

15.1.6 *N* + Prepositional Phrase

bdiwi min gabiilt š-šeex	'a Bedouin from the Shaikh's tribe'
9ayyaal min d-duwaasir	'a (male) dancer from the Dosaris'
sammaač min 'ahl l-firiij	'a fisherman from the neighborhood'
Hyuul min ðahab	'bracelets of gold, gold bracelets'
barnuuṣ min ṣuuf	'a blanket of wool, a wool blanket'
baHar min l-hamm	'a sea of grief'
zooj min š-šuwaahiin	'a couple of falcons'

15.1.7 *N* + š-

In this type of noun phrase *š-* is prefixed to a verbal noun with a suffixed pronoun which refers to *N*. Examples:

rayyaal š-kubra	'a very old, big man' or 'What an old, big man!'
Hurma š-kuburha	'a very old, big woman' or 'What an old, big woman!'
bint š-Halaatta	'a very beautiful girl' or 'What a beautiful girl!'
šaari9 š-ṭuula	'a very long street' or 'What a long street!'
fluus š-kuθurha	'a whole lot of money'

15.2 Adjective Phrases

An adjective can be modified by such particles (see 12.4.C) as *waayid* (var. *waajid*), *killiš* 'very,' *kaθiir* 'a lot, a great deal,' *šwayy* 'a little,' etc. Examples:

waayid zeen	'very good, fine'
laġwiyya killiš	'very talkative'
Haaff kaθiir	'very dry'
gaṣiir šwayy	'a little short'

As adjective modifiers, *waayid, killiš, kaθiir,* and *šwayy* can be either pre-posed or post-posed to the adjective modified. No other adjective modifiers have been recorded.

15.3 Adverb Phrases

15.3.1 Time

Among adverb phrases of time are those that are introduced by an adverbial particle of time (see 12.4.A). Examples:

ybannid gabḷ s-saa9a xams.	'It closes before five o'clock.'
čifta gabḷ ams.	'I saw him the day before yesterday.'
nsiir 9ugub baačir.	'We will leave after tomorrow.'
čint hini min gabiḷ.	'I have been here before.'

Others are made up of two nouns compounded together, e.g., *ṣabaaH ams* or *'ams ṣ-ṣabaaH* 'yesterday morning,' *'ams l-masa* or *'ams fi l-leel* 'last night,' etc. Some others are made up of the demonstrative *ha-* and a noun, e.g., *ha-l-Hiin*[19] 'now' and *ha-l-Hazza*[20] 'now, this time.' A few are made up of N + Adj., e.g., *s-subuu9 l-maað̣i* 'last week,' *s-sana l-maað̣ya* 'last year,' etc.

15.3.2 Place

Adverb phrases of place are usually introduced by an adverbial particle of place (see 12.4.B). Examples:

riHt ṣoob l-baHar.	'I went toward the sea.'
yilasna yamm š-šeex.	'We sat by the Shaikh.'
yximm taHt l-xeel.	'He sweeps under the horses.'
raaH la-wara.	'He went in reverse.'
tawni yiit min hnaak.	'I have just come from there.'

15.3.3 *Haal*[21]

ya raakib buṭbuṭa.	'He came on (lit., "riding") a motorcycle.'
dašš Hamgaan.	'He entered in anger.'
yaana mbaarik.	'He came to congratulate us.'
yruuH maaši kill yoom.	'He goes every day on foot.'
tsaafir b-ruuHHa.	'She travels alone.'

---

19. *ha-l-Hiin* in this transcription is shown as *halHiin*, sometimes reduced to *'alHiin* or *l-Hiin* in rapid speech.

20. *ha-l-Hazza* is transcribed as *halHazza*, sometimes reduced to *'al-Hazza* or *l-Hazza* in rapid speech.

21. See 14.3.

16. VERB STRINGS

This section deals with strings of two, sometimes three or more, verbs with the same subject. In GA the tenses of the strings of verbs with the same subject could be any of the following:[22]

1. Perfect or Imperfect + Imperfect
2. Perfect or Imperfect + Imperfect + Imperfect
3. Perfect or Imperfect + Imperfect + Imperfect + Imperfect
4. Perfect or Imperfect + Perfect
5. Perfect or Imperfect + Perfect + Perfect
6. Perfect or Imperfect + Perfect + Imperfect

Strings of three verbs are not very common; those of four verbs are rare. The strings **Imperfect + Perfect* and **Perfect + Imperfect + Perfect* are ungrammatical in GA. The first verb in such strings of verbs may be an auxiliary verb, e.g., *gaam* 'to start to do s.th.,' or another kind of verb that expresses a desire, e.g., *baġa* 'to want to do s.th.,' an ability or capability, e.g., *gadar* 'to be able to do s.th.,' or continuation, e.g., *ð̣all* 'to continue to do s.th.,' etc., as shown below.

16.1 *ð̣all, ṣaar*

ð̣all	'to remain, continue to do s.th.'
ṣaar	'to become, turn into s.th.'

These verbs and a few others are usually known as linking or incomplete verbs.[23] They require a complement, which might be nominal, adjectival, prepositional, or verbal. Examples:

ṣaar waziir.	'He became a minister.'
ma ṣaar šayy.	'Nothing happened.'
ṣaar maynuun.	'He became insane.'
ð̣all fi l-beet.	'He stayed at home.'
l-hawa ð̣all Haaff.	'The weather continued to be dry.'

---

22. Examples are given in the discussion below.

23. See, e.g., Cowell, *op. cit.*, pp. 452-453.

Examples of verbal strings with *ð̣all:*

A. Perfect + Imperfect

1.	ð̣all yištaġiḷ wiyya ADMA.	'He continued to work for ADMA.'
2.	ð̣alleena nadris.	'We continued to study.'
3.	l-yahhaal ð̣allaw yil9abuun.	'The children went on playing.'
4.	ð̣allat tabči.	'She went on crying, weeping.'
5.	ð̣alleet anaam fi haaða l-'uteel.	'I continued to sleep in this hotel.'
6.	ð̣all ybuug.	'He continued to steal.'
7.	ð̣allaw yjiibuun simač waayid.	'They continued to bring a lot of fish.'

Both *ð̣all* and the following imperfect verb agree with the subject.

B. Perfect + Imperfect + Imperfect

8.	ð̣all yibġa yištaġiḷ.	'He continued to have a desire to work.'
9.	ð̣alleena nriid nadris.	'We continued to have a desire to study.'
10.	ð̣all yHaawil yittaṣil fiik.	'He kept on trying to contact you.'
11.	ð̣all yruuH yadris.	'He continued to go on studying.'
12.	ð̣all yigdar yadris.	'He continued to have the ability to study.'

The verbs in such a string, as those in any other string in this section, have one subject and agree with it in gender and number. The meaning expressed by the imperfect verb *yadris* in sentence 11 above is *purpose.* The sentence can be paraphrased to read: He continued to go *so as to study,* or *for the purpose of studying.* In GA this meaning of purpose is expressed by all imperfect tense verbs after a verb of motion. Other examples are given below.

Examples of verb stings with *ṣaar:*

13.	ṣaar yṭarriš xṭuuṭ.	'He got to the point where he sent letters.'
14.	l-bank ṣaar ybannid s-saa9a xams.	'The bank got to the point where it closed at five.'
15.	ṣirna nruuH nadris.	'We got to the point where we would go to study.'

16.	ṣaarat tHaawil tadris.	'She got to the point where she tried to study.'
17.	ṣaarat tHaawil taji tadris.	'She got to the point where she tried to come to study.'

čaan (var. *kaan*) can be prefixed to any verb string to switch it from present to a past time-frame:

yruuH	'he goes'	čaan yruuH	'he used to go'
raaH	'he went'	čaan raaH	'he would have gone'

Other examples:

18.	čaan yibġa yaji yištaġiḷ.	'He wanted to come to work.'
19.	čint aHaawil 'aji 'aštaġiḷ.	'I was trying to come to work.'
20.	čaan raaH.	'He would have gone.'
21.	čaan riHt.	'I would have gone.'
22.	čaan dirasna.	'We would have studied.'

čaan in such strings is invariable. The meaning expressed (in 18-22) is that of a result clause in a conditional sentence (see 13.5).

23.	čaan raaH diras.	'He would have gone and studied.'
24.	čaan gaam ragad.	'He would have gone (lit., "stood up") and slept.'
25.	čaan raaH yadris.	'He would have gone to study.'
26.	čaan gaam yargid.	'He would have gone (lit. "stood up") to go to bed.'

Examples 23 and 24 can be paraphrased: *čaan raaH w-čaan diras* and *čaan gaam w-čaan ragad,* respectively. The imperfect tense verbs in 25 and 26 express purpose. Among the verbs in this section only invariable *čaan* can be followed by a perfect tense verb. The imperfect of *čaan, ykuun,* is not used as the first verb in a verb string.

16.2 *baġa, raad, gadar, Haawal, jarrab*

baġa	'to want, like to do s.th.'
raad	'to want to do s.th.; to feel like doing s.th.'
gadar	'to be able to do s.th.'
Haawal	'to try to do s.th.'
jarrab	'to try to do s.th.'

The verbs that belong to this subgroup express a desire, an ability, or an effort to do something. Like the verbs in 16.6 above they can be followed by one, two, or more verbs in the imperfect tense. Examples:

27.	baġa yaji.	'He wanted to come.'
28.	baġa yaji yadris.	'He wanted to come to study.'
29.	baġa yġarrir yaji yadris.	'He wanted to decide to come to study.'
30.	baġa yistarxiṣ yaji yadris.	'He wanted to get permission to come to study.'

raad, gadar, Haawal, or *jarrab* may occur in the same position as *baġa.* Unlike *čaan,* these verbs cannot be followed by a perfect tense verb:

31. *baġa ja.

32. *baġa ja yadris.

Like *ð̣all,* the imperfect tense of these verbs can be used:

33.	yigdaruun yajuun yadrisuun.	'They can come to study.'
34.	triid taji tadris.	'She wants to come to study.'

Haawal and *jarrab* are not used interchangeably in all positions. As far as meaning is concerned, *Haawal* expresses the idea of 'making an attempt to do s.th.'; *jarrab* expresses the idea of 'making an effort to do s.th.' with the implication of testing or trying it out. Thus:

35.	baġa yjarrib yadris.	'He wanted to try to study.'
36.	baġa yHaawil yadris.	'He wanted to try to study.'
37.	baġa yjarrib š-šuġuḷ.	'He wanted to try out the job.'

but:

38. *baġa yHaawil š-šuġuḷ.

16.3 *ga9ad, gaam*

ga9ad	'to begin, start to do s.th.'
gaam	'to begin, start to do s.th.'

ga9ad and *gaam* express similar meanings. Like *ð̣all, ṣaar, baġa, raad, gadar, Haawal,* and *jarrab,* they can be followed by one, two, or more verbs in the imperfect tense. Examples:

39.	gaam (or *ga9ad*) yadris.	'He began to study.'
40.	gaam (or *ga9ad*) yHaawil yadris.	'He started to try to study.'
41.	gaam (or *ga9ad*) yHaawil yaji yadris.	'He started to try to come to study.'

If followed by a perfect tense verb, *ga9ad* and *gaam* cease to function as auxiliaries; they become finite verbs with different meanings:

42.	ga9ad soolaf.	'He sat down and chatted.'
43.	gaam širib.	'He stood up and had a drink.'
44.	gaam ragaṣ.	'He got up and danced.'

Like *ḓall* and the verbs in 16.2, the imperfect tense of *ga9ad* and *gaam* can be used to imply a state, condition, or habitual action:

45.	yguum (or *yag9id*) yadris kill yoom.	'He studies every day.'
46.	yguum (or *yag9id*) yadris baačir.	'He will study tomorrow.'

The progressive meaning is expressed only by the present participle of *ga9ad,* i.e., *gaa9id.* Examples:

47. gaa9id yadris. 'He is studying.'

but:

48. *gaayim yadris.

According to the preceding discussion in 16.1-16.3, we can say that:

1. a perfect tense verb may be preceded by *čaan;* if it is a verb of motion, it may be followed by another verb, in which case the perfect tense verb expresses completed action and the imperfect tense verb expresses purpose:

raaH.	'He went.'
čaan raaH.	'He would have gone.'
raaH diras.	'He went and studied.'
čaan raaH diras.	'He would have gone and studied.'
čaan raaH yadris.	'He would have gone to study.'

2. an imperfect tense verb may be preceded by any combination of the following, but in the following order:

	čaan	modal	auxiliary	imperfect
or:	(čaan)	(modal)	(auxiliary)	imperfect

ṣaar	baġa
ð̣all	raad
	gadar
	Haawal
	jarrab
	ga9ad
	gaam

3. if the imperfect is a verb of motion; it may be followed by an imperfect verb with the grammatical meaning of purpose:

čaan	ṣaar	yibġa	yaji	yadris.	'He would have begun to want to come to study.'
			X		'He comes.'
		X	X		'He wants to come.'
	X		X		'He got in the habit of coming.'
X			X		'He used to come.'
X		X	X		'He wanted to come.'
X	X		X		'He would have started coming.'
	X	X	X		'He began to want to come.'

Time Marker *čaan*	Modal	Auxiliary	Main Verb	Complement (after verb of motion)
X			Perfect	Perf. (compl. action) Imperf. (purpose)
X	X	X	Imperfect	Imperf. (purpose)

Note: The position of *Main Verb* on the chart above can be filled by a verb phrase *modal + verb*, so that we might get a sentence like:

čaan saar yibġa yHaawil yð̣all yištaġiḷ.

'He would have wanted to try to keep on working.'

čaan ṣaar yigdar yHaawil yẓ̌all yištaġiḷ.
'He would have been able to try to go to work.'

16.4 *laazim*

This section deals with verb strings that are formed with the help of the auxiliary *laazim. laazim* is uninflected and expresses one or more of the following meanings: 'should,' 'must,' 'have to,' 'ought to' if followed by one, two, or more imperfect tense verbs. Examples:

49.	laazim aruuH ašuufa.	'I have to go to see him.'
50.	laazim tistaHi min nafsak.	'You ought to be ashamed of yourself.'
51.	halHiin kill waaHid laazim yruuH l-mu9askar.	'Nowadays everyone has to go to the (army) camp.'
52.	laazim yẓ̌all yištaġiḷ.	'He must, has to continue to work.'
53.	laazim yHaawil yẓ̌all yištaġiḷ.	'He must, has to try to continue to work.'
54.	laazim yilzam seeda.	'He should, must stay in his line.'

The negative form of *laazim* is *mu(u)(b) laazim,* which expresses either a negative obligation, i.e., 'shouldn't,' mustn't,' 'ought not to,' or a lack of obligation, i.e., '. . . not have to.' Examples:

55.	muub laazim yilzam seeda.	'He shouldn't, mustn't, stay in his line.' 'He doesn't have to stay in his line.'
56.	mu laazim yẓ̌all yištaġiḷ.	'He mustn't continue to work.' 'He doesn't have to continue to work.'

If one of the verbs after *laazim* is negated, only a negative obligation is expressed:

57.	laazim ma yilzam seeda.	'He shouldn't, mustn't stay in his line.'
58.	laazim ma yẓ̌all yištaġiḷ.	'He mustn't continue to work.'
59.	laazim yẓ̌all ma yištaġiḷ.	'He must continue not to work.'

If *laazim* is followed by a perfect tense verb, it expresses a deduction or an inference:

60.	laazim saar.	'He must have gone.'
61.	laazim ya ysallim 9aleek.	'He must have come to greet you.'
62.	laazim raaHat rgadat.	'She must have gone and slept.'
63.	laazim raaH štaġaḷ ams.	'He must have gone and worked yesterday.'
64.	laazim Haawlaw yittaṣluun fiik.	'They must have tried to contact you.'

The imperfect of *čaan, ykuun,* may follow *laazim* in examples 60-64 with no change in meaning. In such cases, *ykuun,* like any other verb in the verb string, agrees with the same subject:

65.	laazim ykuun ya ysallim 9aleek.	'He must have come to greet you.'
66.	laazim ykuunuun raaHu štaġḷaw ams.	'They must have gone and worked yesterday.'

The perfect of *laazim* is *čaan* (var. *kaan*) *laazim,* in which case *čaan* (var. *kaan*) is uninflected. The negative of *čaan laazim* is made by prefixing the negative particle *ma:*

67.	čaan laazim yruuH.	'He had to go.'
68.	čaan laazim tsaa9id 'umha.	'She had to help her mother.'
69.	ma čaan laazim yruuH.	'He did not have to go.' 'He did not need to go.'
70.	ma kaan laazim tsaa9id 'umha.	'She did not have to help her mother.' 'She did not need to help her mother.'

The negative particle *mu(u)(b)* may be used before *laazim* to negate *čaan laazim:*

71.	čaan mub laazim yilzam seeda.	'He did not have to stay in his line.'
72.	kaan mub laazim yǝ̣all yištaġiḷ.	'He did not have to continue to work.'

If one of the verbs after *čaan laazim* is negated, only a negative obligation is expressed (see examples 57-59 above):

73.	čaan laazim ma yilzam seeda.	'He shouldn't have stayed in his line.'
74.	čaan laazim ma yǝ̣all yištaġiḷ.	'He shouldn't have continued to work.'

According to the preceding discussion, we can have the following verb strings with auxiliary *laazim:*

	Time Marker	Auxiliary	Verb
1.		*laazim*	(*ykuun*) Perfect = Probability
2.	(*čaan*)		Imperfect = Necessity

1. = laazim (ykuun) ya (yadris).
   'He must have come to study.'
2. = (čaan) laazim yaji (yadris).
   'He had to come to study.'

17. CONCORD

The parts of speech that show inflectional agreement are nouns, pronouns, personal and demonstrative, adjectives, and verbs. Nouns are the governing or determining elements, and the other parts of speech are the governed elements.

17.1 Adjectives

17.1.1 Positive Adjectives

Positive adjectives are post-posed. They ususally agree in gender, number, and definiteness with the noun they modify:

9igd yidiid	'a new necklace'
čiswa yidiida	'new clothing'
l-9igd l-yidiid	'the new necklace'
č-čiswa l-yidiida	'the new clothing'

Positive adjectives show either a two-fold distinction, or a three-fold distinction for each of these categories.[24]

a. Gender:	masculine and feminine
b. Number:	singular and plural
c. Definiteness:	definite or indefinite

24. The general rules given in this section are modified by more specific ones given later.

For these three categories, an inflected adjective has the following forms:

A. Gender-Number

Adj.$_1$ are unmarked; these are called masculine singular forms:

rayyaal 9ood	'a big, old man'
9ayyil ṣaġiir	'a little child'

Adj.$_2$ are unmarked; they are feminine singular forms:

Hurma Haamil	'a pregnant woman'
mara 9aqiim	'a sterile woman'

It should be noted that in the case of animate nouns the real sex of the referent determines grammatical gender, regardless of the grammatical form of the word, e.g., *rayyaal* 'man,' *b(i)9iir* 'camel' and *šeeba* 'old man' are all masculine, and *Hurma* 'woman,' *'umm* 'mother' and *gaṭwa* 'cat' are all feminine. As for inanimate adjectives, grammatical gender serves as a means of indicating agreement between noun and adjective:

Haakim l-'imaara l-yidiid	'the new ruler of the Emirate'
Haakim l-'imaara l-yidiida	'the ruler of the new Emirate'

Examples of unmarked feminine singular nouns are (see 9.1.B):

šams	'sun'	'arð̣	'earth, ground'
Harb	'war'	čatti	'short note'
9een	'eye'	'iid	'hand'
siččiin	'knife'	boṭiḷ	'bottle'

Adj.$_3$ are marked by the feminine morpheme *-a* and are feminine singular:

Hurma 9ooda	'a big, old woman'
naaga dijiija	'a thin, skinny camel (f.)'

Adj.$_4$ are sound masculine plural forms. These are marked by the ending *-iin;* the referent is male human:

9yaal waṣxiin	'dirty children'
kuuliyya ð̣amyaaniin	'thirsty workmen'

Adj.$_5$ are sound feminine plural forms; they are marked by the morpheme *-aat;* the referent is female human:

na99aašaat zeenaat	'good female dancers'
Hariim yamiilaat	'beautiful women'

Adj.$_6$ are marked by internal vocalic patterns. They are known as broken plural forms:[25]

wlaad mtaan	'fat boys'
mwaẓẓafiin yiddad	'new employees'

NOTE THE FOLLOWING:

1. Adjectives modifying human masculine dual nouns are masculine plural.

9ayleen ṣġaar (or *saġiiriin*)	'two little children'
mudiireen zeeniin	'two good directors'

2. Adjectives modifying human feminine dual nouns are either feminine plural or masculine plural; the latter form is more commonly used:

binteen 9imyaan (or *9amyaat*)	'two blind girls'
Hurmateen mxabḷiin (or *mxabḷaat*)	'two crazy women'

3. Adjectives modifying non-human plural nouns are usually feminine singular, but may be plural; the latter form is not commonly used:

ġraaš matruusa (or *matruusiin*)	'filled bottles'
tuwaanki čibiira (or *kbaar*)	'big (water) tanks'
ba9aariin ẓamya (or *ẓamyaaniin*)	'thirsty camels'
gtaawa sooda (or *suud*)	'black cats'
gawaaṭi mingaṭṭa (or *mingaṭṭiin*)	'discarded cans'
hduum ġaalya (or *ġaalyiin*)	'expensive clothes'

B. Definiteness

As for definiteness, all the forms of the adjectives given above may be definite, i.e., marked by the article prefix *'al-*or indefinite, i.e., unmarked:

r-rayyaal l-9ood	'the big, old man'
l-Hurma l-Haamil	'the pregnant woman'

---

25. Some of these adjectives also have sound masculine plural patterns. See 10.5.2 Major Broken Plural Patterns above.

l-kuuliyya ḏ̣-ḏ̣amyaaniin	'the thirsty coolies'
9yaali ṣ-ṣġaar	'my little children'
mudiir l-maktab l-yidiid	'the new office manager'
hduumha l-ġaalya	'her expensive clothes'
'abu ḏ̣abi l-qadiima	'the old (section of) Abu Dhabi'

17.1.2 Elative Adjectives[26]

The comparative form of the adjective is not inflected for gender or number:

rayyaal 'amtan	'a fatter man' (m.s.)
rayyaaleen 'amtan	'two fatter men' (m.dual)
rayaayiil 'amtan	'fatter men' (m.p.)
Hurma 'amtan	'a fatter woman' (f.s.)
Hurmateen 'amtan	'two fatter women' (f.dual)
Hariim 'amtan	'fatter women' (f.p.)

The superlative is formed either by making the comparative definite

r-rayyaal l-'amtan	'the fattest man'

or by putting the comparative in a construct (see 10.2) with no concord; this latter pattern has a higher frequency of occurrence in GA:

'amtan rayyaal	'the fattest man'
'amtan Hurma	'the fattest woman'
'amtan l-Hariim	'the fattest (of the) women'
'aqdam l-9awaayil	'the oldest (of the) families'

17.2 Pronouns and Verbs

There is no gender distinction in the first person pronouns and verb forms; modifiers agree with the referents of *'aana* 'I' and *niHin* 'we':

'aana yiit.	'I (m. or f.) came.'
niHin yiina.	'We (m. or f.) came.'

---

26. See also 10.2 Elative Constructs and 10.5.1.4 Elative Adjectives above.

but:	'aana Harraan.	'I (m.) am sweating (m.).'
	'aana Harraana.	'I (f.) am sweating (f.).'
	niHin Harraaniin.	'We (m.) are sweating (m.).'
	niHin Harraanaat.	'We (f.) are sweating (f.).'
	'aana l-mudiir.	'I (m.) am the director (m.).'
	'aana l-mudiira.	'I (f.) am the director (f.).'
	niHin l-mudiiriin.	'We (m.) are the directors (m.).'
	niHin l-mudiiraat.	'We (f.) are the directors (f.).'

When the second and third person pronouns are used, verbs agree with them in gender and number:

'inta riHt.	'You (m.s.) went.'
'inti riHti.	'You (f.s.) went.'
'intum riHtaw.	'You (m.p.) went.'
'intin riHtin.	'You (f.p.) went.'
huwa raaH.	'He went.'
hiya raaHat.	'She went.'
hum raaHaw.	'They (m.) went.'
hin raaHan.	'They (f.) went.'

If the subject of a verb is an expressed nouns, verb agreement is as follows:

A. If the noun is singular, the verb agrees with it in number and gender, whether it precedes or follows the noun:

š-šeex rammasni.	'The Shaikh talked to me.'
'ixti raaHat l-madrasa.	'My sister went to school.'
l-mi9ris yištari ṣ-ṣoġa.	'The bridegroom buys the jewelry.'
l-9aruus(a) tištari li-hduum.	'The bride buys the clothes.'
s-siHH ma yistawi zeen halHiin.	'Dates are not good now.'
l-9eeš yinbaa9 bi-l-yuuniyya.	'Rice is sold by the sack.'
l-yiHHa haaði ma tinwikil.	'This watermelon cannot be eaten.'

B. If the noun is dual or plural and refers to human beings, the verb is plural and agrees with its subject in gender:

l-9ayyaaḷa yarguṣuun b-l-bindig.
'(The) male dancers dance with rifles.'

n-na99aašaat yin9išin ha-š-šikil.
'(The) female dancers dance in this manner.'

raaHaw taqaddaw li-9yaaḷ.
'The children went and had lunch.'

l-waladeen gaamaw yadrisuun.
'The two boys started to study.'

l-9aruusateen Haṣṣalan hadaaya.
'The two brides got gifts.'

ma gaṣṣaraw d-duwaasir.
'The Dosaris did their best.'

C. If the noun is dual and does not refer to human beings, the verb is masculine plural:

s-sayyaarateen ddaa9amaw.	'The two cars collided.'
l-baabeen nṣakkaw.	'The two doors were closed.'
d-diriišateen tbaṭṭalaw.	'The two windows opened.'
ddaa9amaw s-sayyaarateen.	'The two cars collided.'
maataw l-gaṭween.	'The two cats died.'

D. If the noun is plural and does not refer to human beings, the verb is usually feminine singular:

t-tuwaanki farġat.	'The (water) tanks were empty.'
li-Hyuul nbaagat.	'The bracelets were stolen.'
ṭṭarrašat li-xṭuuṭ.	'The letters were sent.'
l-yiwaani ṭaaHat.	'The sacks fell down.'

A masculine plural form of the verb is less commonly used. If the noun refers to animals, a masculine plural form of the verb is normally used, regardless of the gender of the subject:

li-gṭaawa šridaw.	'The cats ran away.'
l-ba9aariin xaafaw.	'The camels became afraid.'
n-nyaag xaḷḷafaw.	'The (female) camels gave birth.'
li-ṣxaḷaat kalaw.	'The young goats ate.'

If the subject is indefinite and occurs in a post-verbal position, the verb is masculine singular. Examples:

yaana xuṭṭaar.
'Some guests came to us.'

yaa bint.
'He had a baby girl.' (lit., "A baby girl came to him.")

wiṣil jamaa9a min li-kweet.
'A group of people arrived from Kuwait.'

maḏ̣a muddat sana.
'A period of one year has passed.'

ma baga 9indana šayy.
'We did not have anything left.'

ṣaarli hini sana.
'I have been here for a year.'

ṣaarli mudda w-aana yaalis hini.
'I have been sitting here for some time.'

18. NEGATION

See also 12.5 for the meanings and uses of *la, ma,* and *mu(u)(b).*

18.1 Negating Verbs

18.1.1 Perfect and Imperfect

The perfect and the imperfect tense forms are usually negated by *ma,* less frequently by *la.* Examples:

leeš ma fahamt šayy?
'Why didn't you understand anything?'

wal̤l̤a ma dri.
'Honestly, I don't know.'

l-mudiir ma ygaṣṣir.
'The director does his best (towards others).'

ma gaṣṣart.
'You did your best (towards others).'

ma raaH.
'He did not go.'

ma yistawi fiiha l-maHaar.
'Oysters cannot be found in it.'

ma yṣiir ha-š-šayy.
'This thing cannot be, cannot happen.'

ma yirham.
'It cannot work.'

Imperfect tense verbs that denote a passive-potential sense are negated by *ma* only:

l-9eeš ma yingaṭṭ.
'Rice cannot, shouldn't be thrown away.'

karš ma yintiris
'a belly that cannot be filled' (i.e., a bottomless belly)

ṣ-ṣagir ma yinšiwi.
'a falcon cannot, shouldn't be roasted.'

guuṭi ma yitbaṭṭaḷ
'a can that cannot be opened'

zaam ma yitqayyar
'a (work) shift that cannot be changed'

Two verbal constructions with a perfect or an imperfect tense joined by *wa-* 'and' are negated by *ma . . . w(a)-la* or *ma . . . w-ma.* Examples:

ma yindara w-ma yin9araf.
'It can neither be comprehended nor known.'
(i.e., it is impossible for s.o. to know.)

ma yindara w(a)-la yin9araf.
la yindara w(a)-la yin9araf.
*la yindara w-ma yin9araf.
la riHt w(a)-la yiit.
'I neither went nor came.'

ma čaan hini w(a)-la(čaan) hnaak.
'He was neither here nor there.'

la ragad w(a)-la xaḷḷa 'aHad yargid.
'He neither slept nor let anybody (else) sleep.'

In constructions with *'illa* 'except' *ma* is used to negate the verb. Such constructions have the meaning of 'nothing or nobody . . . except' or 'not . . . anything or anybody except':

ma baga 'illa hduuma.
'Nothing remained except his clothes.'

ma Haṣṣal 'illa hduuma.
'He did not find anything except his clothes.'

ma yfill l-Hadiid 'illa l-Hadiid.
'Nothing blunts, dents iron except iron.'

ma čaaffum 'illa mHammad.
'Nobody saw them except Mohammad.'

ma čaafaw 'illa mHammad.
'They did not see anybody except Mohammad.'

'illa may be followed by a prepositional phrase:

ma ysiiruun 'illa fi l-leel.
'They do not go (at any time) except at night.'

ma tHaṣla 'illa fi s-suug l-yidiid.
'You will not find it (anywhere) except in the new market.'

In classicisms *la* is used to negate indefinite nouns, in which case it has the function of MSA *la* of absolute negation:

la šakk	'no doubt'
la šukr(a) 9ala waajib.	(lit., "No thanks for (one's) duty.")
la budd min s-safar.	'Travel is inevitable.'
la mafarr	'no escape'

18.1.2 Negating Pseudo-Verbs

Prepositional pseudo-verbs are negated by *ma:*

ma fii fgaa9 halHiin.	'There is no mushroom now.'
ma 9indi fluus.	'I do not have (any) money.'
ma 9indič šayy?	'Don't you (f.) have anything?'
ma 9alee dyuun.	'He does not have any debts.' (lit., "Debts are not on him.")
ma lak qeer xašmak lo kaan 9away.	(lit., "You do not have (anything) other than your nose, although it is crooked.") (Meaning: Do not be ashamed of your folks.)

The negative forms of Kuwaiti *'aku* 'there is; there are' and Qatari and Bahraini *hast* 'there is; there are' are *maaku* and *ma hast* (or *ma miiš*), respectively; the corresponding negative perfect forms are *ma kaan 'aku* (or *kaan maaku*) and *ma kaan fii* 'there wasn't; there weren't,' respectively (see 13.2).

Two prepositional pseudo-verbal constructions are usually negated by *la . . . w(a)-la* or *ma . . . w(a)-la* 'neither . . . nor.' A lot of examples are found in proverbs and idiomatic phrases:

'illi ma la 'awwal ma la taali.
(lit., "He who does not have a beginning does not have an end.")
(Meaning: Everything should have a sound beginning.)

la la walad wala talad.
(lit., "He has neither a son nor old furniture.")
(Meaning: He has nothing; he has left nothing for his heirs.)

la la mara wala Hmaara.
(lit., "He has neither a wife nor a donkey (f.).")
(Meaning: Similar to the above proverb)

la la maalin yinfa9 wala waladin yišfa9.
(lit., "He does not have wealth that benefits him nor a son who pleads on his behalf.")
(Meaning: Similar to the above proverb.)

The last three proverbs can be used without the prepositional pseudo-verbal construction *la* 'he has,' e.g., *la walad wala talad, la mara wala Hmaara,* etc., without any change in meaning.

18.1.3 Negating Imperatives

A negative command (or request), which is used to tell s.o. not to do s.th., consists of the negative particle *la* followed by the imperfect tense of the verb.

la tbaddil Hduumak!	'Do not change your clothes!'
la titfaṣxiin!	'Do not take your clothes off (f.)!'
la dduuxuun hini!	'Do not smoke here (m.p.)!'
la tsiirin halHiin!	'Do not go, leave now (f.p.)!'

Two negative commands joined by *wa-* 'and' have *la . . . w(a)-la:*

la tbuug w(a)-la txaaf!
(lit., "Do not steal and do not be afraid!")
(Meaning: If you do not steal, you should not be (you don't have to be) afraid.)

la thaawšiini w(a)-la thaawšii!
'Do not quarrel (f.s.) with me and do not quarrel with him.'

18.2 Negating Other Parts of Speech

Nouns, pronouns, adjectives, adverbs, particles, and prepositional phrases are negated by *mu(u)(b). muu* is usually used before words with initial double consonants or two-consonant clusters; *muu, mub* (or *muub*) are used elsewhere. Examples:

huwa muu d-dreewil.	'He is not the driver.'
muu l-laHad, l-laθneen	'not (on) Sunday, (on) Monday'
'aana muu mxabbal.	'I am not crazy.'
guuḷ ṣabi muu sbayy!	'Say "Servant" not "young boy." '
l-hawa muub Haarr.	'The weather is not hot.'
mub 'aHsan čiði?	'Isn't it better this way?'
muub čiði?	'Isn't it so?'
š-šeex saar, muub hini.	'The Shaikh has left; he isn't here.'
mub mirtaaHiin hnaak.	'(They) are not comfortable there.'
haaði šeen, mub zeen.	'That is bad, not good.'
muub zeen.	'(It is) not good.'
mub ṣoob 9umaan,[27] ṣoob l-baHar	'not toward Al-Ain, toward the sea'
'inta muub ḍ̣amyaan?	'Aren't you thirsty?'
mub taHat, foog	'not below, above'
muub 9aleehum, wiyyaahum	'not against them, with them'
muu s-saa9a xams	'not (at) five o'clock'

Either *mu(u)(b) . . . w-mu(u)(b)* or *la . . . w(a)-la* is used to mean 'neither . . . nor':

muub Haarr w-muub baarid la Haarr w(a)-la baarid	'neither hot nor cold'

ma . . . w(a)-la 'neither . . . nor' is also used, especially in idiomatic phrases:

---

27. *9umaan* is usually used in the U.A.E. to mean Al-Ain, the second largest city in Abu Dhabi.

ma kill sooda fHama w(a)-la kill beeḏ̣a šHama.
(lit., "not every black (thing) is a piece of charcoal, and not every white (thing) is a lump of lard.")
(Meaning: Do not judge people by their appearance.)

Independent pronouns are usually negated by *mu(u)(b);* however, the following negative forms are used rarely:

minta	'not you'
minti	'not you (f.)'
maani	'not I'
mintu	'not you (m.p.)'
mintin	'not you (f.p.)'
miHna[28]	'not us'

The negative form of *'aHad* 'somebody, someone' is *maHHad* 'nobody, no one,' usually as the subject of the sentence:

	maHHad čaafa	'Nobody saw him.'
	maHHad ydišš hini.	'Nobody enters here.'
but:	ma čift 'aHad.	'I did not see anybody.'
	*čift maHHad.	'I saw nobody.'
	ma riHt ma9 'aHad.	'I did not go with anybody.'
	*riHt maHHad.	'I went with nobody.'

A negative response to a yes- or no-question is either *la* 'no' or *'abdan* (lit., "never") or both *la 'abdan* for emphasis:

'inta dduux?	'Do you smoke?'
la.	'No.'
tišrab biira?	'Do you drink beer?'
la 'abdan.	'No, never.'

The phrase *mu(u)(b) čiđi* 'isn't it so' is appended to a statement to form what is known in English as a tail question; *mu(u)(b) čiđi* is usually known as a question tag; it is invariable. The phrases *mu(u)(b) 9adil* and *mu(u)(b) ṣaHiiH* or simply *9adil* and *ṣaHiiH* are also used but *mu(u)(b) čiđi* occurs more frequently. Examples:

l-qada baariz, mub čiđi?
'Dinner is ready, isn't it?'

---

28. Note that only the independent pronouns with an initial '- have negative forms. (*'iHna* 'we,' however, is used rarely.) The negative particle is reduced to *m-* and the glottal stop '- drops.

li-9yaaḷ tqaddaw, muub čiði?
'The children had dinner, didn't they?'

laṭiifa ma tibġa titzawwaj, mu čiði?
'Latifa doesn't want to get married, does she?'

ma riHt wiyyaahum, muu čiði?
'You didn't go with them, did you?'

š-šeex mub hini, 9adil?
'The Shaikh isn't here, is he?'

'inta mub yaay, ṣaHiiH?
'You are not coming, are you?'

PART FOUR

TEXTS

SAMPLE TEXTS

Introduction

This part contains a very small portion of the corpus used for the present work. The whole corpus covers a wide variety of subjects of interest. It includes greetings, getting acquainted, appointments, telling time, weather and climatic conditions, directions, days of the week, months and seasons of the year, systems of education, banking, shopping, mailing letters, etc. Anecdotes, tales, plays, songs, etc., suited to the particular needs of prospective students have also been recorded. The texts and narratives in *A Basic Course in Gulf Arabic* form another small portion of the corpus. The first two texts are dialogs; the third and the fourth are narratives; TEXT V contains some sayings and proverbial phrases. Each of the first four texts is followed by a translation which is not literal but an approximation of the meaning in order to preserve the uniqueness of the Arabic phrase. Each saying or proverbial phrase in TEXT V is followed by an equivalent English proverbial phrase and/or a literal translation in quotes.

TEXT I

ṭalab šuġuḷ

A. tfaḏ̣ḏ̣al! na9am šu triid?

B. salaam 9aleekum!

A. 9aleekum s-salaam.

B. fi šuġuḷ 9indakum?

A. 'ii na9am fii šuġuḷ. tfaḏ̣ḏ̣al stariiH.

B. 'aani bu-sanad. 'abġa 'aštaġiḷ.

A. bass niHin 9indana 9iddat 'ašġaaḷ. kill šaġla miHtaaja la šruuṭ w-mu'ahhilaat m9ayyana.

B. 'aana 9indi kill š-šruuṭ w-li-mhalhalaat. 'aana 9arf 'agra w-'aktib, bass 9ala gadd l-Haal.

A. l-'ax l-kariim šu smak min faḏ̣lak?

B. 'aana 'asmi bu-sanad.

A. 'ahlan wa sahlan! 'isma9 ya bu-sanad! 'iHna miHtaajiin Hagg 'ašxaaṣ yjiiduun l-qiraa'a w-l-kitaaba w-yilzam fi ba9ð̣ l-'aHyaan 9inda 'ingiliizi.

B. ya9ni laazim ayiib ma9aay ingireezi!

A. la ya bu-sanad. ya9ni ykuun 9indak ilmaam b-l-luġa l-'ingiliiziyya.

B. gilt-li riṭna b-l-'ingireezi ma 9arf. 'aana 9arf 'aštaġiḷ šuġuḷ kumblaayaat.

A. kumblaayaat!

B. 'ii na9am. kumblaayaat maal li-bnuuk.

A. 'aa. gaṣdak l-kumbyaalaat. bass iHna daayra mub bank.

B. 'aani 'adri laakin 'abi 'aziidak ma9luumiyya 9anni.

A. ṭayyib ba9ad šu t9arf? niHin nabġi šaxṣ 9inda mu'ahhilaat 'akθar min haaði.

B. čuuf ya ḷ-mudiir! 'aani 'aHaṣṣil šuġuḷ 9indakum fii 'að̣umm w-'afanniš w-'aamur w-'anhi, ham zeen.

A. šu tguuḷ?! tabġi šuġuḷ ð̣ð̣umm w-tfanniš . . . 'aguuḷ xooš! muub 'aHsan-lak tguuḷ tabgi maHalli?!

B. 'amma haaði yirja9 la šiimatk.

A. 'isma9 ya bu-sanad! niHin mit'asfiin. ma fii 9indana šuġuḷ.

B. halHiin ṣaarli mudda w-aana yaalis 9indak w-9ugub haaða killa tguuḷ ma fii šuġuḷ.

A. š-šuġuḷ illi 'inta taṭluba ma 9indana.

B. nzeen ya mudiir! maškuur. fi 'amaan illaa.

A. ma9 s-salaama. 'aḷḷa wiyyaak.

TRANSLATION I

Application for Work

A. Come in! Yes, what do you want?

B. Peace be upon you!

A. Peace be upon you.

B. Do you have work?

A. Yes, there is work. Please sit down.

B. I am Abu Sanad. I would like to work.

A. Well! We have several jobs. Each job requires certain conditions and qualifications.

B. I have all the conditions and qualifications. I know how to read and write, but to the extent of my own abilities.

A. My dear friend! What's your name, please?

B. My name is Abu Sanad.

A. Welcome! Listen, Abu Sanad! We need people who read and write well, and sometimes they must have English.

B. In other words, I have to bring with me an Englishman!

A. No, Abu Sanad. That means you must have a general knowledge of the English language.

B. You tell me I must have gibberish in English. (That) I don't know. I know how to work with (bank) drafts.

A. Drafts!

B. Yes, bank drafts.

A. Oh! You mean bank drafts. But we are a department, not a bank.

B. I know, but I want to give you more information about me.

A. Fine. What else do you know? We want a person who has more qualifications than these.

B. Look, director! If I get a job with you where I employ, terminate, order, and proscribe, . . . that's fine.

A. What do you say?! You want a job to employ, terminate, order, and proscribe. I say, "fine!!" Isn't it better for you to say that you want my place!?

B. This is up to your character.

A. Listen, Abu Sanad! We are sorry. We do not have work.

B. Now I have been sitting with you for some time and after all of this you say there is no work.

A. We do not have the kind of work you ask for.

B. Fine, director! Thanks. Good-bye.

A. Bye. God be with you.

TEXT II

min mašaakil z-zawaaj

A. haluw! minu? 'ubu yuusif?

B. 'ii na9am.

A. marHaba massaak aḷḷa b-l-xeer! 'aamir! tmurr 9aleena l-leela?

B. nšaaḷḷa.

A. zeen. s-saa9a tisi9 'aana 'akuun fi l-beet.

A. 'umm naaṣir! 'umm naaṣir! ya 'umm naaṣir!

C. labbeek! ha! weeš 9indak ya bu-naaṣir?

A. 9asa laṭiifa jaat min l-madrasa.

C. tawha halHiin daašša l-beet.

A. w-li-9yaal yaaw kullahum? nšaaḷḷa l-qada baariz.

C. kullahum hni. l-qada baariz. ṣaarlana mudda w-iHna nintað̣rak.

A. yaḷḷa naadi li-9yaal xaḷḷiina nitqadda.

A. ya hala w-marHaba! Hayyaak aḷḷa ya bu-yuusif!

B. s-salaam 9aleekum! 'ačuuf beetak sġayyir ya bu-yuusif. ma baneet? ma 9amalt šayy? 'inta min zamaan hini.

A. miθilma t9arf ya bu-yuusif l-ma9aaš 9ala gadd l-Haal. miθil-ma yguuḷ l-maθal midd riilak 9ala gadd lHaafak. 'inta min tarakt l-firiij Hatta marr ma tmurr. Hatta rab9ak naseettum kulhum.

B. waḷḷa ya bu-naaṣir halHiin 'aana jaayiik fi mawð̣uu9 yxuṣṣak.

A. xeer nšaaḷḷa?

B. 'aana yaay 'aṭlub l-gurb minnak fi bintak laṭiifa Hagg wildi yuusif. kill illi taṭluba 'awaafig 9alee.

A. haaði ba9deen nittafig 9alee. gabiḷ kill šayy 'aaxið raay laṭiifa.

B. š-tguuḷ ya bu-naaṣir? taaxið raay laṭiifa? waḷḷa ma dareena Hagg l-banaat raay fi miθil ha-l-mawaað̣ii9.

A. waḷḷa haaða mustaġbalha w-Hayaatta hiya.

B. waḷḷa 'aana šaayif kalaamak ma la ma9na.

A. waḷḷa 'aana gilt-lak 'aana raayiH as'alha w-nčuuf.

B. šuuf illi yṣarfak. nitgaabal ba9deen nšaaḷḷa.

A. laṭiifa! laṭiifa! laṭiifa!

D. na9am ya yuba. 'aana hini gaa9da 'adris.

A. baarak aḷḷa fiič! 'aḷḷa ynajHič. ya laṭiifa 'aHibb aaxið raayič fi mawð̣uu9. 'abġiič tfakriin 9adil gabiḷ la tjaawbiin. bu-yuusif, li-mqanṭir, ya yuxṭubč Hagg wilda yuusif. šu tguuliin?

D. walla halHiin ma li raġba fi z-zawaaj. kill hammi 'anjaH w-'aaxið š-šahaada θ-θaanawiyya. ma baga 9alayy qeer ha-s-sanateen. haaða raayi ya yuba.

A. ya binti kalaamič fi mukaana. 'alla ynajHič w-yirða 9aleeč w-ywafjič.

C. ha ya bu-naasir! 'asma9 suwaalfak ma9 laṭiifa. xeer nšaalla?

A. xeer ya 'umm-naaṣir. 'aana ridt 'a9allimč b-l-mawðuu9. l-mawðuu9 bu-yuusif jaay yuxṭub laṭiifa Hagg wilda yuusif.

C. ha weeš gilt-la?

A. bass xalliini 'akammil kalaami. gilt-la gabil kill šayy 'aaxið raay laṭiifa. laṭiifa ma waafagat.

C. ma waafagat! b-tHaṣṣil 'aHsan min yuusif, xeer w-maal?

A. laṭiifa 9indaha raġba tkammil diraasatta, w-hiy ma9ha Hagg.

C. bu-yuusif ma yinradd. b-nHaṣṣil min waraa fluus w-xeer. 'inta ġalṭaan. miθil ha-l-mi9ris mub laagyiin.

A. 'aana ma bii9 binti b-šwayyit fluus. sa9aadat binti foog kill 9tibaar.

A. 'ismaH-li ya bu-yuusif ta'axxart 9aleek. laṭiifa halHiin ma tfakkir fi z-zawaaj. 'intu 9aziiziin 9aleena w-ma9ruufiin min zamaan.

B. šu tguul ya bu-naaṣir! ya9ni bintak b-tHaṣṣil 'aHsan min yuusif? 'aana šaayif 'innak ġalṭaan truuH taaxið raayha. haaði mas'ala beenna niHin r-rijaal. 'aana 'adfa9 kill-ma taṭlub w-ma ngaṣṣir 9aleekum, l-mahar w-ṣ-ṣooġa w-. . . . kill šayy yistawi zeen.

A. 'illi 9inda fluus ti9mii. li-fluus ma tyiib l-9aruus. 'inta lli ġalṭaan.

B. 'aana ġalṭaan lajil ridt 'anaasbak. 'inta ma tistaahil šayy. šuuf illi ynaasbak.

TRANSLATION II

Some Marriage Problems

A. Hello! Who is it? Abu Yusif?

B. Yes.

A. Hello! Good evening! What can I do for you? Will you come to our house tonight?

B. God willing.

A. Fine. I will be home at 9:00.

A. Um Nasir! Um Nasir! Um Nasir!

B. At your service! What do you have, Abu Nasir?

A. I hope Latifa has come back from school.

B. She has just entered the house.

A. And have all the children come back? I hope lunch is ready.

B. They are all here. Lunch is ready. We have been waiting for you for some time.

A. Call the children and let's eat lunch.

A. Hello! Hi! May God preserve your life, Abu Yusif!

B. Peace be upon you! I see that your house is small, Abu Yusif. Haven't you built? Haven't you done anything? You've been here long.

A. As you know, Abu Yusif, the salary isn't much. As the proverb says, "As you make your bed, you must lie in it." Since you left the neighborhood, you haven't even passed through. Even your relations, you have forgotten all of them.

B. In fact, Abu Nasir, I came to see you about a matter that concerns you.

A. What's new? (lit., "I hope it's good.")

B. I came to betroth your daughter (lit., "to seek closeness to you"), Latifa, to my son, Yusif. I will agree to everything you ask.

A. We will decide on this later on. Before anything else, I will ask Latifa's opinion.

B. What do you say, Abu Nasir? We do not know that girls have an opinion with regard to subjects like these.

A. This, in fact, is her future and her life.

B. I see that there is no sense in your talk.

A. I told you that I was going to ask her and we would see.

B. Go see what's best for you. We will meet later, hopefully.

A. Latifa! Latifa! Latifa!

D. Yes, father. I am here, studying.

A. God bless you! God make you successful. Latifa, I want to ask you for your opinion about a subject. I want you to think hard before you answer. Abu Yusif, the contractor, came to ask your hand in marriage for his son, Yusif. What do you say?

D. Honestly, I have no desire for marriage now. My major concern is to succeed and obtain the secondary certificate. I have only two years left. This is my opinion, father.

A. Your words are well put, my daughter. God make you successful and bless you.

C. What, Abu Nasir? I've heard your words to Latifa. What's new? (lit., "I hope it's good.")

A. It is good, Um Nasir. I wanted to tell you about the subject. The subject is that Abu Yusif has come to betroth Latifa to his son, Yusif.

C. And what did you say to him?

A. Just let me finish. I told him that, first of all, I had to ask Latifa's opinion. Latifa did not agree.

C. She did not agree! Can she find a better man than Yusif in property and wealth?

A. Latifa has a desire to complete her studies, and she is right.

C. Abu Yusif cannot be rebuffed. We will get money and a lot of good things from him. You are mistaken. We cannot find a similar bridegroom.

A. I won't sell my daughter for some money. My daughter's happiness is above every consideration.

A. I am sorry I am late, Abu Yusif. Latifa is not thinking of marriage now. You are dear to us and have been known for a long time.

B. What do you say, Abu Nasir! Will your daughter get a better man than Yusif? I see that you are mistaken for going to ask for her opinion. This is a matter between us (men). I will pay all that you ask for, and we won't skimp on anything: the dowry, the jewelry. . . . Everything will be fine.

A. He who has money will be blinded by it. Money does not bring the bride. You are mistaken.

B. I am mistaken because I wanted to be related to you by marriage. You do not deserve anything. Go see what's best for you.

TEXT III

l-'a9yaad

9indana hni fii 'a9yaad diiniyya w-fii 'a9yaad waṭaniyya. l-'a9yaad d-diiniyya 9iid rumð̣aan w-9iid l-Hajj. ba9ð̣ n-naas yguuluun 9iid ð̣-ð̣iHiyya walla 9iid l-Hiyy. ṭaal 9umrak haaði nafs š-šayy. fii 9iid rumð̣aan yisbaHuun n-naas ṣ-ṣabaaH w-yruuHuun 9ala ṣalaat l-9iid w-ba9dma tingað̣i ṣ-ṣalaa yruuHuun yzuuruun ba9ð̣ahum ba9ð̣ w-y9amluun l-'afraaH. yruuHuun l-Hadaayig l-9aamma w-y9amluun r-ragṣaat š-ša9biyya w-yistimirr 9ala haaða l-Haal muddat sab9 ayyaam. l-Hukuuma, Hukuumat š-šeex zaayid, ṭawiil l-9umur, ta9ṭi 9uṭla sab9 ayyaam. fii 9iid l-'að̣Ha, l-'að̣Ha ya9ni ma9naatta hiya 9iid ð̣-ð̣iHiyy miθil-ma nguuḷ b-lahjatna. t9arf ba9dma yHijjuun l-Hijjaaj 'ila makka yingað̣i l-Hajj. n-naas yiðbaHuun ð̣-ð̣aHaaya w-9aadaata ma tixtalif 9an 9aadaat 9iid rumð̣aan. 9iid rumð̣aan ysammuuna ba9ð̣ n-naas 9iid l-faṭir 'aw l-9iid ṣ-ṣagiir. 9indana hini fi lahjatna nguuḷ la ba9ð̣, "9iidak mubaarak!" w-fii naas yguuḷuun, "kull sana w-inta ṭayyib!" 'aw "mabruuk 9aleek l-9iid!" ba9deen fii 9iid s-sana l-hijriyya. 9uṭulta yoom waaHid. fii ba9ad 9iid mawlid n-nabi. fii haðeel l-9iideen n-naas yruuHuun l-masaajid w-yṣalluun w-yigruun l-qur'aan. min l-'a9yaad l-waṭaniyya fii 9iid l-juluus lamma 9að̣amat l-Haakim, ṭawiil l-9umur š-šeex zaayid, yalas 9ala l-9arš w-ṣaar Haakim fi l-balad w-taariix 9iid l-juluus fi θamaanya sitta. ba9deen 9ugubma ṣaar l-'ittiHaad Hagg l-'imaaraat killaha ṣaar 'asma 9iid l-'istiġlaal illi huwa fii θneen Hda9aš illi huw ṣaar fii l-'ittiHaad w-ttaHdat l-'imaaraat. ya9ṭuun 'ijaaza rasmiyya Hagg yoomeen.

TRANSLATION III

Feasts and Holidays

Here we have religious holidays and national holidays. The religious holidays are the Ramadan Feast and the Pilgrimage Feast. Some people say, "Sacrifice Feast," or "Pilgrimage Feast." This is the same, God prolong your life. During the Ramadan Feast people bathe in the morning and go for the Feast prayer, and when the prayer is over, they go to visit one another and have celebrations. They go to public gardens and dance folk dances, and this goes on for seven days. The government, the government of Shaikh Zayid, may God prolong his life, gives a seven-day holiday. During the Sacrifice Feast—*l-'aḏ̣Ha* means *ḏ̣-ḏ̣iHiyya*—as we say in our dialect. You know that after pilgrims go on pilgrimage to Mecca, the pilgrimage is over. People slaughter animals and its practices are not different from the practices of the Ramadan Feast. Some people call the Ramadan Feast the *Feast of Breaking the Ramadan Fast* or *Lesser Bairam.* We here, in our dialect, say to one another, "Happy Holiday" (lit., "Your feast is blessed"), and there are some people who say, "(I hope that) you are well every year," or "God bless you on this holiday," etc. Then there is the Hegira Feast. Its holiday is one day. There is also the feast of the Prophet's Birthday. During these two holidays people go to mosques, pray, and read from the Quran. Among the national holidays there is the Accession Day when His Highness, The Ruler, Shaikh Zayid, the long-lived one, acceded to the throne and became the ruler in the country and the date of Accession Day is June 8. And then when the union of all the Emirates came into being its name became Independence Day, November 11, the day when the union took place and the Emirates became united. They give an official holiday for two days.

TEXT IV

l-'imaaraat

leen nguuḷ "l-'imaaraat" haaḏa ya9ni l-'imaaraat l-9arabiyya l-muttaHida. l-'imaaraat, ṭaal 9umrak, hiya 'abu ḏ̣abi w-dbayy w-š-šaarja w-9ajmaan w-'umm l-giiween w-raaṣ l-xeema w-li-fjeera. haaḏi l-'imaaraat killaha 9ala l-xaliij l-9arabi 'illa li-fjeera 9ala xaliij 9umaan. tidri xaliij ya9ni baHar. 'abu ḏ̣abi, 'aḷḷa ysallimk, hiya l-9aaṣima. l-9aaṣima ya9ni l-madiina lli fiiha l-Haakim, ṭawiil l-9umur, 'illi huw š-šeex zaayid bin sulṭaan 'aal nhayyaan. š-šeex zaayid huwa ra'iis l-'ittiHaad. 'abu ḏ̣abi ṭala9 fiiha batrool min zamaan. yamkin min muddat Hda9šar sana. fiiha madiinateen kbaar humma 'abu ḏ̣abi nafisha w-l-9een.

l-'imaara θ-θaanya hiya dubay. Haakimha š-šeex raašid bin sa9iid, naayib ra'iis l-'ittiHaad. dbayy mašhuura b-t-tijaara w-tṣaddir la l-'imaaraat kullaha li'an l-marfa maalha fii xoor w-l-buwaaxir tarsi qariiba min s-siif.

raaṣ l-xeema tištahir b-z-ziraa9a w-hiya, miθilma t9arf, minṭaġa jabaliyya w-'arḍaha 'axsab minṭaġa fi l-xaliij. fiiha maay waayid. fiiha min jamii9 'anwaa9 l-xuḍaar: fiiha ṭamaaṭ w-filfil xaḍar w-rweed, niHin nguuḷḷa r-rweed 'aw l-fijil miθilma yguuluun 'ixwaanna l-falaṣṭiiniyyiin w-l-labnaaniyiin, w-hamba w-yiHH w-baṭṭiix. . . .

9ajmaan qarya sagiira. hiya 'aṣġar 'imaara. tištahir b-ṣeed l-'asmaač miθil kill l-'imaaraat θ-θaanya. simač l-xaliij, 'aḷḷa ysallimk ṭayyib killiš zeen. fii ṣbeeṭi w-ṣaafi w-hamuur w-čan9ad w-ši9ri w-ribyaan w-ma dri ba9ad. haaḏi 'asmaač l-xaliij.

'umm l-giiween fiiha simač waayid.

TRANSLATION IV

The Emirates

When we say "the Emirates," we mean the United Arab Emirates. The Emirates, may God prolong your life, are Abu Dhabi, Dubai, Sharja, Ajman, Umm al-Qaiwain, Ras al-Khaima, and Fujaira. All of these Emirates are on the Arabian Gulf except for Fujaira, which is on the Gulf of Oman. You know *xaliij* 'Gulf' means *baHar* 'sea.' Abu Dhabi, God protect you, is the capital. *Capital* means the city where the Ruler is; the Ruler, may God prolong his life, is Shaikh Zayid Bin Sultan Al-Nhayyan. Shaikh Zayid is the President of the Union. Oil gushed in Abu Dhabi a long time ago, probably fourteen years ago. There are two big cities in it; they are Abu Dhabi and Al-Ain. The second Emirate is Dubai. Its ruler is Shaikh Rashid Bin Said, Vice President of the Union. Dubai is known for its trade and it exports to all the other Emirates because its wharf has a gulf where (steam) ships anchor close to harbor.

Ras al-Khaima is famous for agriculture, and it is, as you know, a mountainous region and its land is the most fertile in the Gulf. There is a lot of water in it. It has all kinds and varieties of vegetables: tomatoes, green pepper, radish, which we call *r-rweed* or *l-fijil,* as our Palestinian and Lebanese brothers say, mangoes, watermelons, cantaloupes, etc.

Ajman is a small village. It is the smallest Emirate. It is known for fishing like all the other Emirates. The fish of the Gulf, God protect you, is delicious and very good. There are (the following kinds): *ṣbeeṭi, ṣaafi, hamuur, čan9ad, ši9ri,* shrimp, and I do not know what else. These are the kinds of fish in the Gulf.

Umm al-Qaiwain has a lot of fish.

TEXT AND TRANSLATION V

'amθaal w-'aqwaal

1. li-fluus tjiib l-9aruus.
   Money talks. ("Money brings the bride.")
2. gaṭu maṭaabix.
   He eats like a pig. ("a cat of kitchens")
3. 'iðа čift rifiijak Hilu la taakla killa.
   Don't use up all of your credit at once. ("If you think your friend is nice, don't eat him all up at once.")
4. 9aṭi l-xabbaaz xubzak walaw baag nuṣṣa.
   ("Give your bread to the baker although he might steal half of it.")
5. 'illi ma y9arf ṣ-ṣagir yišwii.
   Don't kill the goose that lays the golden egg. ("He who does not know the falcon will roast it.")
6. l-9awar been l-9imyaan baaša.
   In the land of the blind, the one-eyed (one-eyed man) is king.
7. yoom ṣaxxanna l-maay širad d-diič.
   Forewarned is forearmed. ("When we heated the water, the rooster ran away.")
8. ṭ-ṭuul ṭuul nxaḷa w-l-9agil 9agil sxaḷa.
   The mind of a child and the body of a man. ("The length is that of a palm tree and the mind is that of a young goat.")
9. 'igð̣ab maynuunak la yiik 'ayann minna.
   A bird in the hand is worth two in the bush. ("Hold onto your crazy man in case a crazier one comes long.")
10. wild č-čalb čalbin miθla.
    Like father like son. ("The son of a dog is a dog like his father.")

11. killin Haliiba yjiiba.
Like father like son. ("One is brought (or drawn back) by one's own milk.")

12. 'illi ma yiṭla9 9ala 'ubuu naġaḷ.
Like father like son. ("He who does not take after his father, i.e., in looks and behavior, is a bastard.")

13. 'illi yibġa ṣ-ṣalaa ma tfuuta.
Make hay while the sun shines. ("He who wants prayer, won't miss it.")

14. 'illi ma yjiiba Haliiba ma yjiiba z-zuur.
You can lead a horse to water, but you cannot make him drink.

15. 'iða ṭaaH l-bi9iir kaθrat sičaačiina.
When it rains it pours. ("If the camel falls down, its knives will be plenty.")

16. loo fii xeer čaan ma hadda ṭ-ṭeer.
It is a worthless thing. ("If it (e.g., the sparrow) had been of any use, the bird (of prey) would not have discarded it.")

17. lo yadri 9meer čaan šagg θooba.
Ignorance is bliss. ("If Omayr had known, he would have ripped his clothes.")

18. xašmak minnak lo kaan 9away.
Do not be ashamed of your folks. ("Your nose is a part of you although it is crooked.")

19. čaan yabi dibs l-Hasa lHasa.
Where there is a will, there is a way. ("If he wants the molasses of Al-Hasa, he will lick it.")

20. man 9aḍ̣ḍ̣a d-daab yangiz min l-Habil.
Once bitten twice shy. ("He who has been bitten by a snake fears a rope.")

21. l-qird fi 9een 'umma ġazaal.
Beauty is in the eye of the beholder. ("A monkey, in the eyes of its mother, is a gazelle.")

22. l-Hubb 9amay.
Love is blind.

23. killin ymidd riila 9ala gadd l-Haafa.
As you make your bed you must lie in it. ("One can stretch one's leg according to one's quilt.")

24. la Haṣal l-maay baṭal l-9aafuur.
("If water can be gotten, ablution is nullified.")

25. la zzigg fi maa9uun 'akalt fii.
Be good to those who have done you a favor. Don't shit in your own nest. ("Do not defacate in a plate which you have eaten from.")

26. 'illi faat maat.
Let bygones be bygones. The past is dead. ("What has already passed has died.")

27. ḏ̣ulmin b-s-sawiyya 9adlin b-r-ra9iyya.
("Injustice done to all people equally is preferable to justice for some and injustice to others.")

28. z-zeen zeenin law ga9ad min manaama
w-š-šeen šeenin law ġassal b-ṣaabuun
A leopard cannot change his spots. ("A beautiful person is always beautiful even at the time he wakes up, and an ugly person is always ugly although he washes himself with soap.")

29. muu kull beeḏ̣a šHama wala kull sooda fHama.
Do not judge people or things by their appearance. You can't judge a book by its cover. ("Not every white thing is a piece of lard; neither is every black thing a piece of charcoal.")

APPENDICES
AND
BIBLIOGRAPHY

APPENDIX I

1. *j* → *y*
2. *j* → *y* or *j*
3. *j* → *j*

Words which have the *j* sound in literary Arabic usually have the *y* sound in the dialect of Abu Dhabi. This change is not conditioned by any environment. In some words the change j → y is optional; in certain classicisms, borrowings, proper names, and newly introduced words, the *j* sound is preserved.

1. *j* → *y*

yiHH	'watermelons'	finyaan	'cup'
yaryuur	'shark'	rayyaal	'man'
yaahil	'child'	maynuun	'crazy'
weeh	'face'	m(a)siid	'mosque'
riil	'foot'	diyaay	'hens; chickens'
9ayuuz	'old woman'	mooy	'waves'
waayid	'a lot'	falay	'watercourse'
l-yim9a	'Friday'	daray	'stairs'

2. *j* → *y* or *j*

ya (var. *ja*)	'to come'
yaami9 (var. *jaami9*)	'mosque'
yaab (var. *jaab*)	'to bring'
yamaa9ti (var. *jamaa9ti*)	'my folks'
l-yimii9 (var. *l-jimii9*)	'everyone'
yaay (var. *jaay*)	'coming; having come'

yadiid (var. *jadiid*)	'new'
yamiil (var. *jamiil*)	'beautiful'

3. *j* → *j*

jayyid	'good,' as in *jayyid jiddan* 'very good' (from literary Arabic)
jawaaz safar	'passport' (from literary Arabic)
zooj	'husband' (corruption of literary *zawj* or probably from Leventine Arabic)
jooz	'nuts' (from Levantine Arabic)
jibin	'cheese' (from Levantine Arabic)
garaaj	'garage' (from English)
jalbuut	'jolly-boat' (from English)
jigaara	'cigarette' (from Persian)
jaam	'glass' (from Persian)
jimrig	'customs, duty' (from Persian)
juuti	'shoes' (from Hindi-Urdu)
zanjiil	'iron chain' (from Turkish)
taajir	'merchant' (to differentiate it from *taayir* 'car tire' from English)
9ajiib	'strange' (to differentiate it from *9ayiib* 'shameful, disgraceful')
9ajmaan	'Ajman' (proper name)
jamiila	'Jamila' (proper name)
jaam9a	'University' (as in *jaam9at 'arizoona* 'The University of Arizona')

APPENDIX II

1. *q* → *j* or *g*
2. *q* → *g*
3. *g* → *q*

1. *q* → *j*

Literary words with the *q* sound have the *j* sound in GA in the following environments:

a. When preceded or followed by a front vowel: *i, ii, a, aa.* Examples:

Hariija	'fire'	š-šaarja	'Sharja'
jidir	'cooking pot'	jirba	'waterskin, bagpipe'
jiddaam	'in front'	jadam	'foot'
šarji	'eastern'	jaasim	'male name'
jaafla	'caravan'	waafaj	'to agree'
firiij	'small village'	rifiij	'companion'

b. When a consonant sound falls between a front vowel and the *q* sound. Examples:

9irj	'vein'	Halj	'pharynx; mouth'
ṣidj	'truth'	ṣaadj	'truthful'

In environments other than those mentioned above, literary *q* → GA *g:*

gaaḷ	'to say'	guum!	'get up!'
ṣagir	'male name'	goom	'people, folk'
gabiḷ	'before'	'aguuḷ!	'by the way!'

bgara	'cow'	gaṣir	'palace, castle'
gabguuba	'crab; lobster'	gaḷb	'heart'
mabyuug	'stolen'	baag	'to steal'
foog	'above; over'	ruyuug	'breakfast'

2. *q* → *g*

Literary *q* in some forms changes into *ġ*[1] in GA. Examples:

('i)stiġḷaaḷ	'independence'	ġaaḏ̣i	'judge'
l-muġarraraat	'decisions'	faġiir	'poor'
ġunṣuliyya	'consulate'	l-ġaḏ̣a	'justice, fate'
ġarrar	'to decide'	ġamiiṣ	'shirt'
raġam	'number'	manaaṭiġ	'districts'

3. *g* → *q*

Literary *g* in some forms changes into *q* or into a sound between *q* and *g* in GA. Examples:

qani	'rich'	tqayyar	'to be changed'
qanna	'to sing'	yqanni	'he sings'
qayyar	'to change'	mašquuḷ	'busy'
l-maqrib	'Morocco'	qabi	'stupid'

1. This is mainly due to the influence of Persian.

APPENDIX III

1. *k* → *č*
2. *k* → *k*

1. *k* → *č*

Literary *k* changes into GA *č* in two cases:

a. If it is the second person feminine singular suffixed pronoun (suffixed to nouns and particles) or the object suffixed pronoun (suffixed to verbs and participles). Examples:

'ubuuč	'your (f.s.) father'
'ixwaanič	'your (f.s.) brothers'
Haalič	'your (f.s.) condition'
9aleeč	'on you (f.s.)'
fiič	'in you (f.s.)'
wiyyaač	'with you (f.s.)'
9aṭaač	'he gave you (f.s.)'
šaafič	'he saw you (f.s.)'
'aḷḷa ysallimč	'may God protect you (f.s.)'
šaafooč (var. *šaafuuč*)	'they (m.) saw you (f.s.)'
xaabaračč	'she telephoned you (f.s.)'
xabrannič	'they (f.) telephoned you (f.s.)'
baġaač	'he wanted you (f.s.)'
'aḷḷa ya9ṭiič	'may God give you (f.s.)'
mxaabrinnič	'having telephoned you (f.s.)
9aazimč	'having invited you (f.s.)

b. If it is preceded or followed by a front vowel: *i, ii, a, aa, ee.* Examples:

čeef l-hawa?	'How is the weather?'
diič	'rooster'
yabči	'he is crying, weeping'
sammaač	'fisherman; fish dealer'
mu(u)(b) čiǝi?	'Isn't it so?'
siččiin	'knife'
čaǝǝaab	'liar'
čaan hini	'he was here'
suug s-simač	'the fish market'

2. *k* → *k*

a. In the following forms the *k* sound is preserved for the reasons given beside them:

mbaarak	'Mubarak' (male name): because of a backed *a*
ṣakk l-baab	'he shut the door': because of a backed *a*
kbaar	'big, large (p.)': because of a backed *aa*
ykuun	'he will be': because of a backed *uu*
li-kweet	'Kuwait': *k* is followed by a backed *u* in MSA *'al-kuwait*
kill	'all; every': *k* is followed by a backed *u* in MSA *kull*
dikkaan	'store': *k* is followed by a backed *u* in MSA *dukkaan*

b. The *k* sound is also preserved in foreign and loan words:

sikriim	'ice cream' (English)
kabat	'cupboard' (English)
čayyak	'to check' (English)
kalač	'clutch (n.)' (English)
seekal	'bicycle' (English)
stikaan	'tea cup' (Persian)
tanaka	'aluminum can' (Turkish)
banka	'fan' (Hindi-Urdu)
šakar	'sugar' (Hindi)
kaḷoonya	'cologne' (French)
kaaziino	'casino' (Italian)

APPENDIX IV

$$CVC_1C_2 \rightarrow CC_1VC_2$$
$$C = y, t, n$$
$$V = a$$
$$C_1 = x, \dot{g}, H, 9, h$$
$$C_2 = \text{other}$$

Examples:

Literary	*GA*	*Meaning*
yaxdim	yxadim	'he serves'
yaxlif	yxalif	'he succeeds s.o.'
taġsil	tġasil	'she washes; you (m.s.) wash'
taġlaṭ	tġalit	'she errs; you (m.s.) err'
naHsid	nHasid	'we envy'
na9rif	n9arif	'we know'
yahdi	yhadi	'he guides s.o. (to the correct path)'

But:

yag9id	'he sits down'
yatfil	'he spits'
yabriz	'it gets ready'
yargid	'he sleeps'
yiṭbax	'he cooks'
yidri	'he knows'
yilzam	'he sticks to s.th.'

This feature does not affect the following classes of verbs in the imperfect tense:

Class I doubled, since they have initial CCVC-

Class I hamzated, since they have initial CVVC-

Class III, since they have initial CCVV-

Class IV, since they have initial $CVC_1 C_2$- in which V is *u*, not *a*

Class V, since they have initial CVCC-, in which V is *i*, not *a*

Class VI, since they have initial CCVV- or CVCVV-

Class VII–Class X, since they have initial CVCC- in which V is *i*, not *a*

Quadriliterals, since they have initial CCVC-

APPENDIX V

$CVC_1C_2 \rightarrow C_1VC_2$

C = glottal stop '

V = a

C_1 = x, ġ, H, 9, h

C_2 = other

Examples:

Literary	*GA*	*Meaning*
'axḏar	xaḏar	'green'
'axraš	xaraš	'inflicted with smallpox'
'aġtam	ġatam	'mute'
'aġbar	ġabar	'dusty'
'aHmar	Hamar	'red'
'a9war	9awar	'one-eyed'
'a9raj	9aray[1]	'lame, limping'
'a9waj	9away[2]	'crooked, not straight'
'a9ḏab	9aḏab	'having a paralized hand'
'ahbal	habal	'weak-minded'

The *'a-* sound is retained in adjectives of color and defect in which the second consonant is not any of the following consonants: *x, ġ, H, 9, h.* Examples:

1. For *j* → *y*, see APPENDIX I.
2. *Ibid.*

'aṣmax	'deaf'	'ad9am	'light brown'
'abyaḏ̣	'white'	'azrag	'blue'
'aswad	'black'	'aṭlas	'dark blue'
'abḏ̣am	'toothless'	'aṣfar	'yellow'
'aθram	'having a cut lip'	'asmar	'dark'
'ašlag	'cross-eyed'	'amlaH	'grey'

It should be noted that the elative forms retain the *'a-* sound for differentiation:

haaḏa l-gaṣir 'aHmar min ḏaak.
'This palace is redder than that one.'

haaḏi a9way min ḏiič.
'This is more crooked than that one.'

The feminine forms of these adjectives are not affected by this feature; the pattern is *fa9la:*

Hamra	'red'	ṣamxa	'deaf'
ġatma	'dumb'	malHa	'grey'
9oora	'one-eyed'	šalga	'cross-eyed'
beeḏ̣a	'white'	baḏ̣ma	'toothless'

Other elative adjectives are not affected by this feature either:

'a9la	'higher'	'aġla	'more expensive'
'aHla	'sweeter; prettier'	'axyar	'better'

BIBLIOGRAPHY

ARABIC

'aal-nuuri, 9abdaḷḷa, *'al-'amθaal d-daarija fi l-kuwayt,* Part I and Part II, Beirut (n.d.).

'aniis, 'ibraahiim, *fi l-lahajaat l-9arabiyya,* Cairo, 1952.

l-fag9aan, saalim, *'an-nawaaxδa,* Kuwait (n.d.).

maṭar, 9abd l-9aziiz, *xaṣaa'iṣ l-lahja l-kuwaytiyya,* Kuwait, 1969.

——————, *min 'asraar l-lahja l-kuwaytiyya,* Kuwait, 1970.

rafii9, 9abd r-raHmaan, *'agaani l-biHaar l-'arba9a,* Beirut, 1970.

——————, *'awwal l-maHabba,* Beirut, 1973.

——————, *qaṣaa'id ša9biyya,* Kuwait, 1971.

z-zeed, xaalid, *min l-'amθaal l-9aammiyya,* Kuwait, 1961.

WESTERN

(ARAMCO), *Basic Arabic,* Dhahran, 1957.

——————, *Spoken Arabic,* Dhahran, 1957.

——————, *Conversational Arabic,* Beirut (n.d.).

——————, *English-Arabic Word List,* Beirut, 1958.

Cantineau, J., "Études sur quelques parlers de nomades arabes d'Orient," *Annals de l'Instituit d'Études Orientales d'Alger,* ii (1936) and iii (1937).

Cowell, Mark C., *A Reference Grammar of Syrian Arabic*, Georgetown University Press, Washington, D.C., 1964.

Dajani, K., *Spoken Arabic of Qatar*, Beirut, 1956.

Erwin, Wallace M., *A Short Reference Grammar of Iraqi Arabic*, Georgetown University Press, Washington, D.C., 1963.

Johnstone, T.M., "The Affrication of *kāf* and *gāf* in the Arabic Dialects of the Arabian Peninsula," *Journal of Semitic Studies*, viii. 2(1963), pp. 210-226.

——————————, *Eastern Arabian Dialects*, O.U.P., London, 1967.

de Jong, E., *Spoken Arabic of the Arabian Gulf*, Beirut, 1958.

Rabin, C., *Ancient West-Arabian*, London, 1951.

Sobelman, H. (Ed.), *Arabic Dialect Studies*, Washington, D.C., 1962.

Verma, Manindra, "A Synchronic Comparative Study of the Noun Phrase in English and Hindi," unpublished Ph.D. dissertation, University of Michigan, 1966.